VOICES
FROM THE PAST

CHANNEL ISLANDS
INVADED

CHANNEL ISLANDS
INVADED

Simon Hamon

FRONTLINE BOOKS

CHANNEL ISLANDS INVADED

This edition published in 2015 by Frontline Books,
an imprint of Pen & Sword Books Ltd,
47 Church Street, Barnsley, S. Yorkshire, S70 2AS

ISBN: 978-1-47385-159-7

CIP data records for this title are available from the British Library

Printed and bound by CPI Group (UK) Ltd, Croydon, CR0 4YY
Typeset in 10.5/12.5 Palatino

For more information on our books, please email: info@frontline-books.com,
write to us at the above address, or visit:
www.frontline-books.com

Contents

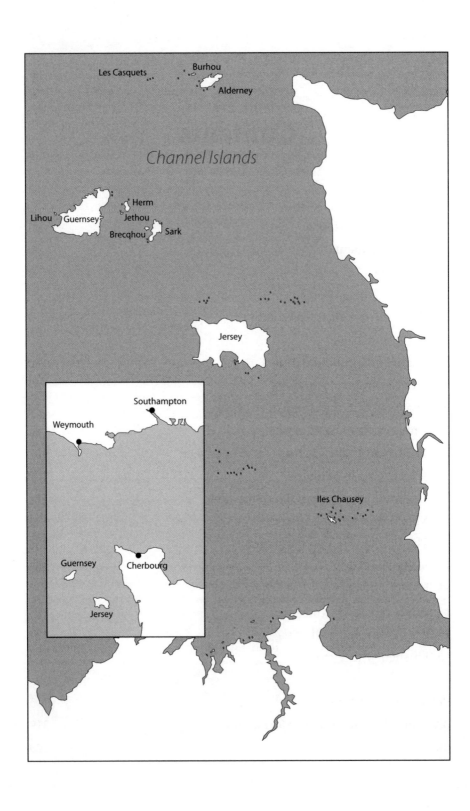

Acknowledgements

The following individuals have been of tremendous help to me whilst compiling this book, and without their help it could never have been completed. Although the list is not exhaustive, those who have been of particular help are: John Goodwin, for his patience in having to listen to my progress, in offering advice, guidance and knowledge and in sharing his extensive research and knowledge on air activity over the Channel Islands and the arrival of the occupying forces; Richard Heaume MBE for his advice, guidance and encouragement throughout the project; David Kreckeler for permitting reproduction of some of his work on the known escapes from German-occupied Guernsey and Alderney; to Pierre Renier for allowing us to use his research into 'Red' Enigma, *Boniface* and the 'Y' Service events of 27 June to 1 July 1940; and to both Pierre Renier and Steve Powell for access to their research on the government files relating to the invasion and occupation of the Channel Islands; to Michael Ginns OBE for kindly allowing reference to his research on Operation *Green Arrow*; Maggie Tablot-Cull for access to her fathers (Bill Green's) records; to Mrs. Bell, widow of the late William 'Bill' Bell, for permission to reproduce excerpts from his books; to Sally Falla for permission to reproduce excerpts from Frank Falla's excellent book *Silent War*; to both Ken Tough and Paul Le Pelley; to the Committee of The Channel Islands Occupation Society Guernsey in allowing me to reproduce excerpts from their reviews and access to the Society's formidable archive; to the Island Archive Services, Guernsey; to Malcolm Woodland; to John Grehan at Frontline Books for his unstinting help and advice whilst compiling information for this book; to Martin Mace, my Publisher, for his guidance, encouragement and enthusiasm for this project; and to my family and friends for all of their support. Lastly, my thanks go to those who took the time to record daily life on the Channel Islands during the Second World War.

Introduction

In the summer of 1940 the British Isles stood isolated and alone facing the might of a seemingly unstoppable German war machine that had compelled France to submit and had driven the British Expeditionary Force off the Continent. Never before had the United Kingdom been in a state of such uncertainty and possible peril. Fortunately the full breadth of the English Channel held back Hitler's armies, and his ambition. Not so for the Channel Islands which stand just a few miles from the French coast.

The British Army and the RAF had lost heavily in the Battle of France. Every man and machine that had escaped back to the United Kingdom would be needed for the defence of mainland Britain. What then would happen to the Channel Islands?

This was the dilemma that confronted the newly-appointed Prime Minister, Winston Churchill, and his War Cabinet. To abandon British territory to the enemy was unthinkable, yet its defence was impracticable, if not impossible. Furthermore, if the Germans attempted an invasion and British troops resisted, the islands would be turned into a battleground, wreaking death and destruction upon the civilian population.

Should, therefore, the islands be completely demilitarised in the hope that the Germans would simply leave the strategically unimportant archipelago alone? But what if they didn't? What would happen to the tens of thousands of Islanders? Could Britain stand aside and watch these people whose lands had been Crown Dependencies for centuries be subjugated by the Nazi regime?

The alternative would be to evacuate the islands and transport their people to the UK. Yet, with a combined population of nearly 100,000, could this actually be done? Would this mass of evacuees then become more 'useless mouths to feed', joining the thousands of others who had already fled from the Blitzkrieg on Continental Europe for the relative safety of Britain. These were difficult questions and decisions that had to be faced and made by the UK Cabinet, Island Governments and every man and woman in the street – and, in those dark days of May and June 1940, they needed to be made quickly.

For the Islanders themselves, the main conundrum was whether they should stay and hope for the best. If the Germans did arrive, what could they expect? The official guidance when it came, perhaps confusing at times, or simply confused through the nature of the prevailing situation, was to keep the islands running, but also, to safeguard the future, that women, children and men of military age were to evacuate. This, though, led to even greater heart-wrenching dilemmas. How could parents send their children away, husbands their wives, and wives their husbands? Conversely, how could they afford not to? Truly difficult times.

The *Luftwaffe*'s bombings of the two principal islands followed and left no one in doubt as to their fate – the enemy was on the doorstep and about to kick the door wide open! How would these foreign troops treat the population on the first, and, as it transpired, only, bit of British soil to be captured?

This for me as a Guernseyman was an important story to be told and for many outside the Islands is a little known story. I myself grew up with a very keen interest in history which was sparked by my grandfather who was the first president of the Guernsey Ancient Monuments Committee, a position he held for thirty-three years. Visits to military installations and museums were a regular occurrence for me. In the 1980s I joined the Channel Island Occupation Society, through which I came to discover what I would describe as 'living history'. I consequently spent many hours talking with people who lived during the German Occupation of the Channel Islands, and from that time I set out to research and record the Second World War history of this part of the British Isles.

There are many scores of books that have been written on this subject and although that history is being expanded and modified as our knowledge increases, the basic story remains unchanged. That story came from the mouths and pens of those who lived through the occupation, the ordinary men and women whose everyday lives were suddenly and irrevocably changed; through the politicians who had to make the, inevitably, invidious decisions and through the newspaper reporters who could freely comment and criticize.

Rather, therefore, than add just another book to the list with my own interpretation of the German invasion, I have sought to relive the drama of those difficult times through the first-hand accounts of those who were there. Only they really knew what it was like to be forced to decide whether to leave behind everything for the safety of the mainland UK or stay and be occupied by the enemy. Only those who endured the indignity of occupation by enemy forces can describe its resultant fears and frustrations.

By replaying the events of the summer of 1940 in this fashion I hope merely to lay before readers the facts about those difficult days and enable them to draw their own conclusions, and allow them to consider how they might have responded in such circumstances.

A tremendous amount of work has been done in the Islands to record the period of the German invasion and start of the Occupation in various ways and I consider the work done by the Channel Islands Occupation Society to record the previously unknown stories and uncover long-forgotten or lost documents and papers, to be of invaluable importance.

It is now more than seventy years that have passed since the evacuation and invasion of the Channel Islands but the interest in what happened increases each year. It is hoped, therefore, that we can continue to tell the story of the rest of the German Occupation of the Islands right up to their eventual Liberation in May 1945 in a series of other books and allow those voices from the past come back to life to tell their stories for future generations.

Simon J. Hamon
Guernsey, 2015

1

'We knew our turn was coming'

The Channel Islands on the Front Line

When the world was plunged into war in September 1939, few could have predicted that the Channel Islands would, in less than a year, be on the very front line between Britain and Germany. Consequently there was little provision for the Islands' defence.

Guernseyman Ralph Durand, who lived through the occupation, wrote after liberation of how the measures taken by the States of Guernsey to defend the Island were, when compared to the subsequent German efforts, somewhat 'ludicrous'. He went on to add:

> In August 1939, while there was still hope that war might be averted, they ordered four guns – two 4.7 guns for coast defence and two Light Anti-Aircraft guns – but cancelled the order after the war had actually broken out. The last of the four guns could not have been delivered until eighteen months had elapsed, by which time, it seemed probable, the Royal Regiment of Artillery would be too busy to be able to spare instructors to train Guernseymen in their use. It was decided instead to concentrate only on providing adequate protection against low-flying aircraft by means of Lewis guns.
>
> Obviously the States' military advisors considered that our danger of attack from the sea was remote and all that we really had to fear was mere nuisance raids from aircraft. For attacks of that kind we needed fire-fighters and stretcher bearers more than soldiers, and the men of the Royal Guernsey Militia – conscripted by immemorial custom for the defence of the island – were released so that they might volunteer for more active service overseas. Their place was taken by a Defence Force – still, however, to be called the Royal Guernsey Militia – consisting of five officers and one hundred men, all over military age or otherwise unfit for active service, who lived in their own homes and were allowed to undertake part-time civilian work on

days when they were not on duty as sentries guarding the oil depot, the telegraph cable and other vulnerable points.

All other defence measures adopted by the States during the first eight months of the war were of the nature of air-raid precautions.[1]

The arrangements for the transfer of men from the Militia and the organising of the new defence force was the subject of a memorandum written by Major (Staff Captain) N.R. Blockley, on behalf of the Major-General Commanding Guernsey and Alderney District, at Fort George, the Military Headquarters. Dated 5 February 1940, the report stated:

Sir, I have the honour to inform you that it has proved impossible so far to fix a definite date for the transfer to units of H.M. Forces of those members of the Royal Guernsey Militia who have volunteered for service overseas. I had hoped that the transfer would be complete by the 28th of January but it now appears unlikely that these men will leave the Island before the 15th of February or perhaps even later.

Those men who did not volunteer were released from their Militia duties on the 28th January, and I am pleased to say that practically all of them have secured civilian employment.

It will be remembered that the Militia Budget for 1940 made provision for the present Militia to remain embodied throughout January and for the reorganised Militia to take over their duties for the remainder of the year, but you will doubtless agree that, in view of the virtual impossibility of obtaining work for an unpredictable but very brief period and of the importance of maintaining the standard and esprit de corps now prevailing, it would be unfair, and inexpedient from a military standpoint, to discharge temporarily to civilian life Militiamen who have volunteered for active service and are awaiting orders to proceed on such service. I therefore propose that, they should remain embodied until the date of their departure.

During the period from the 28th January until they leave the island they will continue with their present duties, and it will not, therefore, be necessary to embody the new Militia until about a week before the end of the period. As the expenses of the present force even when reduced to the 120 men who have volunteered are considerably greater than will be those of the reorganised Militia, it is doubtful whether the total Budget vote for 1940 will completely cover the cost of the Militia for the year and I should therefore be obliged if the permission of the States could be sought for the expenditure of:-

a) any surplus (estimated to be approximately £500) from the Budget Vote for January:

b) an amount to be submitted to the States at a later date when it has been possible to calculate it accurately, to meet the increased expenditure consequent upon the retention of volunteers from the Militia until they leave the Island for service with H.M. Forces.

Leslie E. Roussel lived in Guernsey. He had married in June 1939 just before the outbreak of war and a year later had a baby boy:

In June 1940 the German forces were sweeping across France. My youngest brother Gerald was studying law at Caen University in France at the time. He had to leave suddenly because due to the German advance the university had to close down, so he straightway came back to Guernsey. The first of June heralded a cut in petrol rations to all car owners, and it was agreed to have one meatless day per week.

On June 3rd a curfew from 10 p.m. to 6 a.m. was introduced. This was for all inhabitants except those of British and French nationalities and in order to enforce this more thoroughly armed guards were posted around the island. The next day our new Lieutenant-Governor Major General J. Randell Marshall Ford C.B., D.S.O., M.C. arrived.

On June 5th the growers were asked to refrain from sending flowers. This was due to lack of shipping and two days later potatoes were not allowed to be dug for shipment. On June 14th an appeal was put out for volunteers, as farmers urgently needed help for harvesting.

Four days later the axe came down on entertainment. All theatres, cinemas and other places of entertainment which included dances were closed down. The next day, June 19th, German forces who had still been making headway across France entered Cherbourg. Guernsey people had their first taste of refugees, 120 of them in six small boats from France.[2]

The curfew recalled by Leslie Roussel was also announced to the British public, indeed the world at large, in *The Times* of 3 June 1940, confirming that,

In the Royal Court of Guernsey on Saturday the Lieutenant-Governor was given powers to impose a curfew for Guernsey, Alderney, and Sark if this should be desirable. Guernsey is to have one meatless day a week.

The Channel Islands' economy at that time depended heavily upon its produce. Predominantly for Jersey it was potatoes and in Guernsey it was tomatoes – the renowned Guernsey 'Toms' – although other crops including flowers were all exported. The disruption caused by the war was likely to create considerable problems for these exports and so 'extraordinary' measures had to be taken. On 5 June, W.E. Poat of the States Office on Guernsey, completed a report entitled 'Emergency Measures for Shipment of Produce':

> The States Committee for Horticulture is much concerned with the present difficulties regarding the transport of the island's tomato crop to the mainland. Early in the year the Committee had considerable correspondence with the Great Western and Southern Railways, and as a result, they evolved a scheme which, provided no extraordinary circumstances arose, would have dealt with the export, of tomatoes in a satisfactory manner. It is most unfortunate that, almost at the peak period, the ports to which produce is normally consigned are congested in such a manner as to cause delay in dealing with produce. It is also unfortunate that the peak period for early potatoes should coincide with that of the tomatoes, particularly in view of the fact, that potatoes must be given priority of shipment by the Railway Company's cargo boats, thus lessening the amount of space available for tomatoes.
>
> To deal with this difficulty the Guernsey Growers' Association has successfully arranged for some emergency boats to load for ports other than those served by the Great Western and Southern Railways. But in doing so it is necessary for the Guernsey Growers' Association to guarantee a specified amount of freight or make up the difference. The Guernsey Growers' Association has only a limited fund at its disposal for this purpose. In addition, the Guernsey Growers' Association, which is doing admirable work for the industry, does not include amongst its members all the growers of the island. The Committee feels that the States will agree that this is an island matter and therefore requests that you will be so good as to invite them at the earliest opportunity to grant the Committee a credit, not exceeding £2,000, to enable it to take the necessary steps to secure sufficient boats to deal with the extraordinary shipping difficulties now occurring, and furthermore, to grant the Committee powers to enable it, if necessary to compel growers to transfer to the emergency boats goods consigned to the markets served by such emergency boats.

An early indication of just how desperate the situation was likely to become on the Islands was when refugees from France began to arrive on Guernsey, as Ralph Durant described:

> On May 26th, two French fishing-smacks came into St Peter Port densely crowded with men, women and children refugees from Le Havre. On June 13th three more arrived containing sixty-nine refugees including elderly men, women and children in arms. They were in a pitiable condition of semi-starvation, as owing to persistent calm weather it had taken them no less than three weeks to come under sail from Boulogne.
>
> They had at first intended to go no further than Cherbourg but when they neared that port it was being heavily bombed, so they altered course for Alderney which they had reached on the previous day, and where they had been given money, food and – what they needed more – water.[3]

E.V. Clayton was one of the servicemen facing the threat of invasion on the Channel Islands in the spring of 1940, his unit being posted to Alderney from Guernsey:

> I did not take my camera with me to the islands in 1940, unfortunately. I rather think there was a ban on the use of cameras round military establishments. However, I will try and give you some idea of what life was like at that time.
>
> Our first impressions on landing in Alderney in January 1940 were rather grim. As we staggered ashore from the *Joybell* on to the small jetty in Braye Harbour, most of us under the influence of 'mal de mer'. We found ourselves faced with the long walk to Fort Albert in the drizzling rain. Our luggage went ahead in an ancient army truck circa 1918. I found myself eventually with about twenty other unfortunates in a barrack room in the fort, furnished with iron frame beds, and lit with hanging oil lamps which reminded me of such a room described by P.C. Wren in his book of Foreign Legion life, *Beau Geste*.
>
> There was a Lance Corporal in charge of the room, and its occupants. An old Regular who had served in India at some time, and showed it! His manners and attitude were to say the least basic. We were a motley bunch, from all walks of life, and social backgrounds. The old sweats of the Regular Army had never met chaps like us at close quarters before, and it was a startling experience for both sides.

As you will know, the forts, built in the 1850s, when the French were the main threat, had been disused for many years. Workmen came in daily trying to bring the interiors more to modern standards. The plumbing left a lot to be desired. Showers were icy and this was the coldest winter for forty years. Electricity was to be installed both at Albert and the other forts, but the work was so slow that even when we eventually left [Fort] Tourgis in late May to move to Guernsey the current had not been switched on. No doubt Jerry got the benefit when he arrived the following month.

If the accommodation was basic, the weapons and equipment that the men were supplied with was little better, as Clayton noted:

The rifles and Vickers machine guns we were trained on were all of First World War vintage. We had a few Bren guns which were new. During our second month on Alderney we underwent the M.T. (Motor Transport) Course at Fort Arsenal. There was a great dearth of army vehicles to train on, so a few civilian cars were obtained for training purposes.

I recall my first lesson was on an elderly Flying Standard and I very nearly ran out of road going round the sharp bend near Whitegates. Later I managed to have a go on one of the few Bedford 15cwt trucks which were beginning to trickle in from the mainland. Incidentally, after we had moved on to Guernsey quite a large shipment of 15cwt Bedfords arrived. This was early in June, and less than a fortnight later I heard they were all pushed off the jetty at Alderney after having their engine blocks smashed with sledgehammers. Even then I suspect Jerry would salvage quite a lot of useful parts.

Entertainment in Alderney was sparse. Apart from the pubs 'Rose and Crown' and 'The Divers', I think there was the W.V.S. tea room. I remember there was a young lady called Wilma serving tea and buns. I think she worked for the little Alderney Airline. There was a kind of cinema rigged up in a church hall at weekends. We used to attend church parade in the splendid church in St. Anne's, built of Caen stone. I became very interested in the history of Alderney, and John Le Mesurier the last Governor, and the privateers which used to operate from there.

On Sunday afternoons my friends and I were fond of walking round the island, especially the harbour and cliffs. Sadly, some of those chaps are now buried either in North Africa or Italy. Others I have met from time to time and the talk often turns back to those days of many years ago now.

When we arrived back in Guernsey on Saturday 18th May 1940 and unpacked our kit bags in Fort George it was a pleasant surprise to find the easy discipline which prevailed after the hard training we had undergone in Alderney. My room in Lower Lines had a pleasant view across to Sark, and I used to watch the tidal surges around the rock on which stands the Anfre Beacon. The sea was always blue at this time, and it was incredible to think that across the water in France the last of the B.E.F was being evacuated from Dunkirk.

We saw the black smoke rising from the direction of Cherbourg. Small boats were arriving from France into St. Peter Port harbour. As I described we were maintaining guards on strategic places around the island but it was only a token effort. Our heaviest weapons were Vickers machine guns and they were few in number. No ack ack [anti-aircraft guns] such as Bofors were available. Any German landing at that time would have succeeded within hours.[4]

Living on Guernsey, Winifred Best also recorded the disturbing scene from across the water on the French coast as she looked out towards the island of Herm:

The whole sky was black like the middle of the night! Mixed with this were flames. Cherbourg was on fire! By 4 pm the whole island was in darkness, I will never forget it.[5]

With the British Expeditionary Force being driven back towards the Channel coast, there was mounting speculation about the situation of the Channel Islands, which might soon find themselves quite literally on the front line. On 23 May, two days after the fall of Brussels, Frank Johnson wrote the following which was published in the Jersey *Evening Post*:

We are told that Jersey is the last place the Nazis would attack. It is of neither economic nor strategic importance [but] so far from this being the case, I think – nay, I am sure – that the exact opposite is true, and that at the present juncture on part of the Empire is in greater peril.

Just try to imagine the tremendous effect on the morale of his people, were Hitler able to tell them not only that he had commenced to attack England, but that the oldest part of the British Empire – Jersey – was in German hands. He would proudly point to it as the

7

beginning of the end, the break-up of the Empire … And as I see the position at present, based on this fatal self-complacency, it would be as easy as the proverbial 'falling off a log'.

With the Germans now just a few miles across the water the future of the Channel Islands looked decidedly bleak. R.C.F. Maugham lived on Jersey at that time:

Meanwhile, greatly perturbed, the anxious Jersey people and the equally disquieted residents, awaited with unconcealed misgivings what the future might hold for them. Many, without loss of time, quitted the Island; but the great majority held back until the arrival of some authoritative disclosure of the intentions of His Majesty's Government. Would the Island be defended? That was the vital question which exercised all minds.[6]

One person at least had no doubt what would happen. That person was Ebenezer Le Page, who lived on Guernsey:

Well, when we saw the clouds of smoke in the sky from the Germans blowing up things across the water in France, and boatloads of French came over with horrible stories of what the Germans was doing to them, I reckon we all knew our turn was coming. There was some fools who thought the Germans wouldn't bother about little Guernsey; but I have never been one to hope for the best when the worst is staring me in the face.[7]

For Ralph Durand, the arrival of refugees from Cherbourg, as well as the subsequent fall of the port itself, undoubtedly meant that the writing was on the wall for the Channel Islands:

Up till now, probably, some Guernsey people had taken more interest in local football matches than in the progress of the war, but the pitiable condition of some of these refugees made even the most apathetic and the most illiterate realise that the war and its horrors were coming very near to us and there spread throughout the island a vague feeling of uneasiness that was felt most acutely by those who understood it least.

To those in authority it was obvious that the fall of Cherbourg, which brought this island within forty-five miles of German occupied aerodromes, had materially increased our danger from air-raids. But few people as yet, even among those best qualified to form an opinion, feared anything worse than occasional air-raids.

It was true that the authorities had taken steps – ridiculously inadequate steps they now seem in view of what happened later – to deal with attempts at invasion by air-borne troops, but these precautions the average man regarded in the same way that one regards a fire insurance policy – a provision against a possible but by no means probable event. This optimism was based on the well-grounded belief that under modern war conditions the island was of no military value. The average man failed to realise the great importance that the Germans would attach to the prestige derivable from the possession – however ingloriously won – of one insignificant fragment of the British Empire, and he had no means of knowing to what extent Britain's power to defend the island had been weakened by the enemy's invasion of Normandy.[8]

It was evident that no firm policy had, at that stage, been formulated by the British War Council, as R.C.F. Maugham explained:

In the meantime, the Jersey States authorities, faced for the first time by problems of unexampled magnitude and complexity, lived from day to day in a condition of nervous uncertainty.

Meeting after meeting took place. The harassed chairman of the Committee of Island Defence propounded and carried into effect without let or hindrance (for nobody knew what steps to take) such immediate precautionary measures, a number of perfectly harmless old gentlemen, who would have been much better in bed, spent many hours nightly, in all weathers, guarding gasometers, reservoirs, electrical generating stations and other insular and municipal undertakings from – they knew not what! A body of men largely drawn, I believe, from the Jersey Militia and ranks of the British Legion were placed under the command of long-retired, somewhat aged army officers and drafted to various so-called key-points or danger-zones into which the Island was divided.

These men, I am told, apart from the Militia, were armed with a variety of miscellaneous firearms, but what orders they received, or were instructed to do with their weapons, I never learned, and I consider it extremely doubtful if they did. In any case, they certainly did not spare themselves, and I feel sure that, in so far as they understood them, they carried out their duties conscientiously to the end.[9]

2

'No strategic use'
The Demilitarisation of the Channel Islands

The Channel Islands were, in essence, Britain's most southerly outpost in northern Europe and RAF Guernsey served as an advanced striking base following the withdrawal of the RAF from France.

When Italy joined the Axis and declared war on Great Britain on 10 June 1940, the Channels Islands also played their part. Within hours of the Italian declaration, for example, the airfield on Guernsey was used as a staging post for a raid by Bomber Command aircraft on an aero-engine works in Turin. Islander Bill Green later recalled how he gained advance knowledge of the mission, the source being an RAF Avro Anson pilot, Gerry Smith, who, based at RAF Guernsey, rented a house from Bill's family:

> One day Gerry told me, very confidentially, that there was going to be a heavy raid that night on Italy, mounted from our airport. The information was so confidential that hundreds of people went up to the airport to give a Guernsey welcome to the R.A.F. flying crews as they relaxed on the grass waiting for the 'off'. Thirty bombers landed during the afternoon and were due to set off that night to raid the Fiat works in Turin.[1]

In total, eighteen Armstrong Whitworth Whitley bombers were refuelled on Guernsey, both on the way out to Italy and on the way back on the night of 11 June. Because of engine trouble and bad weather many of them had to cut short their journey and return to Jersey. Mr Charles Roche was the airport controller:

> Then the CO asked if we had airport lights. We had, I replied, but could not use them as the whole Island had been in a state of blackout

10

for months. He gave me an order to switch them on as the airport was a military one, he said. So I switched on, but within two or three minutes a very angry Lieutenant-Governor was on the phone ordering me to turn them off as I was inviting the whole Island to be bombed by the Germans. I managed to get the CO to talk to him and the lights remained on![2]

The raid was discussed in a meeting of the War Cabinet held at 10 Downing Street, on Wednesday, 12 June 1940:

It had been arranged that 12 of our bombers should attack targets in North Italy from the south of France and a further 36 from this country. The latter had, as arranged, refuelled at the Channel Islands. When these aircraft were already in the air, Air Marshal Barratt had received a message from General Vuillemin asking him to call off the operation on the grounds that the French Government objected. Air Marshal Barratt had replied that the operation had been agreed to by the Supreme War Council, that the aircraft were already in the air, and that in view of the lack of warning it would be impossible to comply with the French Governments wishes.

Air Marshal Barratt had telephoned to Major-General Ismay, and through him had received instructions from the Prime Minister that the operation was to be carried out. A protest had subsequently been received from the French Commanding Officer in the South, and Air Marshal Barratt had again got in touch with Major-General Ismay, and had again received from the Prime Minister instructions to carry out the operation. The twelve aircraft which should have taken off from French aerodromes had been prevented from doing so, as lorries had been driven across the airfield.

The 36 aircraft which had refuelled at the Channel Islands had been unfortunate, 14 of them had developed engine trouble and had been forced to land in France, a most unusual occurrence. In this case the trouble appeared to have been due to petrol, and though it was possible that a bad consignment had been used, there was also a possibility of sabotage. The remaining 22 bombers had run into appalling weather, and only five of them had reached their target, on which they had dropped their bombs, though no report of the results had yet been received.

All but four of the 36 aircraft were now accounted for, and it was not certain that all these four had been lost. The majority were dispersed over France. One aircraft had definitely been lost. The decision of the Supreme War Council on this question was quite clear;

while there might well be another explanation, the French action suggested that there might be an understanding between them and the Italians not to take offensive action against one another.[3]

With French attitudes to Britain clearly stiffening following the evacuation of the British Expeditionary Force from Dunkirk, the safety of the Channel Islands was now a question that had to be considered. This was the subject of a detailed report completed by the Chiefs of Staff Committee which was presented to the War Cabinet at the meeting on the morning of 12 June. The report read as follows:

1. We have examined the strategic importance of the Channel Islands in the light of the present situation.

2. Strategic position of the Islands: There are four main islands located as follows

   Distance from the French Coast 10 - 30 miles

   Distance from Portland. 60 - 90 miles

   Distance from Dieppe 130 - 160 miles

3. There are cable-landing points on both Guernsey and Jersey and a repeater station at St. Helier, while in certain places on both islands the cable runs along the shore. This cable is at present of great importance as it is the only telephone cable link to France. The cable lands in France at Pirou (immediately east of Jersey) and then runs via Rennes to Paris. Instructions have already been sent to the District commanders to provide for its protection against sabotage in the Islands.

4. There are aerodromes on both Jersey and Guernsey Islands. The former is used by the Admiralty for training and the latter accommodates the No.1 School of General Reconnaissance of the Royal Air Force. In addition there are many sheltered bays with sandy beaches suitable for the landing of troop-carrying planes. The harbours of the Islands will give complete shelter only to light craft. [Note there was also an airfield on Alderney.]

5. Possession of the Islands would give Germany air, and possibly M.T.B. bases which might be used for the development of an attack on our lines of communication and bases in France, the Western Approaches and our southern coastline, or on Eire. The establishment of any such bases would, however, necessitate the provision of strong defences against attack by sea or air and to establish these a seaborne expedition would be required. Moreover, the enemy's line of communication would be extremely hazardous.

12

6. If the Germans advance further west and a battle develops for possession of the Cherbourg peninsula, the aerodromes in the Islands might be of operational value to us; but their value to the enemy would hardly be sufficient to justify him in the effort needed to capture and use them purely for the purposes of this battle. Similarly, the harbours, though, in these circumstances, they might be used by our small craft, would not be of sufficient value to the enemy for him to attempt to capture them. Should the enemy occupy the Cherbourg peninsula, the Channel Islands cable route would cease to be of value.
7. Should the Germans succeed in occupying the whole north coast of France, the Channel Islands could evidently not be held by us for long; but under these conditions they would no longer be of value to the enemy who would have many better mainland harbours and aerodromes available. On the other hand, it is inconceivable that the Germans would occupy the adjacent mainland and leave the Islands untouched.

There was still clearly some hope that the French would be able to hold the Germans' advance and a second expeditionary force had been despatched to France under Lieutenant General Sir Alan Brooke to support the French and co-ordinate the movements of the large number of British troops that had been left behind after the Dunkirk evacuation. The rapid collapse of the French forces, however, did not bode well and the possibility of the Germans seizing control of France's eastern seaboard had to be seriously considered:

Scale of Attack
8. If the enemy should decide on the occupation of the Islands, he could in existing circumstances land an overwhelming force in troop-carrying aircraft, and there is little we could do to interfere with his initial action. He might also be able to transport troops in fast motor boats. Once in occupation, however, the difficulties of maintenance, though not insuperable, would make his position precarious. It is doubtful therefore if Germany would think it worthwhile to attempt the occupation of the Islands.
9. Germany might well attempt a raid, however, with the objects of:
a) destroying the cable to France; (b) striking a blow at our prestige by the temporary occupation of British territory.

Military Forces in the Islands
10. On the outbreak of war the Militia were embodied both in Jersey and Guernsey (the smaller Islands of Alderney, Sark and Herm are

dependencies of Guernsey). The Guernsey Militia was disbanded in January, 1940, and the present forces in the Islands are as follows:-
Guernsey and Alderney District
The 341st M.G. Training Centre (1500 men) is located in Alderney. This force, combined with the R.A.F. personnel at the training school in Guernsey, is adequate for the protection of the cable and the defence of the Islands against minor raids.
Jersey District
The only defence in this Island consist of some 150 men of the Jersey Militia, who have a proportion of Lewis guns and some 250 rifles. There is also a party of 50 naval ratings at the Fleet Air Arm aerodrome. These latter are only partially trained and may be removed. A local Defence Force against parachutists is being formed some 500 strong, but rifles will not be available locally for more than half this number. There are also small detachments of Royal Engineers in Guernsey and Jersey, and one Army Technical School, for boys in Jersey.
11. There are no coast defences or A.A. guns in the Islands and no considered appreciation for defence is believed to exist.
12. Acts are about to be passed which will render all male inhabitants liable for military service; those of suitable age and fit for service overseas, in the ranks of United Kingdom military forces, and older men and those unfit for service abroad in units for local defence.

It is interesting to read that the Chiefs of Staff Committee saw that the Islands might be occupied by the Germans with the object of 'striking a blow' at British prestige, but thought that this would only be temporary as they would find the maintenance of a force on the Islands difficult. This, of course, did eventually come to pass but not until much later in the war.

Course of Action Open to Us
13. It appears that the following courses of action are open to us: a) To provide the full scale of defence required to prevent the capture of the Islands. With the forces at present at our disposal this is clearly out of the question. (b) To provide forces from the United Kingdom to to [sic] secure the Islands against minor raids; but in no circumstances to involve ourselves in a commitment to reinforce the garrison; we should, therefore, be prepared to evacuate them ultimately. (c) To limit the defence of the islands to local resources. Existing resources are not at present sufficient to defend the island against minor raids. This

course would not ensure the safety of the cable and would not afford a reasonable measure of protection to the local inhabitants. (d) To demilitarize the Islands. This might have unfortunate repercussions on the French. We might be accused of exposing the French Northern flank to a further scale of attack from bases in these Islands. This would no longer apply if the German advance reached a position on the mainland adjacent to the Islands.

14. In addition, the evacuation of the civil population of approximately 100,000 must be considered. The objections to this are: a) The shipping problem would be considerable particularly in the face of probable air attack against which we could not afford to provide fighter protection. (b) We have already too many useless mouths in the United Kingdom. (c) The inhabitants may very well be unwilling to evacuate.

In spite of these objections, we consider that it is our duty to give a reasonable opportunity of voluntary evacuation to those who wish to leave the Islands. This should be done at once since we cannot contemplate the evacuation of large numbers of civilians under heavy air attack.

Having considered all of the above points, the report completed by the Chiefs of Staff Committee included a summary of the situation:

15. To sum up:

(a) The Channel Islands are not of major strategic importance either to ourselves or to the enemy.

(b) They are of minor strategic importance for the following reasons: (i) The only telephone cable to France runs via the islands. (ii) We might require the aerodromes if the German advance penetrates further west. (iii) Germany might make use of the Islands for air and M.T.B. bases. Note: These reasons would cease to exist when the enemy advance reaches the adjacent French coast.

(c) On strategical grounds measures to ensure the security of the Islands against all possible scales of attack would not be justified at the expense of our commitments elsewhere. It is, however, desirable that we should secure the cable as long as possible.

(d) The Islands are no longer safe for training establishments.

(e) We are under an obligation to provide for the reasonable security of the Islands against raids and we feel it is our duty to make available facilities for voluntary evacuation of at least some of the population.

It is obvious that the Chiefs of Staff Committee did not want to commit resources to the Channel Islands which they saw as being of little military value to the UK and, if occupied by the enemy, of no real threat to Britain's security. Equally, there was no desire to evacuate the entire population of the Islands as that would only add the large number of 'useless mouths' consuming valuable resources. The following were the conclusions the COS Committee:

> Action to be taken:
> 16. Accordingly we are arranging:- (a) To despatch immediately two battalions, one to Guernsey and one to Jersey. (b) That after the establishment of (a) above, he [*sic*] should immediately withdraw all training establishments. (c) That preparations should be made in conjunction with the Ministry of Home Security and the Governors of the Islands, for the destruction of all facilities which might be of value to the enemy (e.g. aerodromes and oil stocks), and for the ultimate withdrawal of the garrison if necessary.
> 17. We recommend that immediate consideration should be given by the Ministry of Home Security and other departments concerned to the desirability of offering facilities now for the evacuation of all women and children on a voluntary and free basis. If evacuation on these lines is decided upon, it should be made clear that persons not availing themselves of this offer will not be evacuated at a later date.[4]

The report was discussed by the War Cabinet. The future of the Channel Islands and its people hung upon the decision of the ministers:

> The Chief of the Air Staff explained that, although the Channel Islands had no great strategical importance, the Chiefs of Staff considered that a certain measure of defence should be provided for the two main islands, and therefore had taken steps to send immediately one battalion to Guernsey and one to Jersey. They had arranged for the Prime Minister to be informed of this proposal, but there had not been time to get his formal approval. The Chiefs of Staff had, however, acted in anticipation of it.
> The Minister of Home Security said that he would like to consider, as suggested in paragraph 17 of the Report, whether facilities should be offered for the evacuation of women and children from the islands on a voluntary and free basis. As a first step, he would consult the Lieutenant-Governors. At first sight he was inclined to think that the true inhabitants of the islands would not take advantage of such an

offer, and that the well-to-do settlers could afford to make their own arrangements to leave if they wished to do so. If there should be a desire on behalf of the islanders to be evacuated, the matter was one to be organised by the island authorities.

The War Cabinet (1) Approved the Report by the Chiefs of Staff Committee. (2) Gave covering approval to the orders already given for the despatch of one battalion to Guernsey and one to Jersey. (3) Agreed that, when these battalions had been established, all training establishments should be withdrawn from the islands. (4) Invited the Minister of Home Security, in consultation, as might be necessary, with the Service Departments, to initiate preparations for the destruction of all facilities in the islands which might be of value to the enemy. (5) Took note that the Minister of Home Security proposed to consult the Lieutenant-Governors as to the provision of facilities for the evacuation of women and children from the islands.[5]

The situation in France was deteriorating by the hour with French resistance collapsing. News had also reached London on 12 June that the 51st (Highland) Division had been trapped on the French coast at Saint-Valéry-en-Caux, a small seaside town and holiday resort twenty miles west of Dieppe, and forced to surrender.

With the Germans now just a few miles from the Channel Islands the idea of sending troops to Jersey and Guernsey, units that might suffer the same fate as the 51st (Highland) Division, had to be reconsidered. The decision to send battalions to the Islands had been made at 11.30 hours; by 17.00 hours that pronouncement looked questionable:

> The Secretary of State for War said that the War Cabinet had been informed at their meeting that morning that the Chiefs of Staff were making arrangements to send two battalions for the defence of the Channel Islands. He would like to reconsider the matter in the light of the new situation, and would put his views before the War Cabinet.[6]

If no front-line battalions were to be sent out to Jersey and Guernsey they could not be defended by the limited forces on the Islands. That being the case, there seemed little point in maintaining any military presence. The subsequent decision making process on 12 and 13 June was outlined in a secret 'Memorandum by the Chiefs of Staffs' issued on 18 June 1940:

At the 162nd Meeting of the War Cabinet on 12th of June, 1940, the War Cabinet gave approval for the despatch of two battalions to the Channel Islands – one to Guernsey and one to Jersey. At the 163rd Meeting on the same day the War Cabinet took note of the fact that the Secretary of State for War wished to reconsider the matter in the light of the new situation ...

On reconsideration the Chiefs of Staff at their 178th Meeting on the 13th June decided to recommend to the War Cabinet that the two battalions should not be sent, and that owing to the imminence of the occupation of the French coast it would be better to demilitarise the Islands, and to prepare for the destruction of facilities which might be of value to the enemy. Before this recommendation could be put to the War Cabinet it became apparent that it was necessary to use Aerodromes in the Channel Islands for the protection of the evacuation of the B.E.F. from Brest and Cherbourg. Thereupon orders were given to re-distribute the troops in the Channel Islands, and to reinforce the defence forces with one battery of light A.A. guns ...

The Chiefs of Staff now consider that the policy as to the defence of the Islands when it is no longer required to use the aerodromes should be decided upon.

Their recommendations are:

(i) That all regular British troops should be withdrawn from the Islands.

(ii) That the local forces which remain should be given the role of internal security (including anti-sabotage) only.

(iii) That preparation for destruction of the facilities which might be of value to the enemy, and which he could not equally well obtain on the mainland, (e.g, oil stocks) should be made to be carried out in case of invasion.

(iv) That as the Islands will have been demilitarised it will be unnecessary and undesirable to evacuate women and children, and that the Minister of Home Security should be so informed.

(v) That orders should be issued to the Lieutenant-Governors not to defend the Islands in the event of enemy invasion by sea or air ...

We consider that effect should be given to these recommendations immediately the aerodromes are no longer required. This situation may occur almost immediately.[7]

Following the completion of Operation *Dynamo*, the Dunkirk evacuations which concluded on 4 June, a series of further withdrawals followed. These included Operation *Cycle*, the evacuations from Le Havre, and further evacuations from other ports under the code name of Operation *Aerial*. On 15 June 1940, preparations for the latter began, resulting in a limited two- or three-day operation to evacuate nearly 140,000 remaining troops, vehicles and supplies from Cherbourg, Granville, St. Malo, Brest, St. Nazaire, Nantes, La Pallice and the Channel Islands.

On 17 June the passenger ship *Brittany* arrived in Guernsey and sailed the same day for Southampton with RAF personnel from the School of General Reconnaissance on board – these individuals consisting of thirty-six officers and 136 airmen. *Brittany* sailed that afternoon and arrived in Southampton the following morning.

However, such was the state of flux at that time, whilst some military personnel and equipment was being evacuated from the Islands, more was arriving. On 17 June, for example, *Train Ferry No.1* arrived in Jersey loaded with Government stores; her sister-ship *Train Ferry No.3* was due to sail from Southampton with Bofors anti-aircraft guns for Jersey and Guernsey, but it was apparent by then that, due to the speed of the German advance, the guns would only be installed for a mere twelve hours before the remaining RAF units would be pulled out, so the ship sailed late, on the 18th, without the guns.

Also at dawn on 18 June, the coaster *Fairfield* arrived in Jersey from St. Malo carrying RAF ground staff and stores from 17 and 501 squadrons – their aircraft were flown from Dinard to Jersey on the 17th. These now Jersey-based fighters continued to carry out patrols in the Channel Island area and the Cherbourg Peninsula during the final stages of the evacuation from the latter, which fell to the Germans on 18 June. The fighters stopped patrolling the Channel and evacuated to the British mainland on 19 June. The ground staff and remaining stores left the same day on *Train Ferry No.1* and arrived in Southampton on 20 June.

It was on 19 June that Islander A.C. Robins, a Guernsey resident, made the following observation regarding the military withdrawal in his diary:

> Day of rumour and general unrest ... Evacuation of military commenced during afternoon. The noise and clatter of lorries, the marching of troops continued all through the night; above this din could be heard what sounded like the smashing of glass in Fort George. Impossible to sleep, got up at 5.30 and saw several companies of troops marching down Val-des-Terres to their ships.[8]

At about the same time that the RAF fighters withdrew from the Channel Islands, *Brittany* also left for Southampton carrying students from the Army Technical School, Jersey non-combatants and their families, and general army stores from both Jersey and Guernsey. In addition *Train Ferry No.3* sailed from Guernsey with all remaining RAF personnel from Nos. 23 and 64 Fighter Service Units and the School of General Reconnaissance – three officers and 133 airmen in total. The tanker *Guidesman* also berthed at St. Sampson, Guernsey, and took on board all remaining stocks of military fuel, sailing to Plymouth the same day.

On the day that Cherbourg fell, the fate of the Channel Islands was being considered in a 'secret session of the Royal Court' on Guernsey, wrote Ralph Durand:

> The British Cabinet was then in session debating whether to defend the Channel Islands or to disarm them, and from an early hour an official of the Home Office at the London end of the telephone wire and Mr. L.A. Guillemette, the Bailiff's Assistant Secretary, at the Guernsey end of the wire, were busy transmitting discussions between the British Cabinet on the one hand and the Royal Court of Guernsey on the other hand as to the fate of the island.
>
> The outcome of the discussion was revealed under pledge of secrecy to a few people in the island who were in key positions but it was not known to anyone else until three weeks later when those of us who listened to a B.B.C. broadcast on July 11th learned that, in a statement made to the House of Commons, the Secretary had said that he had offered to arrange for the total evacuation of the Channel Islands, that the Channel Islands Authorities had said that probably many of the inhabitants would be unwilling to evacuate and that, nevertheless, transport for all who wished to evacuate would be provided.[9]

The question of defending the Channel Islands was further discussed by the War Cabinet on 19 June after receiving the Memorandum by the Chiefs of Staff recommending the adoption of a policy of demilitarisation of the Islands as soon as the aerodromes on them were no longer required:

> The Prime Minister said that it ought to be possible, by the use of our sea power, to prevent the invasion of the Islands by the enemy and that, if there was a chance of offering a successful resistance, we ought

not to avoid giving him battle there. It was repugnant now to abandon British territory which had been in the possession of the Crown since the Norman Conquest.

The Vice-Chief of Naval Staff pointed out that the material necessary for the defence of the Islands was not available. It was impossible to provide the anti-aircraft guns and fighter aircraft which would be required for this purpose, without denuding the essential defences of the United Kingdom. The Islands were too far away from our shores and too near the enemy-occupied bases at Brest and Cherbourg for an effective use of naval forces to prevent invasion by sea.

In reply to a question, the Chief of the Air Staff explained that the 'destruction of the facilities,' referred to in paragraph (iii) of the Chiefs of Staff recommendations, included the mining of the aerodromes, which would render them unusable for a period, though not permanently. It was doubtful, however, whether these landing grounds would be of value to the enemy for an attack on this country.

This decision to demilitarise the Channel Islands was not at first announced to the Islanders as a whole, as Ralph Durand noted when writing of the occupation of Guernsey in 1946:

It was apparently at ... [this] time that our local authorities were informed of the British Government's intention to demilitarise the Island, though official notification did not arrive until later. Whether it was necessary to pledge to secrecy the few who were informed of this intention it is impossible for an outsider to judge, but there can be no question that the general public would have been spared much painful anxiety if an official announcement had been made not only that the Island was to be disarmed but especially that the British Government's object in taking this step was to spare us from the ruthless bombardments that were to be expected if troops and munitions remained here.

In any case the secret could not be kept from anyone who happened to be on the White Rock that evening, if he had eyes to see and a brain alert enough to draw conclusions, for harbour officials, dock-workers and the crowds that normally frequented the harbour on fine summer evenings saw lorry after lorry loaded with munitions drive down to the ships' loading berths. Those who knew why these munitions were being returned to England could give no explanation for they were pledged to secrecy, and in consequence a rumour spread

21

that troops stationed in the Island were leaving us and that the Island was to be abandoned to its fate; and that fate – for lack of an official reassurance on the subject – would be, in the fevered imagination of many, a fate such as that from which the refugees of Boulogne and Le Havre had fled. Thus were sown the seeds of widespread unreasoning fear.[10]

Repugnant or not, the prospect of the Germans invading the Islands had become a very real one. This, in turn, brought into consideration the fate of the Islanders. The evacuation of the Islands had been mentioned as early as 12 June. Now, a week later, the subject was even more relevant:

> The Secretary of State for the Home Department and Minister of Home Security said that the attitude of the Island Governments was that they felt bound to acquiesce in the policy of abandoning active defence, but were most anxious to organise the evacuation of their women and children. This was not recommended by the Chiefs of Staff, but it was doubtful whether it would be possible to continue to feed and supply the whole population. In his view, if it were decided that the Islands could not be defended, the least that we could do would be to give the inhabitants an opportunity of leaving. All arrangements would be undertaken by the Island Governments, who would bear the cost entailed in the evacuation measures.
>
> General agreement was expressed with the view that this country could not refuse to receive British subjects evacuated from the Islands in these circumstances.
>
> The Secretary of State for Foreign Affairs said that, distasteful as the decision would be, especially as it gave the enemy an opportunity of claiming that he had occupied British soil, he (the Foreign Secretary) could not see that the Cabinet could well reach any conclusion other than that proposed by the Chiefs of Staff.
>
> The War Cabinet (a) Approved recommendations (i) to (iii) and (v) set out in paragraph 3 of the Chiefs of Staff Memorandum (W.P. (40) 208). (b) Did not approve the suggestion in recommendation (iv) that it would be unnecessary to evacuate women and children from the Islands. (c) Invited the Home Secretary to inform the Island Governments that we would be ready to receive in the United Kingdom such of the inhabitants of the Channel Islands as the Island Authorities wished to evacuate to this country, under arrangements to be made and financed by them.[11]

It may seem remarkable to us today that the Islanders were expected to finance their own transport to the UK (though this was never widely carried out). What must be considered, however, are the numbers involved. There were, as we have seen, around 100,000 people in the Islands and if all of these chose to leave an enormous strain would be placed upon Britain's resources at a time when the country as a whole faced an uncertain future. The prospect also of the ships packed with civilians being attacked, as the Chiefs of Staff Committee feared, was a frightening one. The fewer who travelled, the less was the likelihood of the ships being bombed and, as the Chiefs of Staff observed, it would mean less 'useless mouths' to feed at a time when rationing was already in force.

Having finally decided to demilitarise the Channel Islands, the British authorities sent three ships to evacuate the last of the military personnel and stores. Subsequently, on 20 June, the passenger ship *Biarritz* sailed with approximately 1,000 men on board, whilst the Island-based vessel *New Fawn* left Guernsey for Southampton, and the passenger ship *Malines* and the cargo ship *Hodder* departed from Jersey. *Malines* headed to Weymouth; *Hodder* first to Weymouth before continuing on to Southampton carrying the 150 active service members of the Royal Jersey Militia. This completed the withdrawal of military personnel and stores from the Channel Islands.

With the situation rapidly changing, on 21 June the States of Deliberation, the Guernsey Parliament, met in order to streamline the government of the Island, as Bill Green later recalled:

[It had been] decided to set up an Emergency Controlling Committee under the Presidency of A.J. Sherwill, His Majesty's Procureur. In practice what was created was a new form of government for Guernsey, with Ambrose Sherwill taking on the role of Prime Minister. He quickly appointed seven members to the Committee, each with responsibility for a particular Department. The island was now run by a Cabinet of eight islanders, with the authority and ability to make quick decisions. In the circumstances which prevailed at that time, speed was of the essence ...

It was a very strong team which was to serve the island well during the occupation. I regarded Ambrose Sherwill as a man of sound judgement with the ability to make speedy and decisive decisions. Ambrose with his typical legal approach, liked twenty-four hours to mull over a matter, before he made a decision, but when made, it was sound and solid. It is often said that the occasion produces the man, certainly Ambrose Sherwill was the man for the occasion.[12]

Having made the decision not to defend the Islands, on 24 June 1940, the Bailiffs of Jersey and Guernsey received a message from King George VI:

> For strategic reasons it has been found necessary to withdraw the Armed Forces from the Channel Islands. I deeply regret this necessity, and I wish to assure My people in the Islands that, in taking this decision, My Government has not been unmindful of their position. It is in their interest that this step should be taken in the present circumstances.
>
> The long association of the Islands with the Crown and the loyal services of the people of the Islands have rendered to My Ancestors and Myself are guarantees that the link between us will remain unbroken and I know that My people in the Islands will look forward with the same confidence as I do to the day when the resolute fortitude with which we face our present difficulties will reap the reward of victory.[13]

Frank W. Falla was a journalist on Guernsey employed by *The Star* newspaper. After the war he would recall the wording of the letter that accompanied the King's message when it was sent to Guernsey's Bailiff by John Anderson:

> Sir, I am commanded by the King to transmit to you a message from His Majesty for communication to the people of Guernsey in such a manner as may seem to you advisable having regard to the interests of national security.[14]

It may have been the last words of this letter that led to the Island authorities making their decision, but, as Falla goes on to state when referring to the King's communication, 'we never saw it':

> At no time did the Bailiff, Sir Victor Carey, or members of the Controlling Committee, think it necessary to tell the people the contents of the letter … I think without doubt that the public should have been informed of this message. Although it is obvious that the British Government knew we would be occupied, at least the message

seems to wish us 'Good Luck'. I don't think we would have felt quite so deserted if we had been allowed to receive it.[15]

The decision to demilitarise the Channel Islands was not accepted of by everyone, especially Lord Portsea who stood up in the House of Lords to declare his disapproval:

The islands mentioned in my question have, up to this, always defended themselves, and have done so for many centuries, although they are in the jaws of a very powerful nation which has generally been hostile to us. Very frequent attacks have been made on them. The island that interests me more than the rest of the archipelago is Jersey. Jersey has never been occupied by a foe except in the case of Cromwell, who sent Admiral Blake and 81 ships and 5,000 men to subdue it. It was only after a great fight and many weeks that the island commander surrendered on the most honourable terms possible. This gave the islanders an idea, which is one that is, fortunately, difficult to shake, that they could, with assistance, at any rate, defend their land. They had in those days, and even in my day, a Militia in which service was universal, obligatory, and unpaid, between the ages of 16 and 65. I am one of those who served at the age of 16, though I regret I cannot now pass myself off as being under 65.

Their drill, if it would not have altogether satisfied the Brigade of Guards, would, at any rate, have reached the standard of a well-known person, and that is Brother Boer, because they were all trained in the use of a rifle, and there were 3,500 of them. They believed they were safe, and they sent all their young men to the war, just as they did in 1914. This morning we were much relieved to read the gracious words of His Majesty, and we derive a great deal of comfort from these words and from that promise. It is a promise that I can say no effort of ours will fail to supplement with all that we have and hold.

The islanders, as I say, thought themselves safe, and, protected by even a small portion of the greatest Fleet in the world, they believed they could have held the islands because, they said, 'If we – England – cannot defend these islands, how can the Germans hold them?' That is a difficult question to answer. Guernsey is further away from the French coast than Hythe or Dover, but one of the reasons given for the evacuation is that they were only a few miles from France. That kind of reason or excuse did not satisfy the islanders. They paid no attention to it. They gave their money and their men to the war. One islander, a rich man, has given £125,000 of his own money to the British Government – not lent it, but given it. They have given their all in blood and treasure. Troops were poured into Jersey from France, and two days later they were all evacuated. The policy was reversed, and the chance was given – and it was only a chance because there were very few ships – of the population being evacuated. I am glad to say there were very few islanders, comparatively, who were prepared to leave their country at the mercy of the Germans.

The islanders at once understood the full meaning of demilitarisation. They found it was a very near relative of abandonment, a breaking of ties that were more than 800 years old, a breaking of ties with the Crown of over a thousand years.

In the debate which followed, Lord Mottistone, a former Secretary of State for War, added his views, which concluded with this statement:

Since I last addressed your Lordships I have spoken to a distinguished officer who won the Victoria Cross in the last war. He said, sadly, 'To think that we sacrificed, more than once, 10,000 men to save one line of trenches in France and yet did not fire a shot to save the Channel Islands.'

The process of demilitarising the Channel Islands took many forms, some of which were acts undertaken at a local level – as the events surrounding some War Trophies from the First World War, presented to the people of Guernsey, testifies.

It was in 1921 that Guernsey received its share of the Allies' spoils of war. The list of items received included four 13.5cm Kanone 09 artillery pieces, two trench mortars, two anti-tank rifles, two machine-guns, a gas gong, six steel helmets, two sets of body armour, an entrenching tool, six rifles, three bayonets, twelve 'Pistols Illuminating', three carbines, and a field gun of unspecified calibre.

On 23 February 1922, a report recommended that the four 13.5cm guns, the two trench mortars and the field gun should be placed on display in the gardens of Victoria Tower in St Peter Port. Located on the opposite side of the road to the Arsenal, the gardens already contained two Russian cannon, trophies of the Crimean War.

After two decades of the guns being on display with no maintenance and in frequently damp conditions, particularly at the western end of the gardens which are normally in shade, the wheels of two guns placed that end of the garden had started to collapse. As children often played on the guns, the potential risk of injury was considered too great and in 1938 the decision was made to call in a local scrap merchant who was asked to dismantle and remove the two western guns.

With the swift advance through France of the German forces and following the withdraw of all military personnel from Guernsey, the States became concerned that the two remaining 13.5cm Kanone 09 guns would be seen by enemy aerial reconnaissance aircraft and misinterpreted as active artillery. They chose to hide them by simply burying them, and consequently large sloped pits were dug in the centre of the gardens and the guns pushed in to the holes and covered over. There they remained throughout the Occupation, the Germans utterly unaware of their presence![16]

Returning to the events of June 1940, the decision to demilitarise the Channel Islands was communicated to the people of Jersey in the *Evening Post* of the 19th of that month under the headline, 'A Grave Decision':

> A decision of the most vital importance to the island was taken today by the British Cabinet and announced to the States of Jersey this afternoon by His Excellency the Lieut.-Governor.
>
> This island is not to be defended; it is to be completely demilitarised and declared an undefended zone. The reasons governing this decision are the concern of His Majesty's Government, and we may rest assured that the most profound attention was given to every aspect before it was decided to take this step. We believe there to be no reason at all for panic; the government of the island will go on, and everything will be done to ensure the smooth working of the administration. Keep calm, obey the regulations issued by the authorities and carry on, as far as it is possible, with one's ordinary business. We believe we can offer no saner or sounder advice.

Likewise, by the evening of 19 June the demilitarisation of the Channel Islands would also be common knowledge on Guernsey. That day the Guernsey newspaper the *Evening Press* carried the following announcement on behalf of the Bailiff, Victor G. Carey:

> I am instructed to inform the people of Guernsey that the Government of the United Kingdom has decided that the Bailiwick is to entirely demilitarised.

Accordingly, the Royal Court hereby gives instructions for the immediate demobilisation of the Royal Guernsey Militia and of the Guernsey Defence Volunteers.

Arms, uniforms and equipment are forthwith to be handed in at the Town Arsenal under arrangements to be made by the Officers Commanding the Royal Guernsey Militia and the Guernsey Defence Volunteers, to be disposed of in accordance with the instructions of the Officer Commanding Troops Guernsey and Alderney District.

All ranks of the Militia and all members of the Guernsey Defence Volunteers will then proceed quietly to their homes.

All other persons in possession of firearms must forthwith hand them to the Constable of their Parish who will take immediate steps to have them transported to the Town Arsenal.

The London Correspondent of *The Star* duly wrote the following report which was then telegraphed to his editor for publication:

Friday night: It was officially announced that the Channel Islands have been demilitarised. The Home Office stated that, in view of the general occupation of parts of France nearest to the Channel Islands, it was decided to demilitarise the islands.

All armed forces and equipment have already been withdrawn.

A military expert writes: 'The Government's decision to demilitarise the islands need surprise nobody familiar with the map. The German occupation of Northern France has deprived the islands of any strategic value they might ever have had. In peace-time the garrison of the whole group consisted of no more than a single regiment. Since the islands are of no strategic use to Great Britain – or for that matter to Germany – there was no further need for their continued fortification which might only have exposed the inhabitants to unnecessary danger from German bombardment.

The demilitarisation, it was pointed out in London last night, is somewhat analogous to declaring Paris an open city.

There need be no fear, military experts declared, of the Germans taking advantage from the British decision to quit. The Nazis could no more hold positions on the islands than we could defend them.[17]

How wrong those military experts were! No-one knew what lay ahead for the Channel Islands and its people. With demilitarisation the Islands might be able to sit quietly aside from world events, or maybe it had opened the door to invasion. Jurat John Leale of Guernsey wrote of this:

The British Government had decreed that the stern demand of that time had made it necessary to throw open the Island to the German invader should he care to come. We stood on the threshold of events not only previously undreamed of by any of us, but unprecedented in our history.[18]

3
'Vague, unspecified dangers'
The Evacuation of Guernsey

Though the Islands were demilitarised, no decision had been taken on evacuating the civilian population. Charles Markbreiter, who was the Assistant Military Secretary at the Home Office, had to consider the consequences and feasibility of a wholesale evacuation:

> Despite the possibility that the Islands may come under German Occupation, I think there are grave objections to any policy of inviting and encouraging the islanders to leave. Apart from the difficulty of absorbing them here, there is the consideration that we might have in the end to adopt some measures of compulsion, because those remaining would be too few to sustain a communal life. Tell Mr Sherwill that we think the present policy must be maintained of encouraging the population to stay.[1]

Despite Markbreiter wishing that the Islanders should stay put, the possible evacuation of Guernsey's schoolchildren was discussed by its Education Council at a meeting held on Monday, 17 June 1940. The following is an extract from the minutes:

> After a very full discussion it was resolved:-
> (a) To support a policy of evacuation of school children should such a course be recommended.
> (b) To advance the summer holiday of the Primary School children and to close all Primary Schools at once for a period of four weeks.
> (c) To close the Intermediate School Kindergarten for a similar period.
> (d) To inform teachers in those schools that they were not to leave the Island without permission.
> (e) To allow private schools of more than thirty pupils to open only if the Commandant A.R.P. approved of their precautions against air raids.

An announcement was made in the Guernsey *Evening Press* on 19 June that the United Kingdom government would provide ships to evacuate women and children, men of military age (i.e. 20-33 year-olds) and, if room allowed, other men. The announcement went on to list the items of clothing that should be taken by children and when, where and how they should report, as well as advising parents as to what food they should provide:

> Arrangements are being made for the evacuation of (1) children of school age and (2) children under school age to reception areas in the United Kingdom under Government arrangement. The evacuation is expected to take place tomorrow, the 20 June, 1940.
>
> The mothers of children under school age will be allowed to accompany their children. Parents of school children are to attend at the school attended by their children at 7 p.m. today to notify their willingness or otherwise for the evacuation of their children.
>
> IF PARENTS DESIRE IT
>
> Parents of children under school age who desire their children evacuated must give the name and address of such children to the Rector or Vicar of their Parish by 8 p.m. today. The Rectors will prepare lists accordingly and will transmit them by 10 p.m. to the Bailiff's Office.
>
> Other persons (other than men of military age) desirous of being evacuated must register their names and addresses with the Constables of their Parish at the Parish Douzaine Room as soon as possible and at latest by 8 p.m. today. All men of military age, i.e. from 20 to 33 years, who desire to be evacuated must register their names and addresses with the Constables of their Parish at the Parish Douzaine Room by 9 p.m. They are very strongly urged to do so.

For those children whose parents' agreed to let them be evacuated, the *Evening Press* announcement went on to detail the 'Articles to Take':

> Children should take with them on evacuation the following articles: Gas masks. Two ration books (current and new one). Besides the clothes which the child will be wearing, which should include an overcoat or mackintosh, a complete change of clothing should be carried. The following is suggested:-

GIRLS	BOYS
One vest or combination.	One vest.
One pair of knickers.	One shirt with collar.
One bodice.	One pair of pants.

31

One petticoat.	One pullover or jersey.
Two pairs of stockings.	One pair of knickers.
Handkerchiefs.	Handkerchiefs.
Slip and blouse.	Two pairs of socks or stockings.
Cardigan.	

Additional for all - Night attire, comb, towel, soap, face-cloth, toothbrush, and, if possible, boots and shoes and plimsolls. Blankets must not be taken.

Signed by Victor G. Carey, Bailiff of Guernsey, the announcement concluded by specifying the food to be given to the travellers:

Rations for the journey: Sandwiches (egg or cheese); Packets of nuts and seedless raisins; Dry biscuits (with little packets of cheese); Barley sugar (rather than chocolate); Apple; Orange. Parents of children to be evacuated must attend at the school attended by their children at 9 a.m. tomorrow, the 20th June, to receive instructions as to the final arrangements to be complied with.

Parents of children under school age will attend at the Parish School of the Parish in which they reside at 10 a.m. tomorrow, the 20th June, to receive similar instructions. Persons willing to accompany evacuated children as helpers should give their names and addresses to any headmaster or headmistress. It will not be possible, on account of the danger of air raids, to permit masses of people to congregate at the harbour and accordingly parents must say au-revoir to their children at their homes or at the Schools. The public will not be permitted to approach the harbour.

Transport to the harbour will be provided as necessary. On registration for the evacuation of children or adults, it must be stated whether or not financial provision can be made for the maintenance of the evacuee in the United Kingdom and whether or not the evacuee can go to a relative or friend there and the name of that relative or friend must be given.

'Before these announcements were published,' wrote Ralph Durand, 'those responsible for the evacuation of the school children had already set to work, in great haste but with admirable forethought, coolness and efficiency':

They had not been taken by surprise, for two days before a sub-committee of the Education Council had already made such carefully thought-out preparations for the evacuation of school children – if such a step should be decided on – that they had even printed for distribution to parents a leaflet reminding them that the children must take their gas-masks and ration-books, and offering sound advice on the subject of what clothes were most essential and what form of food would be most suitable for a long journey. When therefore, on the morning of June 19th, the sub-committee was summoned to the Royal Court and – after being pledged to secrecy – asked to make all preparations for the evacuation of the school children, there was little for them to do except wait for further orders.

They did, however, summon all the head teachers in the Island to meet at 2 o'clock that afternoon. To these – still under the pledge of secrecy – the situation was explained and they were told that if evacuation were decided upon, they and their assistant teachers would be expected to accompany the children to the reception areas to which they might be sent.

After an anxious period of waiting for further instructions, a message came from the Royal Court that all children whose parents wished it were to be evacuated and that the matter need no longer be kept secret.

That message had been sent out at about 16.00 hours on the afternoon of 19 June. As Durand noted, 'there was much to be done and very little on which to do it'. He continued:

A first contingent of two thousand children were to be assembled by 4 o'clock next morning ready to be taken to the White Rock for embarkation on three ships due to arrive before that hour. The head teachers had to disperse to their respective schools, summon the children's parents and ask them to decide at once whether to send their children away to an unknown destination or keep them under the shadow of an undefined danger that might or might not materialise.

By 9 o'clock that evening they had to inform the Education Office how many children had been registered for evacuation so that it could organise means of transporting them and their luggage to the harbours. In addition to this, voluntary helpers had to be enlisted as it had been decided that no one adult was to have the immediate care of more than fifteen children. As they dispersed the school teachers' hearts must have quailed somewhat at the thought of how much they had to do in so little time.

'That the work was done – and done very efficiently – is proved by the result,' continued Durand, though he went on to add 'To have done all there was to do without a hitch would have been almost miraculous, and the miracle did not happen'. He explained further:

> By 4 o'clock in the morning no less than nineteen hundred children and their escorts were ready to embark, but the first of the promised ships had not arrived and did not arrive until 10 o'clock, so that the children, who can have had no proper breakfast and little sleep during the previous night, had to wait on the jetty for six weary hours. Then three ships arrived in quick succession.
>
> The first two took fifteen hundred and ninety-one children but the third was a collier with no accommodation for passengers better than a choice between the holds and the open decks and the Education Authorities were reluctant to send on her, for a voyage that must inevitably take seven or eight hours, children already overtired with excitement and loss of sleep. They therefore persuaded the Sea Transport Officer to exchange the collier for a vessel, normally used for the transport of produce, which, though now a cargo vessel, had been built for passenger traffic. This vessel sailed at half-past two in the afternoon with the remainder of the waiting children.

Thankfully, according to Durand's account at least, there 'were no more serious hitches', though 'there was sometimes cause for anxiety':

> As for example when, the tide being very low, it was necessary in the dim half light of the dawn to embark from the lower berth of the quay, which was very slippery, some seven hundred children who were only half awake. And the work required of the Education Office staff continued to be difficult and complicated. So far as was possible it was arranged that children embarked on ships that made the journey at night should be drawn from secondary schools who were of an age to endure discomfort better than infants. It was desirable not to summon children from their homes – in some cases from their beds – sooner than was necessary, but on the other hand it was imperative that the ships when they arrived should not be delayed.
>
> Military Staff Officers who have to arrange the transport of troops do not find it a very simple matter but they at any rate have to deal with men who are not asked whether or not they wish to be transported. The Education Office staff were handicapped by the fact

that not only was evacuation voluntary but also that the parents of the children to be evacuated were apt to change their minds several times in as many hours according to whether the last irresponsible person with whom they discussed the advisability of evacuation was an optimist or a pessimist.

Such indecision was trying for the staff but criticism of the parents would be unjust. It was not easy for them to decide whether to send their children to an unknown destination for an indefinite period of time in charge of school teachers and volunteer helpers who, however kind-hearted and trustworthy, were not bound to them by any ties of blood; or whether to keep them at home under the shadow of vague unspecified dangers which might never materialise. Yet the decision had to be made in a few hours and once the child had gone it could not be recalled.[2]

On 20 June, the *Evening Press* reported on the 'Evacuation Scenes', the additional headlines stating that the 'town thronged with people':

The scenes in the town this morning will never be forgotten by any Guernseyman. Thousands thronged the narrow streets, making last minute arrangements prior to evacuation.

Throughout the night school children have been leaving.

This morning crowds besieged the banks long before opening time and the registration centre at the Constables' Office attracted another huge throng.

Everywhere people were asking the same question: 'Where shall we go?' and none could answer. Nevertheless cheerfulness was the keynote of the throng. Good-byes were said with a smile and Sarnians strode on about their own business.

Nowhere in town could a suitcase be purchased. Many shops closed their doors, as it was found that although it was easy enough to dispose of their goods, no money was forthcoming.

On the quays lorry-loads of tomatoes and produce were being distributed. Everyone was busy and worried, but nowhere was there any sign of panic – nothing but anxious, but orderly, queues.

The feeling of uncertainty which was developing across the Channel Islands as June 1940 progressed is vividly portrayed in the diary maintained by the Reverend Robert Douglas Ord. On 19 June he made the following observations:

Is Guernsey to be an 'Open Town'? Much concern on this point. Everyone is asking what it implies. The local papers have headlines 'EVACUATION OF CHILDREN: PARENTS MUST REPORT THIS EVENING'.

There is little time to make the necessary arrangements. Names must be handed in by 8pm to the parish Rectors, who must then prepare and submit within two hours full lists to the Bailiff's office. Evacuation is planned to take place tomorrow. Mothers of children under age are told that they may accompany them. Persons of military age are urged to register by 9pm. Some 1500 have already left the island. Others must register with the Constables – the chief elected officers of Guernsey parishes – if they wish to go to England. Particulars of clothing and rations for evacuees are set out in the papers. Inevitably there is confusion and in some quarters a tendency to panic. The community has sustained a sudden and unprecedented shock, which reports of Nazi conduct in Occupied Territories do nothing to lessen.

Whilst the Islands' civilian populations were considering their options, the military was still withdrawing. 'Demilitarization goes ahead at high speed,' noted Reverend Ord the same evening:

Soldiers, sailors and airmen are moving down to the harbour continually, causing further dismay by recklessly driving of vehicles. The official declaration of demilitarization has been issued tonight by the Bailiff:

'I am instructed to inform the people of Guernsey that the Government of the United Kingdom has decided that this Bailiwick is to be entirely demilitarized. Accordingly the Royal Court hereby gives instructions for the immediate demobilization of the Royal Guernsey Militia and of the Guernsey Defence Volunteers. Arms, uniforms and equipment are forthwith to be handed in to the Town Arsenal ... All ranks of the Militia and all members of the Guernsey Defence Volunteers will then proceed quietly to their homes. All other persons in possession of firearms must forthwith hand them in to the Constable of their parish who will take immediate steps to have them transported to the Town Arsenal.'

After the roar of the military vehicles, tonight will be much quieter, as, with certain exceptions, all cars are forbidden to roads from 10.30 pm to 5 a.m. Boatloads of refugees from Cherbourg continue to arrive with stories of blazing fires, fleeing inhabitants and a port in ruins. The local French Refugee Committee sped them on their way to what they hope will be safety.

To crown the day's anxieties, news has just come of heavy raids on the east coast of England. It all looks like the end of the world – of this little world at least.[3]

Bill Green read in the Guernsey *Evening Press* that an 'announcement' would be made at Victoria Pier that evening at 19.00 hours on the 19th regarding further evacuation details:

I wanted to hear what the arrangements were as my first priority was to get Mabs, Mum and myself away before the Germans arrived.

When I tried to obtain sailing tickets, I soon discovered that only if I was prepared to volunteer for the forces would I get a passage, but even then I would not be able to take Mabs and Mum. I did not want to join up, I wanted to go back to Armstrong Siddeley [in England where he worked] and that meant that I had no priority.

Mabs and I went down to the Victoria Pier to hear the announcement about the arrangements for evacuation. There must have been well over three thousand people milling around on the Esplanade and the Pier waiting for the announcement. We arrived there at 7 pm. and by 7.30 nothing had happened. By a quarter to eight there was still no sign of any speaker or announcement. We gave up and decided to walk up to the shop in Smith Street. When we arrived outside the Press Office there was a crowd, and Ambrose Sherwill was just starting to speak.

He said that he knew nothing about a meeting at Victoria Pier, but that he had been telephoned by the Press and told that there were crowds there and outside the Press office. He understood that they were expecting him to speak. Apparently Mr Sherwill had been working late, but immediately agreed to come and address the crowd outside the Press office, where the necessary equipment had been set up.

That response was typical of the man, he spoke for twenty minutes without notes and then offered to answer questions. I can clearly remember standing, leaning against Lovell's shop front with Mabs, listening to his speech.

'Evacuation,' he said, 'is entirely voluntary, I do not know whether we shall get many away apart from the children and those of military age.'

Mr Sherwill then stressed the need for everyone to keep calm.

'There have been signs that people had almost got into a panic, but we must all carry on as usual. The Bailiff, the Jurats and I are not going away at all, we are continuing our work and we will look after your interests. That there would be times of trouble ahead was possible. There will possibly be economic difficulties, there might be some difficulty over the food supplies, but hold your heads high like men and women,' said Mr Sherwill.

He explained that men of military age should volunteer for the forces and get away as quickly as possible. They, he said, would be given priority.

'Do you mean,' I called out, 'you want me to go and leave my family here?'

'Yes, that is what you are expected to do!' he replied through the megaphone.

'I am sorry,' I said, 'But I am not going to do what I am expected to do, I will go when I can take my family with me.'

Mabs and I went home and held a family conference with Mum. We decided that we would all be evacuated together as a family or not at all.

Within the matter of a few days the evacuation of children and men of military age had been completed and there were empty spaces on the boats.[4]

Six-year-old Tony C. Bougourd's family came to a similar conclusion as Bill Green's family – they would either leave together or stay together:

I can remember being sent off to school one morning as usual, but with a parcel of personal things and a luggage label attached to the lapel of my coat with my name and school written on it … We spent all day at school waiting to be taken down to the harbour to board the mail boat that would take us to mainland Britain. This seemed like a special treat, as I had never been on such a big boat. Nothing happened that day, however, and during the afternoon we were sent home with instructions to be at school at the usual time in the morning.

It then transpired that all the soldiers had been ordered to leave the island on the first boat out the next day, and mothers and children under school age were to leave on the next boat. Because of this, Dad decided that I should not go back to school in the morning, but should stay with Mum so that we could leave together as a family.

38

As it happened, Tony Bourgourd's family was able to evacuate almost all together, eventually reaching St Helens via Glasgow:

> Dad left on the morning boat. We left in the afternoon. I remember very little of the boat journey, although as it was my first trip on the mail boat, I wish I could remember more. I do know that we were packed down below the deck into a room that had two-tier bunks around the side.
>
> We stayed there for the whole trip, finally arriving at Weymouth at night. The soldiers that had left on the earlier boat had been ordered to stay in Weymouth to help with the refugees. By luck, one of Dad's mates, Len Dodd, who was helping at the docks, recognised Mum and managed to give Dad the news that we were there.[5]

One of the Island children was young Malcolm Woodland who was excited with the prospect of travelling to England:

> My mum had had a letter about what we had to take, so a small case was packed, and we had to go to school in the morning. We were going to go on a boat to England, and we would be billeted; and my parents would join us later. So we went off to school ... carrying sandwiches for the journey! We were supposed to leave about 10 o'clock in the morning but nothing happened, so come midday we started to eat our lunch. We were told we should not eat it all as we might need some for the journey. Any rate about 3 o'clock all the lunches had been eaten! I think they tried gas mask drill, we had assemblies in the playground, and about 4 o'clock we were told that the boats weren't in fact coming until much later. So I went home, went to bed, and the next morning when I woke up, it was sunshine, a lovely day, 'right, we're off back to school again, where's this boat?
>
> 'Well,' Mum said, you're not going.'
>
> 'What!'
>
> I was furious, I'd got my case packed, I was all labelled ready to go with my friends! And she said, 'No, they phoned at 4 o'clock in the morning and I went to look for you and I didn't have the heart to disturb you.'
>
> I didn't talk to her for the whole morning.[6]

Another young child was Jill Harris who became separated from the remainder of her family as they sailed for the UK:

Armed with our boarding passes and one small suitcase each, Aunt Ethel came to fetch us all in her car and we duly arrived on the quay. Unfortunately so had hundreds more with no means of getting away. During a long, hot day my Aunt's and my mother's imagination got somewhat overheated. 'You should come with us Ethel,' my mother urged her sister. Ethel thought perhaps she ought to, which came as a severe shock to Uncle Tom, at home and patiently waiting for his wife to get his lunch! 'You will never get on the boat without a child in your arms!' my mother announced dramatically. Ethel was inclined to agree and I was duly handed over.

At that moment the *Stork*, which until very recently had been used for transporting cattle, manoeuvred to the quayside, the gang planks were let down and the rush was on. Swept away in the tide of humanity, Aunt Ethel fetched up against the customs office, was still clutching me. When she had recovered her dignity and her hat, she was startled to hear a boat's siren and looking round, saw to her horror that the *Stork* was already in the harbour mouth and heading for England.[7]

In many families across the Islands there was much angst and deliberation, some of the latter often heated, surrounding the question of evacuation. Guernseyman Edward J. Hamel was a telephone engineer and so was in a position in which he heard lots of the conversations that were taking place over the telephone network across the Island:

'If you stay here, you'll have to work for the Germans' ... 'We're going to help Great Britain – she wants all she can get. Another said: 'Do you want your wife to live under German rule? – remember the reports from the countries which have already been occupied ... and so on, and so on. They had obviously given the matter considerable thought. Not one of them even mentioned home or possessions – welfare came first – the children's welfare.[8]

Roy Burton was born at the Roque a Boeuf Farm just opposite the little Fief Court House of St George on 7 June 1930. Aged nine when war broke out in Europe, he later vividly recalled the moment that war was declared:

We as a family, uncles, aunts, parents and grandparents, went up to Alderney on a day trip at the beginning of September on board the *Courier*.

On the way back, passing the Casquets Lighthouse, the Captain came over the Tannoy and said he regretted to have to tell us that Germany had declared war on Britain. And I have never seen so much panic as on this boat from that day until now. People with binoculars were looking out to sea and those without were asking what they were looking for. There was nothing to see. They said they were looking for submarine periscopes, because they were frightened to be torpedoed. But we got home safely.

In the months that followed, life for Burton 'came back to normal', interspersed with the odd moment of excitement. One main recollection from the Phoney War period was the fact that in December 1940, 'Miss Le Page, the Principal, sent letters home to say that she was giving up the school at Christmas, due to the fact that she didn't want the responsibility of the children should war come to Guernsey'. The beginning of the Blitzkrieg soon changed matters:

About May, there was talk of evacuation and there was always an aircraft flying over us every day. My young Aunt and Uncle, my Mum's twin sister and her young brother came to the farm because my young uncle wanted to evacuate and they wanted to take us two boys with them. There was a lot of commotion and arguing whether we could go or not.

I was in bed in quarantine with German measles or chicken pox and they were arguing below my bedroom window. I said to my brother to go to the stair window and tell them we want to go with uncle and aunt. But I forgot that the window had no sash cords and when my brother opened the latch, the window came down and squashed his fingers and he let out a cry.

My parents came running up the stairs to see what it was all about and to free his fingers. Mum came to me to my bedroom and asked why Len was at the window. I said he came to tell you we wanted to go with Aunt and Uncle. She said 'You are not going and that's the end of it'.[9]

Roy Burton was therefore amongst the many who stayed. Dr Alistair Rose was another. Some years after the war he recorded his recollections of that time:

I remember the wretched little school children standing for hours in queues on St. Julian's Avenue waiting to be evacuated. Some of them

41

did this for several days on end, and in some cases they then had to make their way home at night perhaps five or six miles away. I trust that the arrangements for feeding these poor souls was more satisfactory. One parent told me that he had longed to get his child away, but after several experiences of this kind, he could not bear to 'put his kiddie through it' any more, and so he had refused to let him go on the last occasion.[10]

There was clearly a breakdown in communication between the authorities and the Islanders which meant that many more people could have been evacuated than actually managed to get away, as Alistair Rose witnessed for himself:

> The scramble for the mailboats and evacuee ships had been terrible, and the authorities had warned us that only specified classes of persons need hope to be evacuated, so that I had almost given up hope of sending them away. Then, one evening I was talking to a colleague who calmly informed me that there was a ship almost empty in the harbour at that moment, which might be sailing at any time. I said, 'Has anyone been informed about this? 'Well,' said my colleague, 'the vicar told everybody he met, and has asked them to pass on the news.' I motored down to the harbour at once, and sure enough there was a large steamer at the quay, christened 'Princess Astrid'. She was capable of holding several thousand refugees.
>
> In fact, she sailed with only a hundred or two, including my wife and children on board. Outside the harbour were two more ships, which never even entered port. The rush was over, and these sailors had risked their lives on a wild goose chase. They were furious, and I heard one of them say that the Guernsey folk could whistle before they would return on a similar errand.[11]

Dr Rose put this failure to evacuate more people down to the fear that the Island was being depleted of key men in the stampede for safety, and 'possibly for selfish reasons employers who saw the possibility of trade booming feared they might lose their labour'. Dr Rose believed that 'it was decided to try to stop the evacuation by propaganda. Very wrongly, in my opinion, the population as a whole was accused of being "yellow", and was urged to remain.'

In this way many who had yet to make up their minds were induced to stay – people, Dr Rose claimed, that could have been more usefully employed on the mainland rather than remaining idle throughout the war under German occupation. He also later wrote that:

> People had tired of trying without success to get away, and by far the greater majority had no idea that the boats had come in. Had they been properly informed I believe it likely that those steamers would all have carried a full load. However, to return to the quay. I could get no information of the time of sailing, but managed to find a St. John's ambulance worker on duty at the dock, and asked him to phone me as soon as the *Princess Astrid* was due to sail. In the meantime, I panicked my poor wife and my mother into packing up, and I shall never forget the bitter scene that ensued. Nor can I blame my wife, for I have often felt that had I been in her place, rushed off into the blue with two young children aged seven and four, I should have felt as she did.

It must be stated that the aim of the authorities was to maintain a viable community on each of the islands which meant that wholesale evacuation would not have enabled this objective to have been achieved. Even so, the Islanders were presented with a terribly difficult decision. If they went to the UK they had no idea what the future held for them and it meant leaving behind not just possibly family and friends but also their property and most of their belongings – everything they had worked and saved for. The alternative was the likelihood of invasion and rule by German forces, with no certainty that the property they had stayed behind to protect would not be violated or sequestered. Some indication of the difficulty people experienced in making that decision can be seen in the account of Frank Stroobant:

> Firstly we were advised to register. Then we were told that an evacuation of the total population of the Island to England was certain. Next we heard, on reliable authority, that the wholesale evacuation would not take place; and some notices were displayed urging the people not to abandon the Island. But the notices did not help us, for some were official and the rest were not, and between the two the ordinary man got himself into a shocking tangle.
>
> At one moment I almost gave my business away; it was not worth much in those days. But the next moment I met a man who assured me that the Germans would not waste their time or troops in Guernsey. Passing on down the street I encountered friends as

puzzled as I, who asked me what I thought. I could not tell them, because I did not know what to think myself. As I left them, another man came running up shouting that total evacuation had been decided on.

I went home in complete bewilderment.[12]

With just a few hours to decide whether to leave the Islands or not meant that the first response of many families was to evacuate, but after further consideration they decided to stay, as Guernsey's Education Council noted:

Throughout the evacuation we were greatly handicapped by parents changing their minds. Actually 755 teachers and helpers had registered at the Vale and Torteval Schools but there were many withdrawals at the last moment and we were able to put 76 Alderney children aboard the *Sheringham* in addition to the local schools.[13]

Ambrose Sherwill, who was desperately trying to cope with the unprecedented situation he was placed in, received a phone call early on Sunday, 23 June from one of Guernsey's doctors with some terrible information – the Island must be completely evacuated. A meeting of the Island's doctors was called:

I met them at 11 a.m. The original convenor, who sat close to me, put forward an impassioned plea for a statement by them all that, for the avoidance of starvation, it was essential that evacuation of Guernsey should be total. Our partial evacuation operation had been completed and I knew that total evacuation was impracticable and moreover that, whatever hardships before us, it would be the wrong thing to do. I thought it impolite to express my view at the moment ... I suggested that this doctor should be sent by me to the Home Office to put the case advanced to me by the doctors and ask for total evacuation. I knew he would fail but said nothing of this.[14]

Dolly Joanknecht was a 15-year-old who worked as a nanny in St Peter Port. She lived in Guernsey with her great aunt. She was one of the many who tried to leave but was unable to:

I had two cousins and they both wanted to be evacuated to England, but my uncle didn't. I sat on the stairs, saying again and again 'I want to go.' My cousin Jack wouldn't go because his girlfriend wasn't going,

Aunty wouldn't go because Uncle wouldn't go, so they all decided I should stay. I tried to get in touch with my mother. I phoned her neighbours but they told me she had already gone with my brothers and sisters. I didn't know what to do; it was absolutely chaotic.

The next morning, I got up early and packed my clothes in a brown paper parcel – my cousins had already taken the suitcases. It was 5.30 in the morning when I left the house, and as I walked through St Peter Port to the harbour I tried to imagine what it would be like when all the houses were empty and the Germans were here. At the harbour I sat on the coiled ropes, watching the buses going by to the ships full of schoolchildren. Their parents were carrying all their belongings in pillowslips – they had no suitcases. I stayed until 11.30 a.m. but I couldn't see my brothers and sisters. On my way home I met my cousins and they demanded to know where I'd been. I told them, then my parcel broke and all my clothes spilled onto the street. I was crying as I tried to gather them up.[15]

Though he noted that by 21 June 'over 10,000 had already left by boat', Leslie E. Roussel had yet to make up his mind regarding whether to remain or evacuate:

I still had my car, a Morris Eight, which I had bought in 1936. I decided to go and see what was happening, by driving the two and a half miles from my home to the harbour known as White Rock.

When I got near it, instead of going to the harbour which may have been out of bounds, whilst things were being organised for evacuation, I drove up the hill which is St. Julian's Avenue. This Avenue leads away from the harbour and is about three hundred yards away from where the boats are docked.

People were lined up in threes, most of them sitting on their cases and the line stretched nearly to the top, all waiting to board the next boat to evacuate to England. Some looked very harassed, some looked very worried, but others remained calm.

With such a scene before him, Leslie was faced with the same painful quandary being faced by most people throughout the Channel Islands:

What decision must I make? I had most likely just hours to decide rather than days. I had married in 1939 (June) and had built a fairly large house in the north of the island, one that was modern for those days. I had a baby son just three weeks old.

45

My parents had made various enquiries about leaving the island, but had by then decided to stay. My two brothers had also decided to stay. They were both single and living with my parents, at Rosewood, the house my parents built in 1910. My wife's parents who were farmers and had one of the best herds of Guernsey cattle in the island naturally decided to stay.

Though so many members of his family had opted to remain on Guernsey and face whatever lay ahead, Leslie decided to take his young family to Britain. He was in the privileged situation of having a friend who had managed to arrange a job for him to go to:

Hastily my wife Bertha and I got two medium-sized cases ready. This was all we thought we were allowed to take for ourselves and the baby. Someone had arranged to pick us up and take us to the boat in a couple of hours' time ... Soon the cases were ready by the front door and this would have been half an hour or an hour before we were due to leave the house. Then the phone rang and the person who phoned worked as a Civil Servant in the town of St. Peter Port.

The conversation that followed had a profound effect on Roussel, so much so that he changed his mind on the subject of evacuation:

She gave me the information that all the Statesmen and people in authority had decided to stay. Posters were put up around the town advising people to stay in order to avoid total evacuation or too small a number staying. This was the wish of the British Government that we should continue to run the Island, come what may as well as possible.

The Bailiff made a stirring broadcast speech and received great ovation from the public. He advised everyone to stand firm. Time proved that this was the right decision to make on that day. I took this advice as sound and sensible so we stayed.

Mr and Mrs G. Attenborough were amongst the many who also elected to remain on the Islands, though, as in Leslie Roussel's case, this had not been their original intention. On 30 June 1940, the following entry was made in their diary:

It had been a glorious day with nothing more pleasing to do than sun bathe and watch with ever increasing anxiety the unending stream of shipping on the horizon making away from Cherbourg, Calais, or perhaps England. Great liners shining white in the sunlight, or battleships painted elephant grey, the morning sun, catching now and again reflections from some metalwork, caused bright light to flash as if some Morse message was being sent. Innumerable ships of all sizes, tonnage, and description had been passing incessantly seeking refuge from the coming calamity. This was all accompanied by the tense feeling of awe – for the booming of guns was now very persistent and ever growing nearer.[16]

It was whilst feeling 'that unfathomable something' that Mrs Attenborough 'footed my way up the hill' and headed into St Peter Port:

We went into the hotel and in a few moments broke the awful news. 'You must pack up your suit cases as soon as possible, not more than 28lb. weight is allowed. The women and children are having to register at the Town Hall. The first registered will be the first to go.' The order came out at 6 p.m., it is now 7.30 and we are 8 miles away …

Then there was the question of conveyance to get into town. This was soon negotiated by a few families clubbing together. Our particular car was the village fisherman's, an 8 h.p., with five people aboard and two suit cases piled on our knees. The discomfort was soon forgotten by holding in your breath for capacity sake and the anxiety to get in before the office closed at 10 p.m. …

On arriving at the Town Hall we found a queue of several thousands 4, 5, 6 & 8 deep, stretched over a mile. Hundreds of people were split up into groups – arguing, discussing – the tenseness of their faces spoke volumes. There were no signs of tears anywhere, there was no time, it was a case of clear the decks for action.

What was I to do? Torn between the anxiety of a near parting from my life companion, my home (my one great passion) and all I held dear: doubly so in the face of this terrifying queue and only one hour to go before the Town Hall closed its massive portals on a gaping crowd.

Before going to the harbour to try and board an evacuation ship, Mrs Attenborough went to her bank to draw out her funds:

As we passed the Westminster Bank at 9 a.m. great was our surprise to see a queue of well over 100 persons and there must have been the

47

same number at Lloyds. As the one I was making for was the depository of the not so big and the small investor I felt my heart sink at the prospect of a long wait with an east wind blowing down the narrow street direct to the harbour. Here there were two queues, one of about 150 facing east and another of about 30 from the opposite direction.

I, as you will appreciate, chose the shorter one. As the minutes rolled by so did the crowd roll up. As is usual with waiting crowds they start pushing to make things more compact and less comfortable. Everything would have gone on serenely if some 'jack-in-the-box' had not started a head-on queue, so that now on the bank portals were faced with a surging impatient and angry crowd of arrow formation, several hundred strong.

As the minutes ticked by and the time of opening approached a not too gentle pressure was felt on all sides, the head-on set having the greater power of resistance they acted as both a fulcrum and a wedge. At 10 a.m. dead on time, someone opened the doors. I was but 10 feet away from the entrance. The leaders of all three branches gave a mighty push, the door-keeper was swept off his feet, the doors were rushed and the inner swing doors kept ajar by the heaving mass. Many must have got in for the doors were closed for ages so it seemed. More men were placed at the door and allowed only ten people to enter at a time ... My husband attempted to relieve me in the queue but after half-an-hour he was on the verge of collapse and I had to make my long vigil of three hours having only moved a few feet.

Progressing agonisingly slowly, the queue that Mrs Attenborough was in was composed of mostly elderly people or women with prams and so lacked the strength to push its way forward against the head-on queue:

It is difficult to describe the attitude of these 'voyous' who regardless of crushed, screaming, fainting, and weeping women turned their shoulders to the crowd and literally mowed down the helpless. It took me over a week to recover from the experience of twisted limb and body. I attempted to give first aid, with smelling salts, to a very old lady who had lost all sense of direction and who was being pressed forward and backward. But once my arm was out of position I risked getting it smashed for I could not get it back.

Finally I was pressed in a flamingo attitude against a rather plump woman with a generous bust and there for a little while I found a haven of comfort. Kindly manly arms occasionally encircled me and I could only whisper a word of thanks over my shoulder. I shall never forget the experience of being humanly walled up alive.

After all her struggles, and those of the others, the bank only allowed each person to withdraw the relatively small sum of £5. It was during the long battle at the bank, and then on her way home, that Mrs Attenborough reached the conclusion that she would not evacuate after all. However, having decided not to leave, she thought she would go down to the harbour and watch the evacuation:

> For several days now the continuous groups of families either in cars, vans or pushing prams and bicycles to take the load, pass incessantly, always towards the harbours … we decide to take the same direction.
>
> Thousands of people are compressed behind barriers which close the entrance to the piers. These are the lookers on, who from their vantage witness the most extraordinary scene that has ever been seen in the history of the Island. The North pier is closed to all but those travelling. Within and without the gates well known farmers are sitting on the pavement with their belongings in sacks and suit cases, accompanied by their wives and children. A blazing hot sun at its zenith is adding to the miseries of those who out of precaution with double suits of clothing, greatcoat and raincoat …
>
> A pathetic looking woman is surrounded by seven children not yet in their teens, the babies are crying at the discomfort of the pitiless sun. They have been there several hours awaiting their turn to embark, their prams have been abandoned on the quay with hundreds of others; they have possibly been waiting since the previous day. Very old people sit patiently as old people can, broken hearted and dazed, their bewilderment is written on their wrinkled old faces. They have forgotten how to cry and have no tears to shed. Many are leaving the homes where their ancestors have lived for hundreds of years.

Bill Green also stayed to face the uncertain future that lay ahead for the Channel Islanders but, as he explained, he, along with most Islanders, really did not know what to do for the best:

> The air of normality that had descended on Guernsey was largely a result of Ambrose Sherwill and his colleagues being very successful

in re-establishing public confidence. Slogans like, 'Compulsory evacuation a lie!' 'There is no place like home!' 'Cheer up!' 'Keep your heads!' 'Don't be yellow!' 'Business as usual' were appearing and had their effect.

At one moment I was convinced that the Germans would be unlikely to be interested in our little island. Their target was Britain, not 'off the beaten track' Guernsey. If they were to come, I told myself, it would not be for some time and we would be able to get away. Then when I had convinced myself that I would stay, I thought to myself that the Germans were only just across the water in Cherbourg and they could be here in a matter of hours. I changed my mind time and time again and everyone I spoke to had a different effect on my thinking.

I met one of my friends in Smith Street and asked his opinion about leaving. He was very firm with his advice:-

'Don't talk so silly, the Germans won't come here, there is nothing for them to come for. My family and I are staying.'

Two days later I met him on Fort Road, pushing a pram packed with everything imaginable on his way with his family to the White Rock to catch the boat to England.

Another two days passed and I again met him, this time in the Jerbourg Road. I was surprised to see him as I thought that he and his family had left the island.

'I thought you had left us.' I exclaimed.

'Well' he said, 'on the way down to White Rock, we came across a number of people who were coming back and they said that it was no use going down there as there were no more boats. They said that they had heard that the people going to England are having to sleep on the beaches in Weymouth. They advised us to turn round and go back home, so that is what we did and now we are staying.'

I was totally confused.[17]

Frank Stroobant expected all men of military age to be shipped to the UK to join the British armed forces, not just those who had volunteered. Believing this, his next thought was therefore to ensure that his wife and baby daughter were also evacuated. Assembly points were established around the Island from where the women and children would be collected by bus. He followed the bus his wife and daughter were on down to the harbour:

The harbour was filled with shipping for the evacuation. Some ships had come straight from fulfilling their errands of mercy at Dunkirk to undertake another here. Their decks still bore the marks of what they had gone through.

Crowds, naturally, had gathered at the approaches to the harbour, and to avoid the confusion of fond farewells, barricades had been erected and only essential personnel and those who were to go were allowed inside them. I did not know this, and to bolster my own and my wife's morale I had not said my proper farewells at home.

When the buses had passed the barrier, I approached a constable on duty and told him I had urgent business in the harbour. To support this, while I spoke to him, I kept the engine of my van running. He may have believed me or he may not, but he let me through. His kindness, however, availed me nothing, for by the time I arrived my wife and baby were on board and all we could do was to wave forlornly to one another.[18]

Some on Guernsey claimed that they had been all but forced to leave the island, an issue which Charles Ammon, the Labour Member of Parliament for Camberwell North, raised in the House of Commons, reading a letter from one of those that had evacuated:

> Far from being 'voluntary' the evacuation was encouraged and ARP wardens went round (in my district at any rate) imploring the people to get out before they were blown out! We were told that the Jerries would be here in twenty-four hours and that the men would be taken to Germany to work as slaves in the munitions factories and as for our women – well, God help them!

Those who had made up their minds to leave found that the Guernsey authorities simply were unable to cope with the thousands of people that wanted to leave the Island. This was exemplified by the experiences of Mrs E. Simon who wrote about the evacuation in her diary entry of 19 June:

> Ethel, Eileen, Tony & myself went to town to buy groceries in the cou [sic], the town was in an upheaval, folks were really in a terrible state, saying the Germans would invade at once as we were declared an open town. We went to Beech Vale & they were all registering to leave the island, so Moonie came back with us to register at once at the Town Hall. I shall never forget the site in the Parade, thousands in a queue & we filed in but the Town Hall closed & we could not register after standing for a couple of hours. Ethel, Eileen, Tony and myself

were hoping to go to Scotland, the others did not know where they wanted to settle but certainly in England.

With events on Guernsey moving fast and changing rapidly, the next day Mrs Simon made the following comments in her diary:

> We went to register leaving here at 4.30 a.m. Moonie came down with us & we stood in the queue till 3 p.m. The Bailiff came & addressed us about midday, he said it was terrible to see the local people abandoning their homes & running away & that their duty was here. We decided we would register and see what we should do later ... The evening we went to Beech Vale & we had all decided we would stay & do our part.[19]

P. Girard was a teacher at the States' Intermediate School for Boys in Guernsey. He was at the school to assist with the registration:

> One particular couple really amused me in spite of the depression all around. The father, a farmer, accompanied by his wife, approached me and just as they reached my desk I heard the dear woman say, 'Well of course Bill, I can't possibly leave little Jim to go to England without me.' At this the farmer stopped dead and said, 'And you keep on saying that you are not going without me'. 'Oh! That's right Bill, we must stay together,' remarked his wife. At this Bill grabbed his wife and made for the door saying, 'Well what the H.... are we doing here, you are not allowing Jim to go without you and you are not going without me and I am certainly not going to leave my farm, so home we go!'[20]

It was arranged with London that on Wednesday, 19 June three ships would arrive at St Peter Port to take away only school children. Teachers were told to pass this information on to parents for them to decide whether or not they wanted their children to leave. Mrs. Corvriend chose to send her children away to the mainland, and recalled the moment when they asked when their parents would come to join them:

> We hated telling them the wretched truth that it would probably be years before we saw them again and months before we heard of them again, and said evasively: 'We will if we can, but you mustn't worry about us'.

The small daughter of a friend, told the same thing, comfortably assured her parents that she would do her best to forget all about them.[21]

It has been said in some quarters that the state of panic was far greater on Guernsey than was the case on Jersey due to contradictory advice:

Official notices were misread, words of advice completely misinterpreted and the most grotesque rumours passed for truth. There was a run on the banks, one evacuating publican gave away his entire stock of liquor. One official, at his own expense, had posters with 'Keep Your Heads. Don't be Yellow' printed in black on a yellow background put up all over the town. He then suddenly remembered that he ought to go [to the UK] and did so, without telling anyone in his department.[22]

In his diary entry for 20 June 1940, the Reverend Robert Douglas Ord provides a graphic insight into the situation on Guernsey that day, particularly in view of the fact that, he mused, 'the margin of time for registration proved too narrow last night':

Crowds besieged the Constables' offices and the suggested timetable was thrown out of gear. Under cover of darkness, children have been leaving. Now with coming of day all roads lead to St Peter Port.

Thousands throng the streets. Normal life is completely suspended. Everywhere the same questions are heard: 'What shall we do?' 'Where shall we go?' Long queues formed as early as 6 a.m. in Lefebvre Street, which was so packed with humanity that movement was impossible.

Those that came to register found that a queue four deep filled the length of the street. One might have walked on the heads of the crowd. Those who fainted could with difficulty be attended. A fearful target for aircraft! But no orders for dispersal were issued.

The Registration order was so worded that many supposed it was obligatory. Hence great numbers registered as a precaution, myself included, though, as it proved, unnecessarily. From 8.45 until after 10, I waited my turn. My name, address and willingness to pay passage were duly recorded. A Canadian by my side remarked that he had just got out of Paris in time with what he stood up in. He, too, was registering, 'in case the authorities sour on me later!'

It was with difficulty that I made my way home; people continually stopping me for advice with a naive conviction that wisdom must of necessity repose in any cleric!

In the High Street other immense queues had formed outside the banks. Except for the payment of wages none was allowed to draw out more than £20 in cash. Unable to supply ready money many shopkeepers closed their doors, while those who had suitcases and other travelling gear quickly sold out.

Evacuees now began to arrive from Alderney, while in the opposite direction an unceasing stream of women and children went down to the harbour to embark. Two thousand leave today, while men of military age will be left until tomorrow. A measure of the panic in some quarters is afforded by the Order forbidding the slaughter of cattle. It has been found that beasts have been left in some fields tethered in Guernsey fashion but without arrangements for milking. The vets have put so many pets to sleep that they have run out of the wherewithal to continue this unhappy task.

Many valuable dogs and cats perished, to the distress not only of their owners but of the vets themselves. Amateurs killed their own pets, sometimes, it is to be feared, with unnecessary cruelty. A person in the queue this morning told of a bird fancier who 'wrung the necks of his birds then cleared off to England'. Poultry met the same fate in places. Car-owners gave away their cars to friends – some for twenty shillings. Others did the like with property: 'There's my house and furniture: do what you like with it. I'm off!'

Well may the Press print headlines: NO CAUSE FOR PANIC! 'There IS a panic, and a most unnecessary panic,' said the Procureur, Mr Sherwill. Growers with glasshouse crops have been ordered not to neglect watering, while farmers are urged to maintain the supply of milk.[23]

With an almost overpowering atmosphere of tension and dismay the rumour machine on the Channel Islands was operating at maximum capacity. Continuing his diary entry for the 20th, Ord wrote that 'it is not surprising that one should fall victim to a cruel trick of rumour':

Before midday it was being said that Russia had declared war on Germany and was already far into East Prussia. I heard a man say he had got this on the wireless at 10 that morning. The effect was amazing. People contemplating evacuation changed their minds and began to go home convinced the situation was saved. Bitter reaction followed when there was not a word of this on the 1 o'clock news. The rumour was stigmatized in the *Guernsey Evening Press*, as well it might be. Instead the headlines struck fear into all hearts. 'NAZIS APPROACH ST MALO!'

Now many took swift decisions. Leaving beds unmade and tables uncleared they made a dash for the boats. Among these are some who will one day have regrets. One of the stampeders – an official on the island – was hailed by an acquaintance as he ran up the gangway 'You don't make me think of Burgomaster Max!' Such rebuke was just, but ought not to be applied to all who went. Many evacuated because they had no special ties of responsibility, or because they could offer their services in some way to the Country.

At a time like this, however, motives are misjudged; there is much ground for pride in the bearing of people, those who went on board and those who said Goodbye on the quay. There was great patience amid the distress and perplexity, high courage in parting from loved ones, especially children, and calmness in facing an unknown future. Nevertheless, it was hard to see the boat warping her way out leaving one behind in an Island where one had no relatives – only friends and duty.

Despite the fact that he had earlier registered for evacuation, for Reverend Ord his mind was made up. He had made up his mind. He knew where his duty lay:

> At home we have quietly discussed the position. Unless evacuation is universal and compulsory, I cannot leave. In any case not until the sick or the aged had been embarked could clergy and ministers leave their posts. G. refused to accept my suggestion that she should go herself, though she was apprehensive of what the Nazis would do with those of my calling. So we made our final decision and found essential peace.

During the day, 'Mr Victor Gosselin Carey, Bailiff, was sworn in as Lieutenant Governor in place of Major Gen. Telfer-Smollett, recalled to England for duty' continued Ord, adding, 'This evening the Bailiff makes his first pronouncement in his new capacity'. Ord recorded the speech verbatim in his diary:

> 'In these grave and anxious times I strongly exhort one and all to remain calm and avoid panic. It behoves us to behave as true and loyal men and women of Guernsey, and to apply ourselves to our duties with that quiet determination which has always characterized all Islanders. I therefore implore you not to be alarmed by reason of the precautionary steps which the authorities are taking. Let us

55

remember that evacuation is voluntary. There is no compulsion. Beyond teachers, children of school age and under, with mothers or other relations in charge, as well as men of military age, it is impracticable for others to hope to be evacuated.'

'Had this announcement been made a day earlier, much misunderstanding and wretchedness [could] have been avoided', Ord wrote, though he did have some sympathy with the Island's leadership: 'Few people can know how hard-driven our local statesmen and officials have been. For those without knowledge criticism is easy. A rumour had indeed been circulated that the Bailiff and Island Administration had already decamped!' Ord then went on to provide an example of the 'wretchedness' he had mentioned:

One unfortunate contretemps occurred at the Victoria Pier this evening owing to a newspaper announcement that further arrangements for evacuation would be given publicly there at 7 pm. A vast assembly congregated in expectation. Under cloudless skies they waited – a perfect target for the *Luftwaffe* had they chosen to fly over. For half an hour at least they waited and then began to disperse on acid comment on official bungling.

Meantime another crowd filled Smith Street outside the Press Office. The Procureur was told and came at once to speak. He declared that he knew nothing of any such arrangement as had been announced. Grave responsibility rests upon whoever convened such crowds. We might have had a thousand casualties in that least sheltered of places.

Only yesterday the Bailiff had said that it would 'not be possible on account of the danger of air raids to permit masses of people to congregate at the harbour. Accordingly parents must say "Au revoir" to their children at their homes or in the schools where they were to assemble. The public will not be permitted to approach the harbour.'

Yet this very thing took place within a short distance of the boats. So Mr Shewill did his best and spoke of arrangements that were being made, adding that it was most unlikely that the mass of Guernsey folk could hope to evacuate. Men of military age, while not compelled, should go to England and do their duty there. To remain would be to court the possibility of 'slave labour', though in the speaker's opinion that would prove unlikely. He said he really did not know if the Germans would come to the Island. Perhaps we might escape the rigours of an occupation after all. The food problem would be the most serious thing they would have to face. Hence the evacuation of the young. And so with further cheering words he sent the people away.[24]

So hurried was the departure of a number of families that it seemed they had, quite literally, rushed out of their houses without even bothering to shut the door behind them:

> Some houses were left open, beds unmade and remains of a hurried morning meal on the table. Other houses were so securely locked that men authorised soon afterwards to collect perishable goods from abandoned houses had difficulty in entering. A tobacconist gave away his entire stock before closing his premises and a publican before leaving invited his neighbours to go into his bar and help themselves to the liquor there. Panic is bad enough when the panickers are otherwise sober, but panic inflamed by drunkenness degenerates into sheer madness.[25]

It was not only the Channel Islanders who had just a few hours to organise themselves for the evacuation. Those on the mainland who were expected to deal with the sudden influx of thousands of people also had little time to consider how they were going to handle the newcomers, as one Guernsey evacuee described in a letter to Charles Ammon MP:

> The evacuation arrangements such as they were, were deplorable. I came over on the *Antwerp*, a troopship, licensed to carry and with lifebelts provided for seven hundred, and there were two thousand men, women and children aboard to be chased by a submarine half-way across. We reached Weymouth at 5 p.m. and we were left there without food or drink until 10 a.m. the next day when people started fainting in all directions and officialdom woke up at last.

The evacuation arrangements were so bad that they actually deterred some people from leaving, as Islander Bernard Haswell explained:

> I got as far as the boats. A lot of people turned back at the last moment; it was hell. June 1940 was the most hair-raising and frightening month in the history of the islands. All one could hear was, 'What are you

going to do?' People were crammed in those ships to be evacuated and the mind boggled at the idea of them crossing the Channel without escorts. On seeing those teeming pots of worms, my brother and I decided not to go.[26]

A young Jerseyman, Mr McLennan-Jones, was working in the office operated jointly on Guernsey by the Great Western and Southern railways and was involved in helping organise the evacuation:

All the staff were told they could go on the *Isle of Sark* but when they got to the White Rock there was a big crowd expecting to get aboard the *Duke of York,* another evacuation boat. However this was to be used only for children under school age and their mothers so it was decided that the GW staff would help with the boarding of the mothers and children. The captain of the *Duke of York* said he could take 1,200 people and ordered that we should count them as they went aboard. Some of the staff helped to carry the baggage and the children up the gangways but as the tide rose these got steeper and more difficult. Many of the children were wailing in alarm and as soon as they were set down in the saloon started running around looking for their mothers. As the morning wore on, the ship was in an uproar, children crying, running around, being sick, yelling for food, or just yelling.

At about 10.30 the captain arrived and checked the number loaded. It was about 1,000 and he insisted we stop at 1,200. Even then the line of buses full of children stretched right up the quay past the Weighbridge, so we mechanically went on loading. Some time later the captain returned and discovered that we had loaded nearer 1,500. He then ordered that the surplus be unloaded but a few minutes later realised that would be an impossible task ...

At 3 am Saturday morning the rush slackened and we were advised to go home but most of us just lay down on the office tables to sleep for a few hours. All day Saturday the evacuation went on, but easier now because it was all adults. I went to the Post Office but it was closed so I went into the mail entrance at the side. Only two men were on duty and they were overwhelmed with work as telegrams had been pouring in all day and they had no way of delivering them as all the messengers boys had already evacuated. I was allowed to look through the large stack of telegrams and found one that told me the *Duke of York* had arrived in Weymouth. She had taken 22 hours to cross instead of the normal six.

We in the GW & SR offices had interminable arguments about whether we should stay on or leave. Four of the staff did leave but the rest of us stayed on until the last minute.

The telephone engineer Edward J. Hamel was one of those who managed to evacuate from Guernsey on board the ship *Antwerp*:

> The queue for the ship stretched for a hundred yards or so. We unloaded the boy and his parcels. The pushchair was parked by the refuse bin at the top of the slip, and we joined the queue. Looking around, life seemed much as usual. A search for friends in the 'line' drew a blank. A man was addressing the queue from the upper promenade of the harbour. Though I couldn't hear all he said, the substance was clear. He was, in fact, telling us that there was no need for panic, and we would be well advised to return home!
>
> There had indeed been talk of panic in the past two days. I am not suggesting that the rumour was false, but I had not met up with a single case in all the conversations I had with people at that time.
>
> In view of the extremely short notice of the evacuation arrangements – in particular – as they affected the children, it was only to be expected that urgent and immediate consultation between relatives and friends would be island wide. Was this panic?
>
> In my experience, which, by the nature of my work, went far beyond the close circle of relatives and friends, I found that the agonising problems facing everyone – especially those with young children – were being tackled in a tense but adult manner. It may be that the idea of panic emanated from a few people, who, at heart, wished to leave, but could not face up to the decision to abandon all their possessions in cold blood, and, to bolster up their weakness, upbraided those who could – and did!
>
> Nobody left the queue! As far as I was concerned, he only served to harden my will to carry on![27]

It was not only residents who were evacuated. Some of those involved in the Islands' administration were also withdrawn or departed. On 19 June 1940, the Lieutenant-Governor of Guernsey (the representative of the British monarch), Major General John Minshull-Ford, received the following message from the British Home Office:

> Sir, I am directed by the Secretary of State to say that, in the event of your recall, it is desired by His Majesty's Government that the Bailiff

should discharge the duties of Lieutenant-Governor, which would be confined to civil duties, and that he should stay at his post and administer the government of the Island to the best of his abilities in the interests of the inhabitants, whether or not he is in a positon to receive instructions from His Majesty's Government. The Crown Officers also should remain at their posts.

The very next day Minshull-Ford was indeed recalled to London, but rather than place all the responsibility to of running the administration on the Bailiff, a 'Controlling Committee' was formed with the Attorney General, Ambrose Sherwill, as its President.

The angst of those who deliberated whether to stay or go, is perhaps best summed up by Frank Hubert, who, as a young lad, lived with his family in Doyle Road, St. Peter Port:

No one had any idea that the Germans would stay as long as they did and many fled, leaving their homes and pets behind, thinking they would be able to return after 'the trouble' was over. One family I heard about drove down to the harbour to catch a boat, found to their surprise that they were allowed on board, promptly sold their car for £1.00 and left. Another emptied a bag of corn in their garden for their chickens to feed on, while they were away and also left …

During the few weeks it took to evacuate the Island in 1940, vets in the Island became so busy they just could not cope, I helped to clear some of the animals that had been abandoned. I recall at least 57 cats and one dog. One family left a saucer of milk and some food, in the side passage of their house for their cat, closed the door and left. Some days later, I rescued the animal, when I opened the door; the poor thing went wild, jumping a good three or four feet into the air. The only way to catch it was to smother it with a blanket.[28]

The moment finally came when husband and wife, mother and son, brother and sister, should part company, as Frank's family broken up in the face of the German Blitzkrieg:

My mother and sister, Margot, together with three of my aunts, two cousins and both my grandmothers … left with the first wave of evacuees … One of my aunts had a friend in Galashiels, Scotland who owned a house, which was standing empty at the time. He invited the family to live there, whilst Guernsey was occupied.

Unfortunately, my blind maternal grandmother, was finding the whole experience of the war and evacuation from the home and surroundings she knew, very difficult. But the added experience of a local air raid, was all too much for her frailty and whilst on their way to Scotland, she died of shock in a village called Burford, near Oxford. It was very sad for us all.

It was actually my sister's ninth birthday on the 20th June the day they left, she didn't celebrate very much. We saw them all off at the harbour, they were upset but Dad and I kept a stiff upper lip thinking, as many did, that it would not be long before we saw them all again.

As we waved good bye to my mother, sister and other family members, I remember my father saying to me, 'Half the people of Guernsey have been evacuated and the other half have stayed behind. I wonder son, when all this is over, which half will we better off? Will it be a peaceful end? What will happen to us?'[29]

4
'Women and children first'
The Evacuation of Jersey

In the Jersey *Evening Post* of 19 June 1940, there was a short notice which appeared to be provided by an official source but was not signed or attributed. It was headed 'Evacuation':

> Shipping facilities are being provided by His Majesty's Government for the immediate voluntary evacuation to the United Kingdom of women and children. Similar facilities will also be available for men between the ages of 20 and 33 who wish to join His Majesty's Forces and, so far as accommodation permits, for other men.
>
> The names and addresses of all women and children (and of all such men other than persons for whom tickets have already been bought from the Southern Railway) should be handed in at the special office at the Town Hall before 10 o'clock tonight, Wednesday June the 19 or between 6 a.m. and 10 a.m. tomorrow, Thursday.
>
> Information will in the case of women and children be required to be given as to whether arrangements have been, or will be made privately, for the accommodation and maintenance in the United Kingdom or whether accommodation and maintenance should be provided for them by the appropriate United Kingdom authorities.

R.E.H. Fletcher lived in Jersey and witnessed the anguish of the people suddenly expected to make what was likely to be a life-changing decision in the space of just a few hours:

> Families, although possessing the necessary permission to leave the Island, gathered in their homes until a very late hour before making their fateful decision and the matter was discussed in every detail.
>
> It must be agreed that it is not a simple matter to know if one is doing for the best by leaving in jeopardy all one's possessions, by

taking his family to unknown difficulties and danger. When we made our decision to get away it was well past midnight so we naturally expected to meet with some difficulty in getting to our respective homes and this proved to be the case as our car was stopped no fewer than four times by armed sentries to whom we had to give our names together with a full explanation of our being out so late. We managed to satisfy them all as a certain licence was allowed under the exceptional circumstances. Bed was most welcome after experiencing such a distressing day.

Next day we had all derived much benefit from our rest and were able to give time for clear thinking and although it might seem strange we had all changed our minds by deciding to remain and keep an eye on our possessions.

Instructions were issued that only 28lb of luggage could be taken by each departing passenger, money was also difficult to obtain. Those who decided to leave had to endure much discomfort, many having to travel in the holds of small cargo vessels and barges crowded to capacity.

Those who could afford it were able to travel by the Mail Boat which must have carried its record number of passengers all anxious to get away.

A few wealthy people were more fortunate being able to get away in chartered yachts and planes whilst others who possessed small boats fitted with motors used them to reach the UK.

The Colonel commanding the Militia asked permission to take all his men to England and so help in any way possible. Permission was readily given and they sailed the next day.

Many people were in such a hurry to leave that they were quite at a loss to know what to do with their domestic pets and as a result many thousands of cats and dogs were destroyed at the Animal Shelter. Cage birds were liberated with the result that Canaries and Budgerigars were to be seen looking for food in most lanes and hedgerows.[1]

A degree of panic and confusion was inevitable, given that people had just a few hours to decide whether to stay or go. The following account gives some idea just how chaotic the situation was in Jersey:

Twenty-three thousand people, out of a population of fifty thousand, queued up at the Town Hall to register their names for embarkation, but such was the disorganisation that the next day people who had registered were bundled on to the boats indiscriminately with those who had not, whilst hundreds more waited on the quays in the glaring sun with their weeping and hungry children for twelve to twenty-four hours before they were taken aboard small boats, mail boats, coal boats and potato boats. Without food, without water, these poor devils endured sea passages ranging from six to twenty-four hours.[2]

Another story comes from Guy Porter who, living at 24 Regent Road, St Helier, addressed the following comments to a friend:

We were told on the 19th that all who wanted to leave must register at the Town Hall. Immediately there was a long queue. I went there at 4.40 the next morning and waited until 11 o'clock before I could register. I then went to the GPO and two of the banks but could not get near these places for the crowd.[3]

A baker's roundsman, George Bird, who was aged 20 at the time, remembers the 19th because it was the day his customers told him they wanted no more bread because they were leaving the Island. After giving the bread away he joined the queue at the Town Hall but it was so long that he was in Gloucester Street (not far from the Opera House) at 20.00 hours and by 22.00 hours he had moved only a short distance.

People in the queue were then told that the Town Hall was closing and would open again at 05.00 hours in the morning. Bird was there by that hour, but, in the end, the Town Hall did not open until 07.00 hours! In the meantime, he says, Ned Le Quesne, who was a prominent member of the States, came along and was telling people they should not leave the Island:

'But can you guarantee we'll have food?' someone asked. Le Quesne replied, 'No, I can't guarantee food but I can tell you that towns in England are being heavily bombed so I don't advise you to go there.'[4]

Bob Le Sueur had decided to leave Jersey, even though his father had no intention of becoming 'a penniless refugee'. Bob, a young insurance clerk, went to the Town Hall on the morning of 20 June to register before going off to work:

The queue was already six hundred yards long at 8.30 a.m. and I couldn't possibly be late for the office. When I got into work, there was only one typist and she was inundated by requests from people. There were huge queues outside our office. It took me two days to get through to our branch manager in Southampton.

When I eventually explained the situation to him, he asked me if I had been drinking. Then he said that, 'If this cock and bull story is true and the Jersey manager turns up in Southampton, we'll send him back. Meanwhile you're to wait there until he does'. I waited five years.[5]

As Arthur Kent on Jersey wrote in his diary, he felt most deeply for those parents with small children and for those who had invalid or aged family members who simply could not escape:

What overwhelming, heart-aching scenes there were in those next few hours! The boats were due early next morning. Imagine it if you can! Twelve hours in which to decide whether you would leave behind the home and work of a lifetime and, with just a few articles of clothing, join the melee in England or stick to your native soil to face the problems and uncertainties of the future as stoically as possible. I will never forget that day, its confusion, its tears. Everyone was waiting for the local newspaper for official information about the evacuation. When it came out there were big 'Women and Children First' headlines, and the confusion became chaos!

Donald Journeaux had only been married a matter of months when he and his wife were faced with painful dilemma of whether to evacuate or not:

My wife and I joined the queues for the few boats that were available. There was widespread confusion and many who queued did not get away, while others somehow bypassed the waiting and got onto the boats.

Everyone was bewildered. People were going around visiting friends and family and trying to decide what was best, and constantly changing their minds, so that when about 14,000 people did leave the Island, houses were abandoned, cars left stranded on the pier and, in some cases, cattle were left unmilked in the fields.

Eventually, Irene and I decided that we should stay in Jersey. My father-in-law, M.H. Newland, was a sick man and would not have survived the journey on a coal boat, which seemed to be the only thing available. We felt we should not leave him.[6]

Whilst the Journeauxs had eventually opted to remain, many of those who did not had used their cars to drive to the harbour and, having no further use for them, simply left them there, as R.E.H. Fletcher saw:

> As one can well imagine it did not take long for a very large accumulation of deserted cars to be seen blocking up all the roads near and leading to the harbour. Before much time had elapsed thieves were busy helping themselves to any which appealed to their taste ... The Police were not long in getting to work, the registration numbers helping them to secure those cars which had been removed ... The States very wisely gave the Police instructions to enter all vacant houses and seize all foods and perishable goods left in them.[7]

For some of those who left, the reasons for doing so were compelling, even if it meant leaving behind immediate family members, as Roy Bullen on Jersey recalled:

> My father left the Island to join his regiment on the last mail boat to leave here. We didn't see my father, all of us in the family, until five years or so later. However, there was a photograph always above my mother's bed of my father in uniform.[8]

Many may have got away, but it was not without some misgivings. Mrs Harman had left Jersey, but her father had remained in Jersey:

> I am completely at sea as to whether we really should have stayed. Everything was such a frightful nightmare those two days. I wish to God there had been more time to think before he came away ...
>
> Audley spent two hours at the Town Hall in the evening trying to register, and then from 4 a.m. to 11 the next morning and after all that we might just as well not have registered at all as nothing whatever was asked for. Just imagine that ghastly, panicky crowd on the quay and me with Rosemary in her Karricot, and as much of our belongings as we had managed to get into two small cases and a rucksack. I'd never even contemplated such a quandary in all my life.

Betty Harvey was another who, as a child, left with some regret and, like many of the evacuees, eventually settled in Britain rather than return to the old life in the Islands:

On the day of leaving … our animals had been turned loose to fend for themselves – my black Labrador, some cats, chickens and rabbits. At the harbour everyone was weeping, wives and husbands were being separated and older children were leaving without parents.

We crossed the Channel in a cargo boat, and there were cattle in the hold. The crossing was very rough and many people were seasick. I think there must have been about a dozen of us crammed into a small crewman's cabin. My mother was about six months pregnant and I can remember a nurse popping in to check her several times during the crossing …

We arrived at Weymouth and were met by my mother's youngest brother George. At Weymouth my mother was approached by a radio reporter who referred to us as 'refugees' which my mother did not like at all. 'We are not refugees, we are evacuees, and we shall be going back as soon as we can.' Sadly this did not happen; my mother died when I was 13 and it was to be 60 years before I was able to make the trip back.[9]

One man given the job of suddenly having to find shipping at a time when Britain's resources were stretched to the limit was Reginald Poulton Biddle who, in 1935, was appointed Docks and Marine Manager at Southampton. Later in 1940 he was Deputy Director of Ports at the Ministry of War Transport:

The night of June 19th/20th was a busy one. Special and immediate measures had to be taken to send all available and suitable tonnage to the Channel Islands to bring away those who desired to leave.

The whole of the resources of the Railway Company's staff and facilities were unreservedly placed at the disposal of the local authorities. Entirely on my own initiative I sent [some] of the S.R. [Southern Railway] Company's steamers to the islands. They had only peace-time certificates to carry 12 passengers but between them they brought over nearly 3,000 evacuees.

The evening of Wednesday June 19th in Jersey, and no doubt in Guernsey, saw much chaos and confusion. The worst was expected at any moment. Indeed, I was told in a telephone message from Jersey at 10 o'clock that the Germans were expected to arrive the next morning, and what was I going to do about it?

I endeavoured to create an atmosphere of greater calm by the information that the steamers referred to above had already sailed.

My own staff in Jersey were not unnaturally anxious about their families and within an hour or two yet another steamer had been commissioned and had sailed for Jersey. The number of telephone messages I received for news of people in Jersey and for particulars of the evacuation arrangement was astronomical!

As we have already seen, the main period for the embarkation of the evacuees was between 20 and 22 June, though the flow of people was, noted Biddle, much less by the 22nd, a Saturday:

> On the Saturday there were steamers alongside the quays at Jersey but only a few evacuees presented themselves for embarkation, whereas at Guernsey there were literally thousands waiting at the harbour and insufficient vessels to deal with them.
>
> Arrangements were made to make public announcements in the streets of St Helier, and by various other means, that ships were waiting at the quay, but in the late afternoon it was decided to send them to Guernsey where they were immediately besieged by waiting passengers.
>
> It would appear that of nearly 20,000 who registered under the Jersey States evacuation scheme not more than 10,000 availed themselves of the facilities, whereas at Guernsey the original number of 13,000 registered quickly rose to 20,000, all of whom had been embarked by the Sunday night.
>
> It was very desirable, in order to maintain an atmosphere of confidence in those who had decided to remain in the islands, for the mail boat service to and from the islands to be continued as long as circumstances permitted. This was the wish of the government on this side and the Southern Railway agreed on the understanding that they would be kept advised of developments. With great courage and a loyal sense of duty the staff in Jersey readily agreed to continue at their posts. It was a bitter disappointment that the subsequent march of events developed with such tragic suddenness that those splendid fellows were unable to leave the island.
>
> They set a fine example which will never be forgotten.[10]

No sooner had the evacuations begun, then some of those who had left were starting to have second thoughts and regrets:

> There are indications that a number of those who have left the Island [Guernsey] are desirous of returning. The wife of one of our well-known northern tradesman 'evacuated' during his absence on business, and so farewells had to be expressed by correspondence.

In another case, a wife left to join her husband, and finding she could not do so on the mainland, has written to relatives to come and fetch her back.

It seems clear that very many of our islanders migrated under the impression that they were compelled to go. No such order was ever issued, of course, but there are evidences in the stories told that many received wrong advice on the matter, given by those whom they consulted.[11]

One 20-year-old woman, who chose not to leave Jersey with her elderly and unwell mother, wrote what she had been told about the crossing in a letter that was published in the *News Chronicle* of 1 July 1940:

After we had finally decided not to cross, mother slept properly for the first time in three weeks. Certainly she would not have survived the journey.

Conditions were appalling – women and children – some separated – were packed in the holds and on the decks of trawlers, potato-boats and even a coal boat. Several boats were only 30 ft long and expected to be at sea 55 hours and even those that went to Weymouth took over 24 hours, as we know from telephone calls by people who travelled.

Women with day-old babies and women who were expecting within twenty-four hours travelled in these conditions … There was no food or drink, except ship's biscuit and water. Those of us who remain live in a world of suspense.

5

'Snatched out of the grip of the Boche'
Alderney, the Abandoned Island

John Glasgow was just a young boy when his mother, Edna, pulled shut the front door of their home on Alderney. Having left with all the other evacuees on Sunday, 23 June 1940, Edna would never see her house again. In fact, she would never return to the Island. Seventy years later, John still has some recollection of his departure:

> Six ships came and church bells rang to tell people it was time to go. They were allowed one bag per person – pets were left behind to fend for themselves or be shot. We spent June 24 travelling and my mother was already ill.[1]

The mother's and son's journey took them to Glasgow, where they arrived at the Holy Cross Church in Knightswood in the city's West End. The evacuees were medically screened, at which point it was discovered that Edna was suffering from advanced tuberculosis. She was immediately admitted to Ruchill Hospital. It was to be the last time that John would ever see his mother.

Alone and without any family member for support, John was taken to Castlemilk Children's Home where he remained for around three months until he was finally reunited with his father Ian who was a serving soldier. Edna passed away on 4 October 1940, and, with her husband away in the forces, was buried in a pauper's grave in Sighthill Cemetery. It was only in 2014 that John was finally able to locate and visit his mother's final resting place:

> I can only assume that as a serving soldier, my father had little time to make arrangements for her burial and taking me out of Castlemilk Home to bring me to Winchester near where he was posted. My father

70

kept nothing and it took me fifty years to find out what my mother looked like.

Frederick George French, who had been the Judge of Alderney since 1938, was the civilian head of the most northerly of the Channel Islands. With his domain being the closest to the coast of Continental Europe, French was acutely conscious of the predicament he and his people found themselves in as the German juggernaut rolled relentlessly westwards. As a result, on Saturday, 22 June 1940, he wrote, and signed, a handwritten notice to Alderney's population:

> I have appealed to Admiralty for a ship to evacuate us. If the ship does not come it means we are considered safe. If the ship comes time will be limited.
>
> You are advised to pack one suitcase for each person so as to be ready. If you have invalids in your house make arrangements in consultation with your doctor. All possible notice will be given.

Just twenty-four hours later the evacuation began. The process was recalled by a Mr Bury, who was appointed as the Island's temporary Sub-Postmaster after the regular one, Captain Marriette, had been recalled to the Army after the outbreak of war. It was Marriette who had interviewed and appointed Mr Bury. The latter had arrived on Alderney on 13 May 1940. His employment only lasted a matter of weeks:

> Many of the island folk were getting away to Guernsey and to England, my night telegraphist among them, and a girl clerk. The situation was certainly alarming and chaos reigned complete … Our transmitting set was working at full speed. A young sorting clerk and telegraphist was sent from Guernsey to take the place of our South African [who performed the night shift]. The young man stuck to his post night after night, and we expected 'Jerry' might land at any time.
>
> Every day I made up a registered bag containing the office stock and cash, locked it in the safe and entrusted the key to him with the instructions that if 'Jerry' came he was to drop the bag over the garden wall, into the churchyard, so that I could pick it up if possible.[2]

Finally, on the morning of that fateful June Sunday, the long-expected day of departure arrived. Mr Bury's short tenure as Sub-Postmaster was over:

The Church bells rang out and the people came into the streets shouting 'The ships are here! The ships are here!' Everyone started packing. All dogs were killed by humane killer at the hand of the local butcher, cats were left behind, cattle untethered, and a general exodus was made to the harbour. The bedridden were carried, and the whole pathetic scene was such that I will never forget.

Mr Bury, in his official capacity, still had a few last-minute duties to perform before he could join the throng boarding the ships in Braye Bay:

I attended the office for the last time to gather up the bag of stock and cash ... and called up the Guernsey Head Office, informed them of the evacuation, and that I was about to wreck the wireless set. Back came the query, 'On whose authority?' I replied 'Judge French', and with the 7lb parcel weight smashed up the set completely.

The scene at the harbour was never to be forgotten. I had previously told the Judge that I must go to Guernsey to hand over my stock and cash, and also to take my wife and daughter to England. He said 'Oh yes, I know you want to go to Guernsey. I had arranged for you to go in the French lifeboat (*Croix de Guerre* which was in the harbour) but we can't find the crew! We believe that they have stowed away on the boats. You must make your own arrangements.'

I said goodbye to many, including my good friend and chief clerk Miss Audoire, and began to look around for transport to Guernsey. In the inner harbour, I saw a fisherman and his son getting his boat ready for sea, and I asked him if he would take my young telegraphist and myself. Said he, 'I'm going to Brixham! But ...' After a few minutes' reflection he said 'If you help me to get this gear aboard, I'll take you!'

The weather was now hazy, and there was a good sea running, but we made the White Rock, Guernsey, by 6p.m., and handed over the stock and cash to the Assistant Superintendent of the G.P.O., who paid the fisherman for his journey.

A mail van took Bury to his daughter's house in Havelet. The following day he and his family boarded the mailboat heading for Southampton. 'Only just in time,' he duly noted.

After the evacuation was completed on the 23rd, Alderney was left deserted except for a 'handful of seafaring men who had last duties to perform', as the historians Michael St. J. Packe and Maurice Dreyfus noted when writing in 1971:

Nick Allen [the Alderney Pilot] went to Casquets to destroy stocks of fuel oil; and the Jennings, father and son, carried official documents to Guernsey before continuing to England in their own boats. There remained, in addition, nineteen persons who utterly refused to leave. The Bailiff of Guernsey, who was also acting Lieutenant-Governor, gave orders for them to be brought at once to Guernsey, and that same evening the Guernsey lifeboat put out, but met with little or no success.

It was not just people who had to be evacuated from Alderney. As Bury mentioned, when the Island's entire population of around 1,500 residents was evacuated, the livestock was left behind. With no-one to tend to the animals, they too had to be evacuated, rather than being shot or abandoned in the way some had in Guernsey. The party that organised the evacuation of the livestock was led by a Mr P.A. Mahy, who arrived to find the Island gripped by a sense of lingering desolation:

I was in charge of the party of farmers and farm hands which evacuated the cattle from Alderney from June 25th to 28th, 1940, and was told that the inhabitants had evacuated on the morning of June 23rd.

We left Guernsey on the 25th June at about 9 a.m. and travelled by the S.S. 'Courier', arriving at Alderney at about 11.30 a.m. On arrival we found a number of cars, lorries, and a motor bus on the quay. All these had been put out of commission in various ways. I went straight to the Grand Hotel, where I had decided to make our headquarters, and on the way noticed that public houses and shops had been broken into, that there were houses with windows open and a few with doors half open.

Later, I went into some of these and found handbags and suitcases half packed and garments lying about the floor. On making enquiries of the remaining inhabitants as to what had happened from the time of the evacuation on the morning of the 23rd to the time of my arrival, I found that no one seemed to know. Some stated that boats with French refugees had been seen in the harbour; others thought that a French lifeboat had called, but no one seemed certain of anything. I had been given a list of eight persons who were said to have remained in the Island, but we actually found 12, including 4 children.[3]

Having established that Alderney was devoid of almost all of its human inhabitants, Mahy was able to turn his attention to main reason he had been despatched to the Island:

> We found a number of cattle, horses and pigs running about loose, but there were a number of these in closed back yards and styles, without water or food. There were a number of young calves tied up in stables, and sows with litters of young pigs in styes – half dead, presumably from want of water and food.
>
> The cows in full milk were naturally all overstocked and could at first only be milked with difficulty and in small quantities at a time. The cows were gradually eased of their milk, which was thick and sour. All cattle, pigs and poultry were turned loose, and food and water were given to the sows with litters of pigs. The young calves would have needed more attention than we could possibly have given them, and I ordered them to be shot as soon as found.
>
> In the meantime, the S.S. 'New Fawn' had arrived and brought seven men whom I did not know but who offered me their services. I accepted their offer and sent them out in various directions to help the farmers and those men who were collecting cattle and driving them towards the harbour. Two of these men proved very unsatisfactory, and I sent them back to Guernsey – one on the first day and the other on the second. The two boats were loaded with cattle, the first leaving for Guernsey as soon as loaded. Getting the cattle aboard was a very difficult task, inasmuch as they had to be driven down steps to the lower landing stage, and many of them had to be pushed and slid down. The cows were being constantly milked, and it was nearly dark when our milkers returned to the hotel.

The task that faced Mahy and his team was far from complete. They returned to it the next morning once the two boats had returned:

> [They] were again loaded, one of them coming into the Old Harbour, where the cattle could be walked from the quay to the ship, and was loaded with 85 head of cattle in 35 minutes.
>
> On Thursday, the 27th, the two boats again returned to Alderney. One was again loaded with cattle which had been collected from the more distant farms, the younger cattle having been put in a stable near the harbour and others in fields nearby. The other boat was loaded with 21 horses, a number of pigs, pork and various other miscellaneous articles, some of which had been collected by various

tradesmen who had come for this purpose from Guernsey. The farmers and their men left by this boat.

During the 2½ days the party were on the Island 400 head of cattle, 21 horses, and a number of pigs, as well as pig carcases, were sent to Guernsey. On the 27th another steamer came into the Harbour to load Government stores, bringing men who were under the charge of a Government official.

Our two boats returned on Friday morning. Our experienced men were gone, and the bringing of the pigs to the harbour and getting them on board the boat proved a most difficult and arduous task, quite contrary to precedent. They would not go down the steps, and in many cases had to be carried into the ship. About 175 were shipped on the 'Courier'.

We had collected on the quay four tractors, some agricultural implements, cattle food, harness and cow ropes, as well as a large safe belonging to the Alderney Agricultural Society. Most of this was left over for shipment the next day with the sheep and pigs that were still remaining. The 'New Fawn ', however, left light at 11.15 p.m. that day.

Nothing, it seems, was to be left for the enemy. Such was the scope of Mahy's instructions, that, sadly, no animal was to be left alive if it could not be evacuated:

Besides the calves that I had ordered to be shot as soon as found, I had ordered the shooting of most of the dogs in the Island, a certain number of cats, a few horses that were either too old to be of any use and diseased or vicious, and an old boar. There were left on the Island a few cows and steers, 30/40 sheep, all the poultry, a small number of dogs and quite a number of cats. During our stay in the Island, and more especially on the last days when visits of aeroplanes over the island became more frequent, the greatest care was taken to prevent the cattle being herded in large numbers or the grouping of cars and lorries. Signals were put up so that the ship's Captain could be informed if any change in the general situation in the Island had taken place.

When we left Guernsey on the 25th we had with us a Sister from the Alexandra Hospital and a few men of the St. John Ambulance Brigade. I understood they were to see to the transport of the invalids who were left in the Island and collect goods, stores and medicines from the Mignot Hospital. This party (with the exception of the Sister) had their meals with us at the Hotel but slept at the Hospital. All members of my party slept and had their meals at the Hotel. They had to be in by 10 p.m. No lights were permitted and I saw that all of them were in their rooms before I retired. I also opened the door of the hotel each morning.

The Guernsey tradesmen and their men had their meals at the Hotel and returned to Guernsey the same day as they arrived. The British Government official and his batman stayed at the Hotel with us while in Alderney.

It has been said that men under my charge were guilty of looting. I told them on the first day that looting was punishable and that they would be searched on their return to Guernsey. There was no doubt some pillaging, but it cannot have been on a large scale as they were kept busy from morning till night and had no means of disposing of any goods. There was some pillaging done by the crews of the boats, of course. These men had the advantage of being able to take their loot to the ships. There certainly could have been no furniture taken or any large articles as the ships were not in the harbour during the night, with the exception of the Government boat, which remained on the Thursday evening.

Reginald Blanchford was with the Guernsey St John's Ambulance party that was sent to Alderney to try and persuade the handful of remaining individuals who had refused to be evacuated to leave, as well as salvage stores and equipment from the Mignot Memorial Hospital:

It was very traumatic. There were cows roaming the streets with udders bursting and an old gentleman was trying to chloroform them to kill them. Going into the houses, you'd find a sandwich with a bite taken out of it and half a cup of tea drunk. We heard a noise in one house, there was an old lady there dressed in curtains and she thought I was the SS because I was in my uniform. She was demented, she thought the Germans had arrived. We got her back to Guernsey.[4]

Another of the St John's Ambulance party later recalled the difficulties encountered in trying to induce the few recalcitrant inhabitants to leave:

One man refused to leave until he had finished packing some personal property which he valued at several thousand pounds. Another, surprised eating his dinner, saw no reason to leave the home where he had lived for more than ninety years. A woman locked herself and her children in her house, under the impression that it was a German uniform they were wearing. And at another house they were threatened with a shotgun.[5]

In the end, despite all the endeavours of the St John's Ambulance team, there were still seven people who refused to budge. They were left behind, their names being listed in a file in the Bailiff's office. There was at least one other individual who decided to remain – a man by the name of Alf Martell who went to Alderney with Mahy's party. Martell had seemingly decided to take advantage of the situation on the abandoned Island:

He was a big man, tall, very strong, daring, and completely fearless. His dark skin was usually unshaven, he had a loud gruff voice and a louder laugh. When the party of men left Alderney for home Alf decided to stay on alone. 'I'll be King of Alderney'. His brothers in Guernsey were anxious when they heard the story, so they boarded one of the boats and went to look for him. They found him fully dressed on a luxurious bed in one of the hotels and surrounded by bottles of whiskey. It was with difficulty that they persuaded him to come home![6]

Judge French went to London where he continued act as Alderney's representative. He was now sure that they had done the right thing in evacuating and he expressed his gratitude for the swift response of the Admiralty in a letter dated 8 July:

Now that the Island of Alderney has been completely evacuated and all but a handful of its people safely snatched out of the grip of the Boche, I write to thank you first and foremost on my own personal behalf and secondly in the name of all the people of the Island for your action in forwarding my request to the Ministry of Shipping and to the Admiralty. The present safety of us all is due entirely to your prompt action and to nothing else ... As you may know six vessels arrived in less than twenty hours.[7]

Many of the various excursions to Alderney during the evacuation period had been made under the auspices of the Royal Guernsey Agricultural and Horticultural Society, who kept a record of the animals removed and of their subsequent disposal:

They amounted to 224 cows, 150 heifers, 5 bulls, 20 steers – some 400 head of cattle altogether, besides 20 horses, 3 ponies, 30 pigs and 36 pig carcasses. The horses and two of the ponies were brought over at a later date.[8]

Having collected its last cargo of livestock from Alderney, the steamer *Courier*, under Captain James Ingrouille Senior, was ordered to head for Plymouth, calling at St Peter Port, Guernsey, en route. The short crossing from Alderney was an eventful one and was described by Ralph Durand, whose account of the Occupation was published in March 1946, shortly after his death on 22 December 1945:

> The raiders also attacked the local steamboat 'Courier'. She was on her way from Alderney, bringing salvaged stores and a few people who had remained in that Island after the bulk of the inhabitants left, and was near the entrance to St. Sampson's Harbour when a plane sprayed her deck with machine-gun bullets and dropped a bomb that fortunately missed her. The captain beached the ship and when she was aground some members of her crew launched her boat, rowed ashore, and ran away, leaving those still on board, eleven of whom were wounded, to get ashore as best they could.
>
> Two men and two women, one of whom was wounded in the leg, swam ashore and were taken to the First Aid Post for bandages, blankets and hot tea. Fortunately for those who still remained on board a young dock hand had more grit than some members of the crew. He swam ashore and brought back the ship's boat so that all reached the shore. The 'Courier' was refloated next day ...[9]

Courier eventually made it into St Peter Port, at which point P. Girard went to speak to Captain James Ingrouille:

> When we arrived the ship was tied up at the New Jetty and the pigs were loose and crowding the deck of the vessel ... The vessel had actually left the Jetty when several running figures were seen approaching. One was in Air Force uniform, the other wore a military uniform and accompanying them were two or three civilians one of whom I recognised, dishevelled and unshaven he was, as a friend, and a very well known figure in the business life of the Island.
>
> The Captain drew the bow of his ship back towards the Jetty enabling these men to jump on board and I still retain a mental picture of my friend's flying leap to the deck of the ship. He was probably the last civilian passenger to leave Guernsey by steamer before the

Occupation proper began. Apparently he did not remain a passenger for very long as he and his companions were immediately enrolled as deck hands for the duration of the trip during which three of the wounded animals died.[10]

Alderney is unique as being the only British dominion to have been fully evacuated of its civilian population and then occupied by German forces for the duration of the Second World War.

6

'Unnecessarily hasty action'
Reactions to the Demilitarisation and Evacuation

On Sunday, 16 June 1940, the Reverend Douglas Moore had taken a holiday-preaching appointment in Manchester, fully expecting to return to the Channel Islands. However, he soon found himself becoming involved in efforts to evacuate the Channel Islands. This is what happened to him:

> I had hoped to return to the Channel Islands by a boat leaving Southampton on June 21. I heard that arrangements were being made for the demilitarisation of the Islands ... The following morning I learnt that the Government were encouraging a scheme of evacuation, and had authorised the Lieutenant-Governor to give financial help to evacuees whenever necessary. This was reassuring.
>
> That evening I expected to leave Waterloo by the boat train, but found the Friday night mail service had been cancelled. Making a trunk call to my wife in Guernsey, I succeeded in getting through at 5 a.m. on Saturday. The information revealed that evacuation was proceeding with great rapidity.
>
> Still hoping to get back to Guernsey, I went to Southampton later that day, but was turned back at the dock gates, finding that sailing had again been postponed. However, on the Sunday evening I succeeded in getting on board the *Isle of Sark*. Twenty minutes before sailing, the *Hantonia* arrived from the Channel Islands with a party of evacuees on board. To my great astonishment she carried no more than a quarter of her complement of passengers.
>
> When I reached Guernsey the following morning (June 24) I found that measures taken by the authorities of the Island had not only succeeded in allaying panic but had checked evacuation altogether. The ancient 'States of Guernsey' had been suspended and all administrative functions were now in control of a small emergency

committee. St. Peter Port was plastered with posters, such as: 'Don't be yellow' 'Evacuation is not compulsory,' etc. Cargo boats were at work again; shipments of tomatoes once more in full swing ...

This brought us to the evening of Monday 24. By the next day the nervous strain was plainly increasing; nothing approaching panic, but everyone was conscious of terrible perplexity, and people were waiting for a lead. At that time the only way of leaving the Islands was by the ordinary mail boat – reduced to two a week – or by cargo boat due to sail June 27. As we had received no satisfactory reply from the representative of the doctors, the ministers decided to send one of their own number, and I was asked to go to London on the Thursday, and with the help of our connexional [sic] authorities see what could be done to re-start the evacuation scheme. Arriving at London at midday on Friday I was able to arrange an interview at the Home Office.

The presentation of our case was received with the fullest sympathy. I was assured that the question was still under consideration, but whether anything further could now be attempted was doubtful.[1]

The evacuation of those civilians who wished to leave the Islands had not been an insignificant achievement. At 10.00 hours on 19 June the passenger ship *Antwerp* left Guernsey with 1,154 children from Amherst, St. Sampson's and St. Joseph's School. It was followed by the cargo ship *Felixstowe* with 437 children from Vauvert School. At 14.30 hours, the cargo ship *Haselmere* sailed with approximately 300 pupils, including those from Notre Dame School. Then, just before midnight, the Dutch passenger ship *Batavia IV* sailed with pupils from the boys' and girls' Intermediate Schools, the Ladies' College and Elizabeth College.

This day saw the start of the main departure of the rest of the civilian population with another thirteen ships leaving Guernsey; a further sixteen ships sailed with evacuees from Jersey. Carrying 475 passengers, *Antiquity* sailed from Jersey during the afternoon of the 20th, by which date a total of 23,000 civilians in Jersey alone had registered for evacuation.

The cargo ship *Sheringham* left from Guernsey the following day – at 03.30 hours. On board were 750 schoolchildren from the Vale and Torteval Schools. Soon after at 07.00 hours, the passenger ship *Viking* embarked an additional 1,880 schoolchildren. Two thousand more evacuees – made up of 1,000 infants and expectant mothers – embarked on the passenger ship *Duke of York*. This would be the biggest departure day for the Islanders with a fleet of another twenty-five ships embarking more of the civilian population from Guernsey alone.

Eighteen ships had also sailed with evacuees from Jersey on 21 June, with *Shepperton Ferry* carrying a cargo considered as military stores aside from 400 evacuees. The naval yacht *Philante* had departed with the Lieutenant-Governor of Jersey, Major General J.M.R. Harrison, and sailed to Portland.

The last official mass evacuations of civilians from Guernsey, involving fourteen vessels, took place on 22 June. The Belgian passenger ship *Prince Leopold*, together with the passenger ship *Royal Daffodil*, having anchored outside the harbour, left empty – probably as a result of the 'Stay Don't Be Yellow!' campaign. The other notable departure that day was the Trinity House vessel *Vestal* with 121 Trinity House employees on board. On 23 June the official evacuation ships ceased to operate from the two principal islands.[2]

As would be expected, *The Times* duly reported on the evacuation. An article, published on 29 June 1940, gives some impression of the way the news was relayed to the people of the United Kingdom:

> The children were sent away first and many thousands of them, in the charge of their teachers, crossed safely to a South Coast port. Among the first party of children was a number of B.E.F. troops who had crossed from a French port to the Channel Islands. After disembarking the children marched to a theatre and public gardens, where W.V.S. workers gave them sandwiches, bread and butter, and tea. Later they went by motor-buses to the railway station, where special trains took them northwards ...
>
> One of the schoolmasters in charge of one party said: 'We came over in a cargo boat packed tightly with nearly 700 on board. The children behaved like true Britishers, and so did their parents when they said farewell to them.'
>
> Shops were putting the shutters up all over Guernsey. The Lieutenant-Governor was withdrawn several days ago and the Bailiff was made temporary Governor with civil authority. After the children came the mothers with babies in their arms, and then the adult population of all classes, leaving crops behind to perish and all their worldly goods locked up in houses with blinds drawn.
>
> Cargo boats were mainly used for getting the people away and for many days they brought a steady stream to a South Coast port. When asked about Jersey's potato crop, only a quarter of which had

been lifted, one exporter said that the farmers had turned their cattle into the potato fields. A Jersey poultry farmer said: 'The last thing I did before packing up and leaving thousands of poultry behind was to throw all the corn to the chickens and leave them to it.' On the quay at St. Peter Port thousands of baskets of Guernsey potatoes were left to rot.

The reaction of the people in the UK at the sudden evacuation was exemplified by the comments of Lord Mottistone during a debate in the House of Lords on 3 July 1940:

Everyone in this Empire was concerned, if not shocked, by the evacuation of the Channel Islands. It has been said: 'Parliament was never told; the first thing anybody heard about it was in the Press.'

I know very well from my own service as Secretary of State that the Channel Islands stand in a peculiar position tactically and strategically, because they are practically a part of the French continent. We never in those days, nor have we in these days, envisaged the fortification of the Channel Islands as an outpost. They are right under the guns of part of France, which is nearer to us almost than they are themselves.

This is no precedent, and we shall be glad if my noble friend could now tell us, as I gather from him he will welcome the opportunity of doing, that this is a totally isolated case of an indefensible and unfortunate character, and that there is no chance whatever that any great fortified place of this Empire shall ever be surrendered without full warning being given to the Privy Council and Parliament. I know that hardly requires stating, nevertheless we should be glad to hear it from my noble friend.[3]

Criticism of the manner in which the Islands were evacuated was voiced repeatedly in Westminster. Mr John Parker, the MP for Romford, added his voice to the debates:

I would like to know from the Home Office whether there was any definite Government policy at all about the question of the evacuation of the Channel Islands. I can quite understand why a certain number of farmers and people who have lived for generations on the Islands would not want to leave, but a large part of the population ought to have been evacuated. The Government should have definitely said, 'We want practically the whole of the population, apart from the farmers in the country districts, to be evacuated,' and should have done all they possibly could to persuade the local people in authority to get the population evacuated …

A letter that I have received from Jersey says: It is remarkable that the self-same authorities who impressed on the islanders the necessity for business as usual stated at a meeting of licensed victuallers on the 28th that occupation by the Nazis must be expected at any time. German reconnaissance planes were in fact then flying over the town. This information was passed to my correspondent over the telephone on 29th June and therefore can be taken as being pretty accurate.

If the Island authorities discouraged evacuation and then suddenly decided at the last moment that a German occupation was inevitable, why were they not informed by the British Government that an early occupation was expected and persuaded to change their minds? Many people who wanted to be evacuated were not evacuated. There are in this country a great many relatives of people who would like to have come from the Islands. There are a great many invalids left on the Islands. Apparently the people in charge of them were told that a hospital ship would be arriving to take them, because the ordinary ships which were used for the evacuation were much too crowded for invalids. No hospital ship ever arrived to collect them.

Another one of my correspondents has stated that his parents stayed behind because they could not get savings bank deposits out on the day on which they wanted to leave. They stayed a day or two, and then there was no ship and they could not get away. There were a great many people who ought to have been, and could have been, removed during the period who were not. I am thinking particularly of elderly people and invalids who will suffer very much during the German occupation.[4]

The explanation that was offered was one repeatedly used by the Home Office, which was that it was necessary for a large proportion of Islanders to remain:

The information before the government indicated that substantial numbers of the inhabitants would be unwilling to leave their homes, and the conclusion was reached that any scheme for attempting by compulsion or inducement to transplant to this country the whole of the population of the Islands, including those who have been for generations settled on the land, would be both impracticable and

Pictured whilst docked at Jersey on 19 June 1940, this is *Train Ferry No.1* about to depart for Southampton. On board are personnel of Nos. 17 and 501 squadrons, as well as other military personnel and equipment. (Imperial War Museum)

Members of the Guernsey St John's Ambulance Service assist an elderly woman evacuee on arrival at Weymouth. (Author's Collection)

The SS *Isle of Sark* in St Helier Harbour on 21 June 1940. This images gives some idea of how busy the harbour was during the evacuation. (Jersey Evening Post)

A postcard from the magazine *Der Adler* showing a Dornier Do.17P flying over the south cost of Guernsey. (Author's Collection)

HAVE APPEALED TO ADMIRALTY FOR A S
O EVACUATE US.
THE SHIP DOES NOT COME, IT ME
VE ARE CONSIDERED SAFE,
THE SHIP COMES TIME WILL BE LIMITE
O ARE ADVISED TO PACK ONE SUITC
R EACH PERSON SO AS TO BE READY.
YOU HAVE INVALIDS IN YOUR HOU
ARE ARRANGEMENTS IN CONSULTAT
ITH YOUR DOCTOR. ALL POSSIB
OTICE WILL BE GIVEN.
JUNE 1940

The original evacuation notice for Alderney signed by Judge French. (Trevor Davenport)

The immediate aftermath of the *Luftwaffe* attacks on Jersey and Guernsey on 28 June 1940, as viewed from Glategny Esplanade. The smoke seen here is coming from White Rock in St Peter Port, Guernsey. (Norman Grutt)

The clean-up after the bombing of 28 June 1940, pictured underway in St Peter Port. (Author's Collection)

Another view of the aftermath of the air raid on St Peter Port, with workmen removing the debris and rubble. This picture was taken by one of the first German soldiers to arrive on Guernsey. (Author's Collection)

A portrait of Harold Hobbs in his Royal Naval Volunteer Reserve uniform. (Tony Hobbs)

Personnel of *Fernaufklärungsgruppe* 3.(F)/123 (Long Range Reconnaissance Group 123). The *Staffelkapitän*, *Hauptmann* Reinhard Liebe-Piderit (also spelt Liebe-Pieteritz), can be seen in the middle of the front row. (John Goodwin)

German troops preparing for their part in Operation *Green Arrow* are pictured at the recently captured airfield at Cherbourg, 1 July 1940. The men seen here, from the 396th Infantry Regiment, part of the 216th Infantry Division, would soon be airlifted to the Channel Islands. (Author's Collection)

Another view of men from the 396th Infantry Regiment at Cherbourg, 1 July 1940. (Author's Collection)

The moment of departure for the Channel Islands has arrived, and the soldiers of the 396th Infantry Regiment, now wearing their life jackets, climb aboard the Junkers Ju 52s for take-off. The *Luftwaffe* crews are already at their positions. (Author's Collection)

Invading German troops pictured shortly after their arrival, by air, at Guernsey on 1 July 1940. It is believed that the motorcycle beyond the troops is a light-weight 350cc BMW R.35 which the occupiers brought with them. The individual with the 'X' above his head is believed to be one *Unteroffizier* Umann. (Author's Collection)

Major Dr Lanz salutes, whilst Dr Maass shakes hands with Ambrose Sherwill outside the Royal Court, Guernsey. (Damien Horn/Channel Islands Military Museum)

Pictured on a BSA police motorcycle, Acting Inspector Arthur Langmead assists *Luftwaffe* personnel with directions. The latter are busy posting the first orders of the German Commandant around St Peter Port. The printed orders can in fact be seen in the hands of the officer on the extreme right. The three men on the left of the image are a machine-gun crew on their way to take up defensive positions at Castle Cornet. (Author's Collection)

Occupiers and occupied on Jersey. They are, from left to right: *Major* Dr Lanz, C.W. Duret Aubin (the Attorney-General), *Kapitänleutnant* Koch, *Oberleutnant* Richard Kern (the first German to land on Jersey), and *Oberstleutnant* Hermann Plocher at Jersey Airport. (Channel Islands Occupation Society)

German personnel in front of the control tower at Jersey airport, pictured during the afternoon of 1 July 1940. (Channel Islands Occupation Society)

A Dornier Do.17P of *Fernaufklärungsgruppe* 3.(F)/123 at Jersey's airport. (Author's Collection)

A newly-installed anti-aircraft gun at Jersey's airport after the German landings. (Author's Collection)

A picture of early German occupation troops outside the Hotel Ommaroo in St Helier, Jersey. The soldier with the 'X' below his feet is, once again, *Unteroffizier* Umann, who had briefly transferred across from Guernsey to consolidate positions and early defences on Jersey. (Author's Collection)

The scene at Guernsey's airport during the early days of the Occupation. The fighters are from *Kampfgeschwader* 53. (Author's Collection)

A sentry outside the German HQ of the British Channel Islands, which at the time this image was taken was located in the Channel Islands Hotel on Glategny Esplanade in St Peter Port, Guernsey. (Author's Collection)

German troops on the White Rock, St Peter Port, waiting to be despatched to Alderney to begin the Occupation there. (Author's Collection)

A member of the *Luftwaffe* speaking to a Police Constable Eugenine Le Lievre on Glategny Esplanade, Guernsey. (Author's Collection)

Major Dr Lanz, the German Commandant, is pictured stepping out of the Guernsey Police Force's Wolseley police car – the only vehicle in the force's fleet at the time – soon after his arrival. The Police Constable seen here was one of three assigned to the Commandant as chauffeurs during the early days of the German Occupation. (Channel Islands Occupation Society)

The first German troops to arrive on Alderney are pictured having taken up residence in their headquarters on the Island, which was established in the Island Hall in Connaught Square, St Anne's. (Author's Collection)

An early shot of German troops en route to occupy Sark. Sitting at the back in the black uniform is a Marine Police NCO. To the latter's immediate right is a member of the requisitioned Guernsey boat's crew, a second member of which can be seen sat in front of the ship's wheel. (Author's Collection)

These men formed part of the first German unit to occupy Sark. The NCO in charge of the sixteen-strong group (not all of whom appear in this image) was *Gefrieter* Obenauf, who can be seen in the centre of the back row. The building in the background is the Bel Vue Hotel which stood at the top of Harbour Hill. (via Mrs Carre)

The first troops to occupy Herm pictured on the island's Harbour Hill. (Author's Collection)

A view of Jersey airport, complete with a Junkers Ju 52 troop transport, taken on 17 July 1940. (Author's Collection)

A *Luftwaffe* sentry on duty outside the former RAF headquarters building on Guernsey Airport as the Occupation gets underway. (Author's Collection)

undesirable. It was recognised, however, that special facilities should be provided for those who wished to leave, and the arrangements which were at once put into operation were based on the principle that priority should be given to women and children and to those men of military age who, under the Island laws, were liable to service with His Majesty's Forces.

The transport made available also enabled numerous other persons to leave the Islands, and as a result between one-fourth and one-third of the total population was brought to this country ... Evacuation was planned on the principle that women and children should be brought away but a sufficient part of the population should remain behind to enable the life of the islands to go on.[5]

Anger at the way in which the evacuation had been conducted was also expressed by the Earl of Radnor in the House of Lords:

When the islands were demilitarised an announcement was made, I believe at six o'clock in the evening, that a voluntary evacuation would take place and that those who wished to be evacuated had to register by nine o'clock the same evening. If anything was calculated to cause consternation among a population of something like 90,000 people; that was bound to do so. There was a seething mass, I believe, outside the various offices where you could register for evacuation, and naturally the wildest rumours and everything which goes with such disorder.

The voluntary evacuation was conducted in that great hurry; it lasted, as far as I can ascertain, for about two days. Very little explanation was given to any of the people concerned. Parents were told that they would not necessarily be allowed to go with their children, wives – the wives of the men under my command – that they would be separated and be a long way from their husbands. Time was very short, and they were in fact separated from the only persons whom they could consult on whether they should evacuate or not.

At the end of two days, voluntary evacuation finished, and the railway companies were asked by the Government to carry on, and did carry on, a commercial service thereafter at a risk which ultimately involved the fact that most of their staff in the islands are still there. But the people with whom I am concerned, when they had their second thought and decided to evacuate, could not afford the fare back to England. An instance was brought to my notice of a woman with three children whom it would have cost £4 to come to this country. All that she had to live on was the family allowance which she received because her husband was serving in the Army. It was not fair on that woman, first of all to make her take a hurried decision, and secondly, when she failed to do so, to expect her to pay the fare back.

Perhaps that is an indictment of the Government, and I may be accused in my turn of causing alarm and despondency; but I cannot see that these facts are going to help the enemy in any way, and my statement of them may stir the Government to take some steps to rectify the wrong that they have done by their unnecessarily hasty action.[6]

While many continued to vent their feelings of anger, frustration or sadness at the Government's decision to abandon the Channel Islands to their fate, the Germans continued in their preparations for the next stage in the Blitzkrieg.

7

'The blackest day
Guernsey had ever seen'
The Bombing of Guernsey

Seemingly abandoned by the British Government, the remaining populations ridden by uncertainty and fear, the Channel Islands awaited the next step in the unfolding drama of the German Blitzkrieg. When it came, it was during the early evening of Friday, 28 June 1940.

At about 18.45 hours that evening, a gaggle of Heinkel He 111 bombers appeared over the harbours of both St Helier and St Peter Port dropping bombs and machine-gunning as they went. One of the crew of the Heinkel flown by *Leutnant* Knorringer (Pilot Officer), Hans Grah, who acted as a *Beobachter* (Observer/Navigator), later recorded his involvement in the raid on the Islands. Serving together in I/*KG* 55 Knorringer and Grah were assigned to 1 *Staffel*. Their Heinkel He 111 was one of nine participating in the raid, forming three *Kette* (flights). Operating out of Villacoublay (located just south west of Paris), they were drawn from both the first and second *Staffel* of *KG* 55. Each aircraft carried a bomb load consisting of twenty 50kg bombs, stored vertically in the internal bomb-bay.

The following is an extract from the diary of Hans Grah, providing a first-hand German account of the events of that day:

> Today, we have also waited a long time. We fixed the rest areas on the field to be somewhat more comfortable, the French have left everything in such a condition, it is hardly believable. Then yet another order comes. With a *Kette,* we shall attack troop embarkations, and ships departing the British Channel Islands. We take off at 18.35 hours. The flight-path was over Caen to the British Channel Islands, Guernsey and Jersey. We look at the interesting northern French landscape, small fields, filled with hedges. From above the coast of the Cherbourg peninsula we already see, lying in the haze, the

islands. We fly on, the first raid against England. Larger troop embarkations should be occurring there. One aircraft attacks a small departing steamer, it goes without saying however that it skilfully avoids the bombs through permanent zig-zag manoeuvres. We then flew over the quays of St. Peter [Port]. Everywhere on the island the glass roofs of the greenhouses light up in the sun, Guernsey is famous because of its tomatoes. On the quay stands a mass of vehicles, troops, also a small ship lies there.

Turning – the other machine has already bombed, hits on a warehouse – we approach, the bombs being aimed at vehicles, the first bomb, the second and so on, marvellous, none are falling wide. Big pieces of debris fly about, a fire burns. Next run, again everything into the vehicles, below its burning fiercely. The small ship will also get something.

We descend to a lower altitude, circling over the island, no defences! Again bombs at the vehicles. I suggest that we should land and occupy the island. *Leutnant* Knorringer has his doubts, I try to convince him, but he doesn't want to, what a pity! (On the next day another aircraft did with complete success!).

A few bombs still remain, so heading to Jersey, it is already burning in the harbour there, the second *Staffel* having bombed there, the remainder are dropped, a steamer the intended target, but unfortunately everything goes into the water – we later found out, that on Guernsey, all the vehicles were loaded with tomatoes, that should have gone over to England, a fine mess that must have been. Troops were already no longer on the island, since some days earlier. It's a pity that we had not landed, that would have been a complete success.[1]

To Islander Miss A. Le M. Mainé, 28 June 1940 was, without question, 'the blackest day Guernsey had ever seen':

It was, of course, the height of the tomato season and, as usual, if perhaps unwisely, dozens of motor cars and lorries were formed up in two rows along the White Rock waiting to ship their produce. It was a beautiful summer's day and the pier presented a very animated appearance. I, myself, spent most of the afternoon on the Jetty seeing about the dispatch of two large cases of books for the Ladies' College, the staff and pupils having left eight days before.

When I returned home I found Elise and Lydie (Figtree) had turned up unexpectedly and stayed for tea. Advocate Sherwill was due to address the public at 6.15 p.m. in Smith Street, but we did not go. After the girls had left I went to College to finish some more work, and Helene and I expected to go and see the mailboat in ...

I was just about to leave College, and had actually opened the door when I heard machine gun fire and bombs being dropped. I at once realised that an air raid was on and quickly closed the door and threw myself flat in the passage where I lay more or less terrified for the best part of an hour listening to the hateful noise of German planes overhead and bombs being dropped at intervals. The concussion in the large empty building was terrific, and it seemed to me that the place might be hit at any moment and collapse. There appeared to be three attacks with a short interval between, but the whole raid lasted about 45 minutes.[2]

As mentioned by Miss A. Le M. Lainé, the regular mailboat was indeed docked in St Peter Port. On board which was Mrs R.J. Stephen:

Three planes with their engines shut off swooped out of the sun ... There was a terrific explosion as the first bomb fell, splinters rattled on to the deck and a man standing next to my small boy sagged on to the deck with blood pouring from a wound in the groin ... some ran to get below, but others less lucky, chose to panic down the gangway plank and make for the sheds and warehouses on the wharf. They were caught by a raking machine gun fire from the second and third Nazi planes and went down in rows like ninepins. The policeman taking the tickets on the gangway was blown to pieces and the shed went up in flames.[3]

Frank Stroobant ran a café in St Peter Port, which was known as 'Home from Home', and saw large numbers of lorries full of tomatoes standing on the north arm of the harbour known as the White Rock:

We were all in the café. The first time I realised it was a raid was when all the windows came in. They were blitzed by machine gun bullets. Looking out, we could see a blaze on the White Rock where all the lorries were burning. In the café it was a genuine panic – everyone on the floor. But after the first burst I managed to get them down into the cellar. I don't think the air raid lasted more than ten minutes at the very most. But we naturally expected them to return and finish the job off – which they didn't do.

The air raid warden came in to see me and said: 'Frank, this is a mess.' And I looked out and saw that by this time the White Rock was a pall of smoke. And that is where the casualties happened because many of the lorry drivers had, for safety, dived under their vehicles and, of course, when they were machine gunned and the petrol tanks exploded.[4]

Ambrose Sherwill had just finished addressing a crowd of anxious Islanders outside the offices of the Guernsey Press Company – the speech that Miss A. Le M. Mainé had decided not to go and listen to – when, as he later recalled in his memoirs, the German bombers attacked:

> The machine gunning of our lifeboat, of the usual distinctive build, and clearly marked on her deck with a large red cross, resulted in one of the crew (the coxswain's son) being killed outright. The long lines of tomato-laden lorries in the harbour awaiting their turn to unload into the waiting ship were machine gunned and bombed very severely.
>
> Bombs were dropped elsewhere in the island doing considerable damage and there was much indiscriminate machine gunning. The raid started just before 6.45 p.m. and one bomb hit the harbour weighbridge and stopped its clock at that time. 27 men and 4 women lost their lives and 38 men and 9 women received serious injuries.
>
> Curiously enough the mailboat 'Isle of Sark', which fired on the planes with her machine-gun – the only such weapon in Guernsey at that time – and the other ships in harbour escaped unscathed. Four British planes, in formation, made a swoop over the island within about half an hour of the end of the raid. It was most reassuring.[5]

Along with his parents, schoolboy Malcolm Woodland was one of those in the crowd who listened to Ambrose Sherwill's speech. They soon found themselves in the thick of the action:

> After the evacuation of the other children in my class, life carried on much as normal, playing with friends, going swimming, packing tomatoes, until my parents said someone was going to give a speech in town and I'd have to go with them as it was important.
>
> We took the bus to town and got off at the North Pier Steps, walked up them to the junction between Smith Street and the High Street between Lloyd's Bank and Boots. The place was packed solid with people. Mr Sherwill gave a speech about whether people should evacuate or not. Anyway, being quite young and not very tall and

being stood amongst these people all I could see were people's legs, so my Dad stood me up on the windowsills of Lloyd's Bank for a better view.

The announcements went on quite a bit, from 6 to about 6.30, and being as we were some of the last to arrive, we were near the beginning of the rush to get out of the town to go down to the bus terminus for the return journey home. We went down the steps and along the harbour front looking for the Baubigny bus, which was there waiting on its stand. We were waiting to get on with lots of our neighbours and people were talking about what Mr Sherwill had said.

I then heard this throbbing of aircraft, so I looked up, and coming up from the south were tiny specks of silver in the sky and they got closer and closer. Dad said, 'Look, there they are!' and I could see them!

We could see by then that they were fairly large aircraft, as far as I was concerned anyway, and they were in a formation. We were just getting on the bus, and I said to Dad, 'Why are they putting ladders down from the aircraft?' He looked up and said 'Oh my God!', and he called to my Mum, 'Quick, get off the bus, we've got to go!' The ladders weren't ladders, they were the vertical descent of the bombs shining in the sun! This was an air raid!

My Dad led us to the Ladies and Gents toilets by the bus terminus as he had spotted that the building had been sandbagged. He said, 'Right, we've got to get over there and shelter in there, quick, run!' Well we were running fairly fast until we got up by the Albert Memorial – then the first bomb landed!

I think we took off then and we got there rather quicker, and so did a lot of other people. We pushed our way in as it was packed, and several clutches of bombs came quite close, and there were some very loud bangs. I'd gone off air raids by then.[6]

Guernseyman Kenneth Lewis avidly recorded his daily experiences in his diary. As he noted in his entry for 28 June, he and a friend had decided to go and listen to the speech:

At about 5.45 p.m. Ralph and I left his house to go to Smith Street and heard the Procureur – Mr. Ambrose Sherwill – speak on the Island situation. After hearing his speech we drove quietly home to the Steam Mill Lanes; on arrival Mrs Le Poidevin went up the road to tell Mrs Bougourd of the substance of the speech, whilst Mr Le Poidevin, Ralph and myself went out on the lawn.

On arrival there we heard the throb of aeroplane engines and on looking up we spotted three Dornier 215s approaching the Island at a height of 5,000 ft. They were flying in a single line abreast. As we watched, the centre plane dropped back and with that we heard bursts of machine gun fire and saw puffs of smoke coming from the plane, at the same time we heard an ever increasing scream which I at once realised was a screaming bomb.

With presence of mind Mr Le Poidevin threw himself on the ground and at the same moment we heard the crump as the bombs burst on the Weighbridge; the first bombs dropped at approximately 6.54 p.m. We then rushed into the garage and on seeing so much glass we rushed out again meanwhile another salvo of bombs had dropped.

We took refuge behind the big chair in a corner of the room and we felt the house shake violently as more bombs were dropped. We then rushed into the front room and saw a large pall of smoke arising from the town, the machine gunning of the aeroplanes did not stop all the time.

Mrs Le Poidevin and Mrs Bougourd then returned and we took refuge under the table singing hymns and praying throughout the raid. It was while under the table that we heard the Air Raid warning sound. Salvo after salvo of bombs were dropped the majority being in the vicinity of the harbour and on the line of produce which was about to be shipped. The only defence we had was a light gun on the Mail-boat which kept the raider to a height of 2,000ft.

At about 7.45 the noise of the engines died away and I decided to make a dash for home as I knew they would be worrying about me, and I eventually arrived home safe and at 7.50 the All Clear went.[7]

Ossie Gallienne, a St. John Ambulance man at the time, vividly recounts the events immediately after he had 'trooped up to the Press Office' to listen to Sherwill:

Afterwards I went to the ambulance station to let them know what it had been about. When I got to the top of the rise, three German planes came in front the East. They must have flown right over the harbour and in line with the harbour. The first plane suddenly started a trail, a small trail and it went straight to the East. I knew what this meant as I had heard that before they ever started [attacking] in a new place, started to raid, they would warn their friends to get out of the way.[8]

Arriving at the Ambulance Station, Gallienne recounted to those on duty what he had just seen, adding that he was certain a raid was imminent. His story was not believed, one of the ambulance crew stating that it was just another reconnaissance flight. Seconds later, Gallienne was proven correct:

> The plane, having turned around, came back from the West, straight along the smoke trail towards the harbour, over the top of the first aid room roof. I could see the plane still approaching the harbour by then, and it dropped a bomb.
>
> The bomb went down about a hundred feet or so, and burst open; the main bomb went down surrounded by incendiaries. Then came the explosion, the phone rang and the air raid siren went off. Charlie Froom (an ambulance colleague) took the call and said, 'We've got to go down to the harbour.' I said, 'Do you want me to come down with you?' 'No, you stop here and take the phone calls, Lionel Taylor (another colleague) and me are going down.'

It was to be the start of a frantic, and fraught, few hours for the St. John Ambulance team. Meanwhile, also in the same crowd as Malcolm Woodland and Ossie Gallienne outside the offices of the Guernsey Press Company was Bill Green:

> Commencing on Monday 24th June, one of the members of the new Controlling Committee spoke each evening at 6.15 pm to the crowd outside the Press Office. On the Friday evening, the 28th June, the President of the Controlling Committee, Ambrose Sherwill, was due to speak and I wanted to hear what he had to say.
>
> There was a large crowd standing outside the Press office in the summer sunshine waiting to hear Ambrose Sherwill, but first we had to listen to Deputy Stamford Raffles who, as Information Officer, read out a procession of statements and notices. I remember him telling us that 500 cattle had been saved and brought over from Alderney, which had been almost totally evacuated. Whilst I did not realise it at the time, those extra cattle must have provided Guernsey with much needed supplies of milk and meat during the occupation.
>
> When Ambrose Sherwill spoke he tried to calm everyone down by saying; 'Whatever else is wrong, it has been a beautiful day.' I recall those words so well and I remember later saying … how wrong he was![9]

With the speeches drawing to a close, Green decided to head off and make his way to his bicycle shop before giving a couple of people a lift home in his car. His journey was soon interrupted:

> As I was returning, driving down St James past the prison, I heard a strange noise. It sounded like the clatter of a machine gun and looking up I saw three German aircraft with bright flashes of fire coming from their wings. It was about ten to seven on the 28th June 1940 …
>
> I abandoned my car alongside what was then St Paul's Church, ran for the protection of the buttresses and threw myself on the ground against the wall of the Church. The ground never felt so comfortable.
>
> There were several other people, including Mr W. Frampton, the States Accountant, and his wife, sheltering around the church. 'I don't fancy being out here,' said Mr Frampton. 'No, neither do I', I replied. So I went around to the rear of the church, broke a toilet window, climbed inside and quickly opened a door and let in Mr and Mrs Frampton and about a dozen other people. My thoughts were, as no doubt were everyone else's, to take cover at all costs. We sheltered in the church, and after a while were relieved to realise that we personally, were not the target for the German planes.
>
> It sounded to us as if all hell had been let loose down in the harbour area. First we heard the whistle, then the thud of exploding bombs. Soon it seemed to us that the sea front was under an incessant bombardment. Jerry planes were shrieking overhead, tracer bullets were pattering down like rain, salvo after salvo of bombs were being rained down on our defenceless island. Soon there was a thick pall of smoke drifting slowly across the sky. The reality of war had come to Guernsey.

After what seemed an eternity to Green, the raid appeared to have ended. Leaving the shelter of the church, he ran across to Smith Street, arriving at his shop to find it full of people:

> Then suddenly the German planes resumed their attack, the whistling and the inevitable thud of the bombs, concentrated everyone's mind on self-preservation. The shop was in some ways an exciting place to be, because every time a bomb exploded, all the tools on the bench would bounce up and down and the bikes in the window would jiggle about.

On the evening of the 27th Frank Collenette and his wife, Hedy, went to St Peter Port to see if they could acquire any of the cattle that had been removed from Alderney, with little idea that the following day tragedy would strike the very place where they had been barely twenty-four hours earlier:

> It was Hedy who saw the bombs at first. Outside of our cottage door she said: 'Look something is coming out of those planes'! Many days before we had seen planes with those awful crosses on them, flying sometimes quite low. But we never imagined this! We were really afraid of the Germans because we had heard how they had treated other occupied countries.[10]

Having only recently witnessed the evacuation of his mother, sister, three aunts, two cousins and both of his grandmothers, the teenage Frank Hubert would have a lucky escape on the 28th:

> It was very sad for us all. For those who chose to stay behind, it was a disturbing and unnerving time. My father was worried about both his businesses … They were his livelihood and he had to try and keep them going. Running an agricultural firm meant that we were actually encouraged and helped to continue trading and as an eighteen-year-old, I decided to stay and support my father and our family business.
>
> Dad's business involved the export of tomatoes to England. Many of his staff were of military age and had already left to join the forces. It was therefore necessary for me to obtain a driving licence quickly to help him out. The times I had spent driving around the vineries and on private land held me in good stead for when I applied for my licence. I only had to drive up the Havelet Road, reverse into the nearby Strand, make a U-turn and I'd done enough to pass my test. I was then able to drive a lorry, collecting and delivering the tomatoes to my father's depot on the White Rock area of the harbour.
>
> We didn't have to wait long before the Germans made their mark on Guernsey!
>
> I had driven a lorry load of tomatoes down to our depot at the White Rock for shipping but there was a queue of lorries all waiting to be unloaded. My father and I drove back home in his car, to Doyle Road, only about 5 minutes' drive away, for a bite to eat, giving a chance for the queue to peter out.

Never had we made such an important and lifesaving decision as this, because no sooner had we arrived home, than we heard bombing and gun fire. It was terrifying![11]

With the harbour under attack, Frank and his father had also sought shelter from the explosions as best as they could:

We pushed the dining room table against the wall and got under it, we did not know how close to our house they would come. It was a bit naive of us perhaps, to imagine that a mere table would protect us, but we felt much safer under it, than above it and it was the only thing we could think of to do.

Surprisingly, the telephone rang, startling us both. Bill Peel, one of dad's staff, just happened to call from England, at that very moment, to ask if he had left the Island too early and should he return to help my father with his business. Needless to say, my father was able to explain about the bombing and that even if he tried, he would not be allowed back into the Island.

Whilst many Islanders recall the damage that the raiders caused on land, Bill Green would also describe the effect on the shipping in the harbour:

The mailboat, the *Isle of Sark*, which had been embarking passengers, had an anti-aircraft gun on its aft deck. This was in action until the gallant gunner was injured in the arm. A cargo boat, the SS *Sheringham*, was also equipped with a gun which was used against the German attackers.

Another vessel, the SS *Courier*, was en-route from Alderney to St Peter Port with salvaged stores, two hundred pigs and some of the last inhabitants, when it was attacked off St Sampson's Harbour. She was machine gunned, by the Germans, causing eleven casualties amongst her crew. The aircraft that attacked her also dropped a bomb, which fortunately missed its target. The Captain beached the SS *Courier* near the entrance to St Sampson's Harbour and many of her crew and passengers managed to make their way ashore. The next day the ship was refloated and immediately set sail for England.

The blast from bombs which were intended for the *Isle of Sark*, caused a number of fishing boats and yachts to sink in the harbour. Neither the *Isle of Sark* or the SS *Sheringham* were hit.

At 10 pm, soon after the air raid was over the *Isle of Sark* left harbour with 163 passengers and headed for England. That was our last mailboat until after the occupation.[12]

According to Ralph Durand the attack marked the moment when, for the Channel Islands, the war had begun, but he was not impressed with the effectiveness of the German pilots and crew:

The marksmanship of the bombers was distinctly poor. Part of a salvo of bombs aimed at the gas-works fell on the Fruit Export Store and the rest on the beach near the Long Store. A bomb aimed at the States Water Board's pumping station near the Forest Road fell in front of, and blew the roof off, a house at La Vassallerie. Bombs aimed at the petrol store on the Castle Emplacement hit a house in the Strand, the west end of the slaughter house, and the rocks near Castle Cornet. A few fishing boats and small yachts were the only sufferers from three bombs aimed at the mail boat … the other two steamers in the harbour escaped with little if any injury. At what target a bomb which fell near a Martello tower at Vazon was aimed it is difficult to conjecture.[13]

After what seemed like an eternity, the raid was over. People gradually emerged from the multitude of places where they had sought shelter to assess the damage. Malcolm Woodland vividly recalls this moment:

Eventually the 'All Clear' sounded and we went out. Well, one of the bombs we heard was very close because just across the road by the Town Church is, it had blown the tobacco factory there to bits and it was all on fire. Of course everything else was smoking and on fire especially at the White Rock.

We went to look for the bus, but there wasn't a bus in sight, every single one had gone. I don't know what had happened, I suppose the drivers had gone as far away as they could. So how were going to get back as we lived at L'Islet, quite a long way from town? Dad said we would have to walk.

Everyone was milling around wondering how they were going to get home. Suddenly along the quay came a lorry which used to deliver the tomatoes and it was our neighbour, our contractor, Mr Sid Vaudin. He had been delivering tomatoes on the White Rock and when he'd finished, he'd gone off, and got as far as St George's Hall when he heard this fearful racket. He stopped, and saw planes coming up around, and realized there was something on, so he parked his lorry and waited until it was all over. Then he turned round and came back because he knew that a lot of his clients for tomatoes in our road, and around L'Islet, had sent tomatoes and were going into town for the speech. So he turned round and came back with his lorry and picked up as many as he could.[14]

P. Girard, whom it may be recalled was a teacher at the States' Intermediate School for Boys in Guernsey, provides this account of the *Luftwaffe* raid:

> Soon after I had arrived home the Air Raid took place and being in charge of the Castel First Aid Post I rushed through the fields to the Castel School with my 'tin hat' on my head.
>
> As I crossed the fields German planes were flying overhead and I could hear the bullets whistling through the air fired indiscriminately or possibly aimed at the buildings at Le Grand Mare which were bombed and destroyed because apparently adjoining race course had been mistaken to be an important airfield.
>
> Looking towards St. Peter Port I could see huge flames soaring upwards and I remember thinking that the Town was on fire.
>
> When our Post members assembled they were eventually ordered to proceed with their lorries to the White Rock and there our members were given the task of conveying bodies to the Mortuary. Later I helped move some of the casualties to and from the Operating Theatres of the Hospital.[15]

Frank Hubert's father was a volunteer telephone operator for the Auxiliary Fire Service, whilst Frank himself had joined the AFS's demolition squad. Formed from volunteers, one of its roles was 'to make buildings safe, after the effects of a bombing'. Both father and son were soon in action:

> Once we had recovered from the initial shock of hearing the bomb attack, we ran straight to the Arsenal headquarters just a couple of hundred yards around the corner from our house in Doyle Road and reported for duty. I was the only member of my section to turn up, so the Chief Officer, Mr. Oliver, found all kinds of odd jobs for me.
>
> The first of which was to take an extra water pump down to the harbour for the firemen already down there, after the air raid.

Fortunately the tide was high enough and in the meantime, they had been pumping the seawater from under the Cambridge berth. I noticed that my father's business premises survived the raid and even the lorry I had driven down there was okay. However, other lorries in the queue had been annihilated and the drivers killed. I saw at least two bodies and found the whole sight very disturbing.

On my way back to the Fire Station, I noticed one of the St. John's ambulances at the top of College Street, by the old prison wall, it had been machine-gunned. I later discovered that the driver, Mr. Joseph Way, had been killed.

As I drove into the Station so did two cars carrying injured people, unfortunately the drivers were unaware that the first aid post had been transferred to the Castel Hospital, in the centre of the Island, which was being used as the emergency hospital. My next job was to collect some stretchers from St. Paul's Church, opposite the police station. A chap, standing nearby at the fire station offered his help, but chose to sit on the back of the new Austin (pickup) lorry I was given to drive.

We had to take the stretchers to the Castel Hospital, but as I drove along the Rohais, my passenger suddenly decided he did not want to stay on the back any more and climbed around, opened the door of the cab and got in alongside me.

Somewhat surprised and not a little shaken up by his bizarre behaviour, my foot slipped off the clutch pedal and the engine backfired. For a split second I thought we were being shot at. Despite this unnerving experience we duly arrived at the Castel Hospital and were instructed to take the stretchers up to the operating theatres. As we did so, we could not help but notice all the people queuing up the stairs apparently waiting to donate blood for those injured in the bombing raid. Such was the reaction of the locals, once they heard about the bombing and that people had been injured, they instinctively offered to donate blood and to help where they could.

It was some time later before I could speak to my passenger properly, I learnt that he was a Guernsey man by the name of Le Monnier, he had been in the forces but managed to escape from France. I never did find out why he jumped into the cab and frighten the life out of me. When our duties at the Fire Station were over, on that horrendous day, we were invited down to the home of one of the men that worked for my father, Mr. C.J. Le Page. He and his wife lived at La Cloture Passee, in the north of the Island, where it was thought to be safer than in Town. Mr. Le Page was a local preacher and had earlier managed to escape enemy fire as he fled along Les Banques from the harbour. I remember before retiring that night, all four of us kneeling at a chair and giving thanks for being spared that day.[16]

As would be expected, it was not just the firemen who were kept busy that day.[17] Dr Alistair Rose played a vital role in Guernsey both before and throughout the Occupation. He left a detailed account of his involvement in treating the wounded after the air raid:

On the 28th June (I remember it was a Friday and a most perfect day) Dr. Gibson, and I went down to L'Ancresse Common for a few holes of golf. It was too hot for exercise and our golf suffered in consequence, so we thought the 19th hole would hold out more attraction and betook ourselves to the new club house. On the way, I remarked what a perfect evening it would be for an air raid. A German reconnaissance plane had passed over the centre of the island on the previous day, flying high and fast, but when I made this remark I did so mainly in jest; and I was soon to prove the old adage that there is many a true word …

We had both gone to the golf course in Dr. Gibson's car and on the way home he suggested we drop in on T. for a drink, the latter's house being situated in the centre of the island. The three of us were sitting sipping whisky and sodas when the noise of approaching aircraft brought us to the windows. We saw three planes flying in formation approaching from the south. T. fetched a powerful pair of binoculars and focussing them excitedly shouted, 'They're Huns!' We all identified the crosses under the wings quite easily.

Soon from under the planes little puffs of smoke appeared, to be followed by a staccato but irregular crackle exactly like the explosion of jumping-jack squibs. T. said, 'They're setting off crackers to scare the people'. The absurdity of this idea did not strike us at the time, for in our state of defencelessness, quite harmless to our enemies, the thought of attack seemed equally absurd. We had forgotten the impression that those lines of lorries would create, and so had the growers, in their anxiety not to miss the market.

The planes disappeared towards the harbour, and suddenly there was a series of distant explosions, and we could feel the concussion of the bombs. We knew now what was happening, and I remember my reaction was one of futile anger. I would have fired even a rifle at the planes if I had had one. However, the only guns available were those on the boats which were loading tomatoes; they did their best

100

but were no real protection against the aircraft which continued to bomb and machine gun the White Rock for more than an hour.

When it was all over, Dr. Gibson and I left for the hospital in order to find out whether or not there had been any casualties. We drove through the winding lanes, and were suddenly brought to a halt by a car standing in the middle of the road with its engine still running. The occupant had abandoned it so hastily that he had even dropped a suitcase which was half resting on the road and half on the running board. I drove the car into a field to clear the road. When we got to the hill above the hospital, we could see a thick pall of black smoke hanging over the town, completely obscuring the horizon. It was merely the burning petrol of the lorries, but it seemed to us that the whole of St. Peter Port was in flames.

As we pulled up at the hospital, the first cases were arriving and we began to get news of what had happened. The toll of dead and injured was very high for a raid of this nature as we subsequently learned. The wounded arrived in a steady stream, many of them seriously injured, and soon we had upwards of fifty cases awaiting operation. The killed, it transpired later, numbered much about the same.

Our A.R.P. arrangements had been considerably upset, if not completely disorganised, by the departure of most of the volunteers, and we had to get busy and improvise a service as best we could. The St. Johns Ambulance Brigade, as could be expected of them, bravely answered the call and went down to the quay to pick up the wounded. While they were there, the planes attacked again and the ambulance was riddled. The driver was killed, and another member seriously wounded; others had narrow escapes. One of the latter told me how he took refuge beneath the ambulance. He heard the whine of the falling bomb which struck not thirty feet away, and he was lifted a foot off the ground by the concussion, and had the horrible experience of seeing the chassis sinking down on top of him. He thought he was done for, but luckily it was just due to punctures in the tyres!

Most of the casualties occurred among the lorry drivers, and those that were sailing on the mail boat that night or friends who were seeing them off. A trained nurse, who was amongst those about to sail, was travelling to England in response to the sad news that her mother and sister had been killed in an air raid on Bristol. She immediately made for the hospital where she worked all night in the theatre.[18]

This nurse was one of many individuals who, staff or otherwise, attended the hospital to render what assistance they could, as Dr Alistair Rose noted:

Helpers, nearly all of them quite untrained and quite unaccustomed to the scenes we witnessed that night, turned up to lend us a hand. Some of them were fishermen who worked feverishly carrying the wounded from the yard to the wards, and from the wards to the theatres. Many of them, once it was over, just quietly disappeared to remain anonymous. The spirit shown by all was absolutely superb, and can never be forgotten.

We organised two theatre teams, and after a spell of preparation which allowed us to give blood transfusions to those most requiring it, and to swallow some sweet tea and biscuits ourselves, we got down to the work in hand. I wish that I could paint a colourful pen picture of the scene that night. Unfortunately, after four years the memory of it remains only like the inconsecutive episodes of a half-forgotten dream.

I carry a vivid mental picture of the dimly lit wards crowded with stretchers, for there were at first far too few beds to accommodate the cases, and of the anxiety written on the faces of the casualties, each hoping to be the first to receive attention. Nurses and helpers scurrying to and fro, and doctors directing and organising the trained and untrained helpers, quickly appraising the nature of the cases, and deciding the order of their urgency.

At one moment I would be called across by a V.A.D. (Volunteer Aid Detachment) to examine a man whose leg was bleeding, 'I noticed the blood dripping beneath the bed', she said. The light was so poor that it was difficult to see where the bleeding was coming from, but the tourniquet had slipped a little and the haemorrhage was soon controlled. The V.A.D. was left to watch the case and report on the pulse.

As I crossed the ward, my name was called out by a figure lying in the shadows. I have no idea to this day who he was, 'You know me, Dr. Rose,' he said, 'take me into the theatre soon, please'. I reassured him that we would operate as soon as we could. Then I had to hurry away to give a transfusion to an old lady, who was in desperate straits. She had a compound comminuted fracture of one leg, which had been reduced to a shapeless mass. Her waxy pallor and shallow rapid breathing told their tale.

When I returned with the blood from the donor, I saw that unfortunately not even a transfusion could help her, and within a minute or two, she breathed her last. She was one of the very few cases we lost.

In his account, Dr Rose went on to describe 'another very tragic case', in this instance that of a French youth who had been brought in from the harbour:

I forget his name now, but I remember he had a companion called Paul. I will call him H., although that was not his name. Paul was not seriously hurt, and made a good recovery, but H. had been taking cover and was just getting up when a bomb fell near him. A piece of the bomb must have entered through his trouser pocket (for there was no hole in the clothing) and penetrated his thigh.

Unfortunately, it damaged the femoral artery, which is the main artery to the limb. H. and Paul, had arrived in Guernsey in order to get to England to serve in the army of General de Gaulle. H. was a brave little soldier. Throughout the frequent relapses from haemorrhages which occurred at intervals during the following weeks, he would always gain courage by singing the Marseillaise. The artery was tied but it was damaged so high up, that ligature was not effective, and the poor lad gradually bled to death.[19]

Having recovered from the initial shock of the German air raid, Miss A. Le M. Mainé was another of the many Islanders who stepped forward to do their part:

After the raid Helene and I, who belonged to the Trinity First Aid Depot, rushed down to see what we could do, as it was obvious that casualties must be numerous. When we arrived at the Depot, I was sent with the first party down to the White Rock where we had a great shock. The raid had been a severe one and the whole area was like an inferno. Fires were raging everywhere, and the roadway was strewn with glass from shattered windows. The Weighbridge was on fire and most of the tomato lorries were blazing, as well as sheds and stores, etc. But worst of all, people were lying about, some dead, others seriously wounded and needing attention.

The mailboat, having arrived from Jersey earlier in the evening, was alongside the Jetty when this brutal attack took place, and the quay was crowded with would-be passengers. Many of these sought refuge on the landing below the Jetty, but many were injured. The mailboat's guns kept the German 'planes, which numbered three, fairly high up, otherwise the result might have been still worse.

When my party got there we found that the St. John Ambulance people had already been busy with the most urgent cases and we were sent to the Country Hospital where most of the casualties were taken. There we helped to carry the stretchers from the Ambulance to the wards, and we were asked to unload lorries full of tomato baskets so that the lorries might go and fetch more casualties, as the Ambulances could not cope with all quickly enough. As a matter of fact, one Ambulance was machine-gunned during the raid, the driver being killed, and the Ambulance itself was stranded up St James's Street. Miss Seabrook and I came back to town in a car and conveyed a patient from the Town Hospital to the Country Hospital, calling at the Depot on the way to see if there were any hospital cases there, but there were none.

Helene had remained at the Depot most of the evening, with one visit to the Town Arsenal. By the time I was free it was 10.30 p.m. and we were all very tired. Some of my party, who had had nursing experience, stayed at the hospital all night to help the staff. The following day we heard that the mailboat left at 9 p.m. strangely not having been hit at all. Ernest, who at that time came home for lunch every day, told us that he was on the South Esplanade during the raid and that a bullet pierced his car. He was lying flat on the pavement and a woman about ten feet away was wounded in the leg. After the raid he took her at once to hospital and she was the first casualty to arrive. Three members of one family, Mr Le Page (Millmount) and his two sons were killed; two sisters, Misses Roberts, were so badly injured that they both died in hospital ...

We all felt rather shaken for some days and I, for one, could not settle down to anything. During the next two days the Air Raid Alarm was sounded a few times and we quickly put on our tin hats and ran to the Depot, but no further raid took place. German 'planes flew over and took photographs of the damage they had done, but no bombs were dropped.[20]

As a newspaperman, it fell to men such as Frank W. Falla and his colleagues to gather the facts and report on the raid:

We had no defence. The tide was low and the crowds rushed for the only shelter available, underneath the pier. This certainly saved hundreds of lives, but others were not so lucky. Some tried to shelter under their vehicles only to be crushed as the fires started and the vans and trucks collapsed. The blood of the wounded and the dying mingled with the juice of the tomatoes, and when I came on the scene just as the last Hun plane faded into the distance the sight was one I shall never forget: the flames, the bodies, the cries of the dying and the injured, and the straggling line of people emerging from their shelter under the pier.

The air-raid warning sirens were not set going until at least ten minutes after the first bomb had been dropped, and even then it was not the ARP officials who set them in motion but three cool-headed telephone operators, the Misses Wilma Guille, Mildred Langmead and Elsie Windsor, at the town and country exchanges. Their instinctive action saved further lives.

At *The Star* office we worked through the night piecing together the story of the raid, getting the names of the victims from police and ambulancemen, answering incessant telephone calls. We heard how the planes had attacked the Guernsey lifeboat on its journey from Jersey to Guernsey, killing lifeboatman Harold Hobbs; how they had machine-gunned an ambulance clearly carrying the Red-Cross roof marking; we heard of the killing of Police Constable Clifford (Chipper) Bougourd and of ambulance driver Joseph Way. The youngest of the victims of this pointless raid was a boy of fourteen, the oldest, a woman of eighty-one.[21]

On the evening of the raids, it was from the nine o'clock news on the BBC that Falla heard a startling piece of news:

The ironic news came over the air, just two hours after the bombs had fallen, that 'The Channel Islands have been demilitarised and declared an "open town".'[22]

Roy Burton, at the time a young schoolboy, and who has already given us his recollections of the events surrounding the evacuation from the Channel Islands, recalls how a family acquaintance was amongst the casualties:

One of our friends who had gone to Alderney that day [see the chapter 'An Island Evacuated'] was Frank Le Page. He and his two sons Frank (19) and Roy (14) got killed at the harbour.

He had told his oldest son Frank to come and meet him at the harbour. Roy also wanted to go but was told by his Mum to stay and help with the cows. But when Frank was leaving, Roy pestered his Mum to be allowed to go, and she relented and let him go. On leaving, Roy ran back to the house. His Mum said: 'What have you forgotten?' He said: 'Nothing. I want a clean shirt.' That was the last thing he ever said to her ...

That was the first funeral I ever attended, just after my tenth birthday. They lowered Mr Le Page's coffin in first, then the oldest son Frank and then Roy last.[23]

8

'A terrifying experience'
The Bombing of Jersey

As six of the nine German bombers set about attacking targets on Guernsey, the remaining three Heinkels continued on towards Jersey. Moments later they appeared over St. Helier, where scenes similar to those experienced in St. Peter Port were played out.

In St Helier, Jersey, Leslie P. Sinel, who was on the staff of the Island's *Evening Post*, wrote in his diary that it had been a quiet and uneventful day until around 18.45 hours, when,

> Bombs were dropped at La Rocque and in the Town Harbour vicinity, the planes sweeping over roads with their machine-guns blazing. Houses were wrecked at South Hill, stores were set on fire in Commercial Buildings and hundreds of panes of glass were shattered in the Weighbridge vicinity, stained-glass windows of the Town Church being damaged. Bombs also fell in the harbour itself, which was primarily the German objective, several small boats and yachts being destroyed. Eleven people were killed and nine injured, either by pieces of shrapnel [bomb splinters] or machine-gun bullets.[1]

R.E.H. Fletcher was sitting in a friend's garden after tea when, at about 19.00 hours, they were both startled to hear a very heavy report some distance away:

> 'What was that?' I asked. My friend suggested that it might be that part of the French Fleet was being destroyed. Before I could venture my opinion a tremendous explosion seemed to lift us from our chairs and much too near to be pleasant so we both jumped up to see if we could discover its cause.
>
> Immediately over our heads appeared three German planes followed by another three and as they were machine gunning whilst

passing we innocently thought we were spectators of an air battle …
In about an hours' time the six planes returned using their machine
guns and fires could now be seen burning fiercely near St. Helier
Harbour.[2]

Dr Averell Darling was the Resident Medical Officer on duty in Jersey
General Hospital that day. He later recorded his recollections:

I was in the male surgical ward dealing with a patient when I heard
the noise of planes. I looked out of the window and saw three Heinkel
bombers. As I watched I saw bombs beginning to fall.

I left the patient and went through the hospital down to Casualty.
And almost as I got there the first victim arrived, He had a great hole
blown in the side of his chest and he died within a matter of moments.
Fifty per cent of those who were admitted to the hospital and who
died were killed by bombs. The other half died from machine gun
bullets.[3]

On 6 January 1940, the first *Luftwaffe* Enigma signals were decrypted by
the staff working at the Government Code and Cypher School, at
Bletchley Park. On 28 June the following Enigma messages were
disseminated to British Military Intelligence and Air Intelligence:

Most Secret CX/JQ/91 - 28/6/40
2) From study of aeroplane negatives (taken at 2000 metres) and
reconnaissance reports, the German command was informed as
follows on 27/6: Aerodromes at Jersey and Guernsey had each one
repair-shop and two hangers. Not visibly occupied. Reconnaissance
at height of 300 metres reported Alderney, Guernsey, Sark and Jersey
still inhabited. No A.A. Fire. Note: Document of 27/6/40 seen by
source dated above photographs and reconnaissance '2'/6/40, but it
seems evident that a figure has been dropped out after the '2'.
3) At 1645, 27/6, Reconnaissance Group 123 had been asked by
Luftflotte 3 to send a motorcyclist immediately with results of
reconnaissance of Channel Islands. An officer, if possible
Staffelkapitän or Gruppenkommandeur, was also to report
personally.[4]

This reconnaissance flight following on from a whole series of earlier
flights, was witnessed by a number of people, and whilst being correctly
identified as a Dornier, was in fact a Do.17, and not a Do.215 as some

108

diarists have recorded. Whilst very similar in profile, the Do.215 was only used in limited numbers by the *Luftwaffe* and at this time were located in Berlin. Further messages were intercepted on 28 June:

Lfl.Kdo.3 Gruppe le - 28th June 1940 at 16.4SHrs - No.S
A.) Air situation
To 2a): Results of reconnaissance - Visual reconnaissance: 11.15hrs in St. Helier Harbour Jersey 2 transports with one embarking or unloading, 200 vehicles on the quay. 11.25hrs in St. Peter Port Guernsey 1 transport, 150 vehicles on the quay. Vehicles in the locale of camouflage on frames.[5]

This *Luftwaffe* summary of the raids was also intercepted and interpreted by the men and women at Bletchley Park:

Lfl.Kdo.3 Gruppe le - 28th June 1940 at 23.30Hrs - No.7
A.) Air situation
To 2a): Report on results: I./K.G.55 with 9 He.III (took off 18.50hrs) raid against the Channel Islands. In St. Helier harbour direct hits on the quay and columns of trucks. In St. Peter Port several hits observed on docks. Large fires, several explosions with black plumes covering the entire island from east to west on return flight, with possibility of hits in fuel tank storage. No losses.
Bombing altitude 1000 – 2500m. Quantity of bombs jettisoned 180 SD50. Observations: Heavy truck and private vehicle columns in St. Peter Port and St. Helier. To 2a): Light anti-aircraft fire on Isle Sark.[6]

Understandably, the German attack was widely reported in the local papers the following day. The following was part of the coverage in Jersey's *Evening Post* on Saturday, 29 June 1940:

The raid started about 7 p.m. An E.P. reporter, who lives in St. Clement's heard the sound of aircraft engines flying low and, going outside with field glasses, saw three medium bombers in formation flying in the direction of St. Helier, low enough for the black crosses under their wings to be plainly seen with the naked eye. Almost as they passed over the F.B. Fields [a sports stadium] the sound of explosions from La Rocque direction were heard and, watching, the reporter saw the machine fly on over the Fort and saw machine-gun fire from the tail of one of them as it obviously fired at the harbour.

More explosions were heard, and then at intervals for an hour or so, Grève d'Azette district was subjected to intermittent machine-gun fire, and the same tale comes from many different parts of the Island.

The first of the German bombs to fall on Jersey exploded at La Rocque on at the south-east corner of the Island to the east of St Helier, as the *Evening Post*'s reporter noted:

One bomb at La Rocque fell harmlessly in the harbour and stuck in the mud, the other fell on the Gorey side of the slipway and it was this which caused the casualties. Mrs. Farrell and Mr. Pilkington were out of doors near Mr. Frank Gallichan, who dived under one of the seats on the front and escaped injury, but the others were so badly injured they succumbed in hospital. Mr. Adams is stated to have gone to the door when he heard the aircraft engines and to have been killed outright by the blast from the explosion.

A resident at La Rocque stated this morning that most of the windows along the front were shattered, cottage roofs partly blown off and doors and windows in a house opposite the harbour were blown out. He also stated that he had seen a sample of one of the machine-gun bullets which were showered freely on the whole district and describes it as very sharp of hardened steel and a little thinner than an ordinary pencil.

What happened on the Albert Pier in St Helier Harbour is best described by one of those who were actually present, a Mr. R.K. Troy, who was the stevedore in charge of the loading of a ship. In the hours after the raid, Troy stated:

We saw machines come over, but we took little notice at first, for we have seen so many German planes lately. Suddenly I heard machine-gunning and realised that they were attacking and that we were the target. I shouted to the men to take cover and I myself got under a crane, and only then realised that there was little or no shelter there, as the crane was one of the high gantry type. The men scattered all over the place, some under lorries and others under stacks of sacks. Coming over as they did from the Fort we had no protection for the high wall of the walk was unfortunately behind us. Mr Truscott and another craneman were hit by machine-gun bullets, and others of my gang, Messrs. W. Tirel, Connors and Wilson, were also wounded, Mr. Tirel having his toes completely shot off.

110

A bomb which burst near the railway sheds was also dropped, and then I heard that Mr. Fallis had been killed. He had come out of his quarters and as the machine went over he laid down under the lee of the S.R. [Southern Railway] passenger shed, but a splinter of the bomb hit him as he crouched down and terribly mangled him. I ran over to his assistance, but I soon saw that there was nothing to be done for Mr. Fallis, so I ran back to the other injured men to try and get them to hospital, but neither my car nor the lorries on the pier would start, every one of them having been hit and put out of action. The ambulance then came down and the injured were taken to the General Hospital, and here I must say a good word for the work of the police, ambulance drivers and A.R.P. men, who worked splendidly and calmly.

After the first raid had occurred I called out to the men who were working for me, 'What about making another start?' and several of them agreed but the planes came over again, this time from the direction of St. Aubin's Bay, and did some more machine-gunning. I saw it was hopeless and told the men to make their way up the pier.[7]

Working alongside Troy on Albert Pier was Mr. J.A. Laurens, whose subsequent account bore out his colleague's statement:

I took cover under a lorry and a fellow alongside me was hit. As we went up the pier after the second raid they started machine-gunning again and Mr. Troy and I, who were then alone, lay down alongside the promenade wall, and I can tell you we hugged it close.[8]

The account in the Jersey *Evening Post* filled most of a whole in the Saturday edition, and continued with the following:

Police Constable Le Gentil was injured by a bullet as he dived for shelter under the railway station entrance and Police Constables Le Blencq and Howe had narrow escapes as they grabbed some children who were passing and rushed them into the comparative shelter of the railway station …

Bombs fell on stores in Commercial Buildings and smoke poured from these buildings high into the sky. Bombs fell on a hotel, striking the wall of the building on an adjoining lane and passing right through the building did a considerable amount of damage.

A small sports car stationed in Mulcaster Street was wrecked and most of the windows in the whole neighbourhood were out, broken glass littering the roadways and pavements.

Another hotel suffered badly, two bombs falling in the court-yard. Other bombs fell in the old harbour destroying six small yachts, while others fell on the Havre-des Pas slopes of Fort Regent; it was one of these which struck Mr Mauger's house, killing him and narrowly missing his wife who was also in the house.

The Fire Brigade, Police, AFS, ARP Wardens and demolition parties were soon hard at work barring off the affected area, rescuing the injured and clearing up broken glass as far as was possible and witnesses are high in their praise of the conduct of the police on duty at the time of the raids …

Brig-y-Don Children's Convalescent Home at Samarès was amongst the places hit by machine-gun bullets last night. 'Seven bullets hit the house,' said the matron this afternoon, "but there were no casualties and very insignificant damage was caused. There is no cause for alarm at all.'

The recently-married Donald Journeaux recalled how a friend of his, Bertram Payn, had been standing outside with his mother at La Rocque, on Jersey's south-east corner, when the first bombs fell:

It was a terrifying experience for them and a miracle that they were not killed. Two bombs fell, one on the water without exploding, and the other on the slipway. The shrapnel caused a vast amount of damage to the cottages nearby, and all the windows in the village were shattered.

Altogether three people were killed and quite a number wounded. It was not possible at that point to get an ambulance as they were all busy in the town. Bertram, assisted by friends, had the painful duty of wrapping the bodies in tarpaulin and lifting them into a lorry. Fortunately a delivery van came to his rescue and the bodies were transferred into it and taken to hospital.

It had all happened in such a short space of time, but it had a lasting effect on the villagers. After that when planes came over they would run to hide in the channel of the dried-up brook behind the houses.

In the aftermath, Donald was able to inspect some of the destruction that was left in the wake of the departing bombers:

Bombs had been dropped in the harbour, damaging many small boats and setting light to nearby stores. The Yacht Hotel and other buildings suffered and many windows were smashed including some of the stained-glass windows in St Helier's Church.

On Mount Bingham the roof of a friend's house was hit, and in a house across the road a man was killed. Bombs also fell on Fort Regent. Ten people were killed and a number injured, mainly by shrapnel. It was fortunate that there wasn't greater loss of life, although the Germans may have considered the raid a failure.[9]

Yvette Coley was working with her father at a potato warehouse on the New North Quay when the bombers struck:

When the explosions came there was falling bits of masonry and bricks from Normans' building which came crashing through our glass roof. The girls who were packing potatoes screamed in the panic and I took them over to Castle Street where most of them lived. They wanted to get back quickly because some had children at home.

On my way back to the warehouse the planes came again, firing their machine guns. I ducked down behind some red boxes that used to stand at the Weighbridge.[10]

Ernest Watson was a reasonable distance from Coley at the time, but he also recalled the destruction caused by the raiders in the area around New North Quay:

I was in Kensington Place when the bombs fell on Normans Ltd. From where I was – about half a mile away – I could see the smoke of a fire and there was a lot of dust just after the bombs. I could hear machine guns. It seemed pretty serious.

I went straight back home to see if my wife and children were all right. As I was head A.R.P. Warden in St Clement I went to our headquarters at the New Era cinema. None of the other wardens turned up. They had all gone to see the fireworks![11]

That said, in the aftermath of the attack there was widespread praise for the emergency services' response, though this was tempered with some criticism about how some members of the public initially responded:

'Considering the skeleton organisation we have I am really proud of the way the A.R.P. Services worked,' said Major W. Crawford Morrison, the organiser, this morning [and quoted in the Jersey

Evening Press on 29 June], 'but do please do all in your power to stress on people that they must keep indoors in case of a raid. Many casualties may be caused by people rushing to see and I cannot too strongly advise everyone to keep under cover and to obey the wardens when they are advised what to do. Last night many ignored the wardens altogether.'

It cannot be too strongly emphasised that people should take cover as soon as they hear the air raid warning, many people stop and gaze upwards and it is emphasized that faces turned upwards show plainly from an aircraft and invite 'frightfulness.' In these days the safest thing to do when aircraft engines are heard is to take cover at once, for the air raid warning was only sounded last night when the damage was done ...

It would seem that people learnt quickly and soon heeded the advice given by the likes of Major W. Crawford Morrison, as the events of the following day suggest:

There was an air raid warning again about the middle of the morning [of 29 June], and in town people quickly got off the streets and sought refuge in shops and offices. A second raid warning was sounded about 12.50 p.m. today and a party of wardens detailed to attend to the fire at Fort Regent reported they had been machine-gunned. There were no casualties.

Once the raiders had departed on the 28th, and the all clear sounded, the authorities were soon able to establish that ten individuals had been killed and nine wounded on Jersey. In respect of the dead, the following detail was announced the next day:

Mr John Mauger, retired plumber, who was killed at his home at Mount Bingham.

Mr. B. Fallis, an ex-Royal Artillerymen, caretaker of the public lavatories on the Albert Pier and collector of the toll levied on persons meeting the Southern mailboats, who was killed by a splinter of a bomb which fell close to him as he took shelter alongside a shed.

Mr. R. Coleman of Byron-lane, a jeweller employed by Messrs. C.T. Maine Ltd, killed on the Albert Pier. Mr. Coleman had come here from London some four or five months ago and leaves a widow and daughter.

Mr L. Bryan, an employee of Messrs. Voisin and Co., who was killed by a bomb splinter as he walked on the Albert Pier promenade with his wife.

Mr E.H. Ferrant, licensee of the Grapes Hotel, Mulcaster Street, who was badly injured and died in hospital as he was being operated upon.

Mrs M. Farrell, Harbour View, La Rocque, a sister of Nurse Dobin. She died in hospital.

Mr T. Pilkington, staying at Harbour View, La Rocque. He was a Manchester man on holiday and was badly wounded, dying in hospital.

Mr Jack Adams, who has been in the employ of Mr J.H. Harper for many years as an engineer and who also lives at Harbour View. He, it is thought, was killed by the blast as he went to the front door.

There was another name on this list, that of Harold Hobbs. The son of the Coxswain of the Guernsey lifeboat, Harold was killed near St Aubin's Harbour. Following this, on 29 June 1940, the decision was taken by the RNLI not to remove the two lifeboats remaining in the Channel Islands to the British mainland. However, the day before,:

A phone message was received about 3.15 p.m. from the Chief Inspector of Lifeboats by the Hon. Sec. Guernsey stating that the Institution wished to evacuate the Jersey Lifeboat 'Howard D' and that the Jersey Hon. Sec. could not raise a crew for the purpose, and asking whether the Acting Hon. Sec. in Guernsey could assist.

The Acting Hon. Sec. agreed to enquire into the possibilities of getting the Jersey boat brought up to Guernsey with our vessel to subsequent evacuation to England of both the Guernsey Lifeboat 'ON 672' and the Jersey Lifeboat 'Howard D'. The Coxswain, F Hobbs, was approached and raised no objection whatever to raising a crew for the purpose.[12]

The crew sent from Guernsey to collect *Howard D* travelled on board the Guernsey relief lifeboat *Alfred and Clara Heath*. This crew of seven, Coxswain Fred Hobbs, Second Coxswain Fred Zabiela, Bowman Bill Gourney, Harold Hobbs, Alec Hobbs, Fred Zabiela Jnr and Gerald Dunstan as Engineer, left the moorings at St Peter Port at 16.05 hours to head across to Jersey.

The intention was to take both vessels to Guernsey and then sail from there to the English south coast, as the Fred Hobbs had access to a large yacht owned by a Mr Tate, a millionaire who had settled in Guernsey. It was suggested that Hobbs sail with his family and Tate's on the yacht, whilst the two lifeboats followed, thereby forming a small convoy. First though, *Alfred and Clara Heath* needed to reach St Helier:

> All went well until they reached Noirmont Point about 15 minutes steaming from the Jersey Harbour, when three German aeroplanes appeared astern and dived down to a few hundred feet above the Lifeboat and machine gunned the Boat and crew. The crew layed [*sic*] flat on the bottom of the boat, the Coxswain to keep a look out.[13]

The Coxswain turned for the St Aubin's breakwater and immediately began zig-zagging before running the lifeboat up onto the beach, in amongst the rocks, in an effort to gain some cover. Everyone immediately jumped over the side of the boat.

Moments later, as the bombers continued on towards St Helier, it was realised that Harold Hobbs had been shot through the head, hit by a bullet which had ricocheted off the nearby rocks. Gerald Dunstan had also been wounded, a bullet grazing his knee. The Jersey *Evening Post* carried the following piece on 29 June 1940:

> Mr Harold Hobbs, who is aged 34, was the son of the coxswain of the Guernsey lifeboat … 'There were six of us in the Guernsey lifeboat and we were off Noirmont when six planes machine-gunned us. They fired enough bullets to kill a battalion, and killed my son outright. He did not suffer, that is one consolation. The rest of us were quite unhurt.'

The lifeboat, meanwhile, was still serviceable, with only a few holes from the machine-gun rounds visible above the waterline. The crew lifted Harold back in the boat and made for Elizabeth Castle, just outside St Helier, where they waited before finally entering St Helier at 19.45 hours.

Fearing more bombing raids, once Harold's body had been taken ashore, both lifeboats were moved out of St Helier and anchored in the lee of St Aubin's Fort until the following morning. The Guernsey crew remained in Jersey for a couple of days, being billeted at the Aurora Hotel, whilst an inquest into Harold's death was held. In the meantime, the RNLI also decided that both *Alfred and Clara Heath* and *Howard D* should now remain in their respective islands. They fell into enemy hands in the days that followed.[14]

In the days that followed careful negotiations were conducted by Harold's mother at the Royal Hotel, Guernsey, with a high-ranking German naval man, believed to be the Harbour Master *Hauptmann* Obermeyer, in an attempt to have his body returned from Jersey. It would appear that the Germans on Guernsey were just as shocked as the locals that an unarmed vessel, and a boat designed to save lives at that, should have been targeted in such a way.

Apologies were duly given by Obermeyer for the actions of the *Luftwaffe* crews on that day and arrangements were quickly made to return Harold's body to Guernsey for a formal burial. As Harold had served in the Royal Naval Volunteer Reserve, his coffin was draped with a Union Flag. The German authorities offered to provide a guard of honour to fire a salute over the grave, but, as the Hobbs family wanted no German presence at the funeral, so this was declined.[15]

Having decided to demilitarise the Channel Islands, to ensure that no further attacks were made, the United States Ambassador in London, Joseph P. Kennedy, was asked to pass a message to the German Government:

> The evacuation of all military personnel and equipment from the Channel Islands was completed some days ago. The Islands are therefore demilitarized and cannot be considered in any way as a legitimate target for bombardment. A public announcement to this effect was made on the evening of June 28.[16]

By then, of course, it was too late.

9

'The Mad Murderer of Berchtesgaden'
Reactions to the Air Raids

No sooner had the sound of the German bombers' Daimler-Benz DB600A engines receded into the distance, then people across Guernsey and Jersey began to emerge from where they had sought cover or safety to assess the damage wrought.

Bill Green later described the scene at St Peter Port, where 'lines of tomato vans and lorries waiting with produce for shipment to the mainland were left as smouldering wrecks'. He added that,

> Forty-nine vehicles were burnt out or seriously damaged. Bomb craters were everywhere. The Weighbridge was extensively damaged and its clock stopped at few minutes before seven … The whole of the front, from the States Offices, where every single window was broken, right along to Les Banques suffered considerable damage, there was hardly an unbroken window to be seen. Well over one hundred windows were broken in the Royal Hotel.[1]

It had not only been the harbour and its facilities that had been targeted or hit by the raiders, as Bill Green went on to recall:

> Whilst the main raid was concentrated against the White Rock, the German Heinkel 111 bombers also dropped bombs in other parts of the island. In the country a bomb was dropped near the St Saviour Reservoir and another at the race course at Vazon. A number of houses were damaged by bombs. In the Strand, Strand Villa, an adjoining cottage and another house received considerable structural damage. Two bombs fell, one in the front and another at the rear of this group of properties.

At the Guernsey Brewery over one hundred windows were blown out. A house in St Andrews, at La Vassalerie, suffered considerable structural damage, all the windows and doors being blown in. Fortunately none of the occupants were injured as they had taken cover. The Germans machined-gunned other areas of the town and haymakers in the fields, without causing any serious injuries.[2]

As already described in the previous chapters, there had been many individuals, both civilians and public servants alike, who had 'done their bit' during the bombing. Some of the latter were noted by Bill Green:

During the raid, P.C. Bob Kimber was in the Watch House at the end of the White Rock. While the bombs were dropping all around, he was on the telephone to leading island officials, giving them a commentary of what was happening. Just as he rang off at the end of the raid, a bomb dropped close by in the harbour. The blast blew him out of the Watch House. Fortunately he was uninjured, but it was a narrow escape.

Charlie Froome, was on duty at the St John's Ambulance Brigade headquarters when the raid started. He immediately responded to the three calls for assistance he received. With colleague Lionel Taylor, he drove the ambulance down to White Rock and parked it alongside the Weighbridge, facing up the Avenue with its rear doors open.

Joe Way, who ran the small garage next to Stainers in the Pollet, was just about to board the *Isle of Sark* and leave the island, when the raid started. Joe at one time had been a St John's Ambulance driver and, realising that there were casualties, he headed back to the area of the clock tower where the Ambulance was parked.

Joe joined Ambulance men Lionel Taylor and Charlie Froome, in attending the injured. He tried to persuade Charlie to drive the ambulance further down White Rock, saying 'There are many injured down there, who need attention'

'I'm sorry' Charlie said, 'we can't be everywhere, there are people here who need attention,' and added 'It is safer for the ambulance to stay where it is, as many of the tomato lorries are ablaze and if we managed to get down, we probably would not be able to get back again'.

As the Heinkel 111s roared in for yet another attack Lionel and Charlie sought cover under the ambulance, while Joe lay flat on the ground. Two bombs exploded between the vehicle and the Weighbridge, causing considerable damage to the ambulance and injuring Lionel in the backside. Charlie was uninjured, but suffered from concussion. Joe was blown, by the force of the blast, into the ambulance and against the partition behind the driver's seat.

Seriously injured, Joseph Way succumbed to his wounds soon afterwards. Police Constable Frank Le Cocq, who was later to become Chief Inspector, was also at White Rock helping the injured when Deputy Police Inspector Langmead ordered him to drive the ambulance and the casualties to hospital. In his account, Bill described the difficulties that Le Cocq experienced:

> One of the ambulance's rear tyres was flat, as was the spare. However Frank managed to drive the damaged ambulance up St Julian's as far as the South African War Memorial before the tyre finally came off the rim. Despite that he continued his 'bumpity, bumpity' progress until he reached St James, where he was stopped by Police Sergeant Jack Harper. It was obvious that the ambulance was no longer drivable, so a passing coal lorry belonging to Stan Collings was commandeered. A tarpaulin was laid over the back of the lorry and the injured were transferred from the Ambulance. The coal lorry was turned around and driven by P.C. Le Cocq to the Castel Hospital. The damaged ambulance was abandoned in St James Street, forty or fifty yards down from the junction with Saumarez Street.

The ambulance was too important to be left where it was. Bill would recall how, later on the 28th, he was asked to help recover and repair it:

> A little later that evening, I received a telephone call from Len Rouget. He had been approached by Reg Blanchford, who was in charge of the St John's Ambulance in those days, to see if he could get the damaged ambulance mobile again. It was felt that it might be needed again before long. Len agreed and wanted me to go down and help him. I saw it as my duty and of course I went. Len and I met in St James Street, where the damaged Ambulance had been abandoned.
>   One of the two rear tyres, they were the old-fashioned balloon type, was totally shredded beyond repair, the other and the spare were in nearly as bad a condition. The rear of the vehicle had been peppered with shrapnel, there were probably in the region of one

hundred and fifty holes, both large and small. Most of the windows were shattered, but the engine and cab were almost un-damaged.

We decided that we would try to drive the Ambulance round the corner into Saumarez Street to Len's repair workshop, less than a hundred yards away. The engine started easily enough, but the vehicle would not move because the rear wheel, without its tyre, was jammed in the gutter. We fetched a wooden stake from Len's garage and after much effort managed to lever the rim of the wheel out of the gutter and away from the pavement. Len then slowly drove the damaged ambulance to his workshop. We worked all night on the repairs and by dawn had managed to do enough so that the ambulance could go back into service.[2]

Though some Islanders, such as Miss A. Le M. Mainé, had believed that the ambulance had been 'machine-gunned during the raid', Bill would write that this had not been the case:

Many claims have been made over the years, that the ambulance was machined gunned by the Germans, but we found no evidence to support that allegation. The damage which I saw and helped to repair was, in my view, caused by shrapnel and lumps of road metal.

Understandably, the raids were heavily reported throughout the United Kingdom. The following was published in *The Times* in response to the air raids. The article, which bore the straplines '29 Killed in Brutal Raid. Channel Islands Bombed. Demilitarized Area Attacked', began with the Home Office announcement from earlier in the day:

Air attacks took place on Jersey and Guernsey yesterday. Material damage was done to property and many civilians were machine-gunned in both islands. At least six persons were killed and several injured in Jersey, while in Guernsey 23 persons were killed and 36 were injured. As stated last night, the Channel Islands have been demilitarized and all armed forces and equipment have already been withdrawn.[3]

The Times then continued with the story in more detail. The indignation felt by the newspaper can be felt, despite its measured wording:

The earlier Home Office announcement referred to stated that in view of the German occupation of the parts of France close to the Channel

Islands, it was decided to demilitarize the islands. Within a few hours of the official announcement that the islands had been demilitarized came the news that German raiders had flown over the islands and dropped bombs. For days past many men, women, and children had been transported to England from the island. Jersey prize cattle, which could not be got away, were turned into the fields to eat what was left of the crops. Thousands of baskets of potatoes were left to rot.

From a military point of view the islands were of no use to Great Britain, and their occupation will bring no advantage to the enemy.

Further coverage was given to the attacks in *The Times* on 1 July 1940, this time under the headline 'The Channel Isles Raid Death Roll of 33':

In the ferocious raids on the demilitarized Channel Islands of Jersey and Guernsey (reported in the later editions of *The Times* on Saturday) the death-roll among the defenceless civilian population was 33.

In Guernsey 23 persons were killed and 36 injured, while 10 were killed and several more injured in Jersey. The raids were made about the same time as it was announced that the bulk of the populations had been safely evacuated a week ago. But for the timely evacuation the casualties would undoubtedly have been very high, for against islands which had not even a gun to protect them the enemy bombers swooped low enough to take deliberate aim as they showered down high-explosive and incendiary bombs and machine-gunned the streets.

Among the particularly revolting acts of the raiders were the machine-gunning of a lifeboat while it was on an errand of succour to Jersey, killing the son of the Guernsey coxswain, and a similar attack on an ambulance taking wounded to hospital.

The demilitarization of the islands began early last week. The seaport was stripped and the soldiers and airmen, munitions, stores, and equipment were safely shipped over to England. Judge French, Governor of Alderney, and his staff have arrived at a South Coast port with the whole of the island's money under armed guard.

Further discussion over the air raids appeared elsewhere in the same edition of *The Times*, though this section of the paper examined a number of different aspects of the war at that point:

The German Air Force on Friday murdered thirty-three civilians in the Channel Islands, which had been made and declared a demilitarized area some days previously. They themselves have felt constrained to issue an unusually mendacious communique, claiming that they made 'very effective' attacks upon troops who were non-existent.

Morally speaking this attack is worse even than those made on columns of refugees in France, because the refugees were at least in the area of military-operations whereas the Channel Islanders were not. It is as if Paris had been bombed after having been declared an open town and after the armies had retired to the south of it. No doubt such a completely defenceless target proved irresistible and a welcome change from the targets which the German air crews have been attempting to attack in this country.

Writing to *The Times* on 29 June 1940, the author and linguist James Bertrand de Vincheles Payen-Payne (of 49, Nevern Square, London), began his letter, which was duly published a few days later on 3 July, in an equally outraged manner:

Sir – The unprovoked and malicious attack by the mad murderer of Berchtesgaden on Jersey has drawn attention to the Channel Isles. They are the last remnants of the Duchy of Normandy to belong to the British Crown. Their government is still feudal. Both Jersey and Guernsey have an English major-general as Governor, but the legislation and government of the islands is in the hands of a Bailiff and 12 jurats. These jurats, together with the 12 rectors, 12 constables, and 17 delegates of the parishes form the governing body of Jersey.

The French made an attempt to seize the island in 1781, but were defeated by Major Peirson, who fell in the moment of victory, as is shown in the well-known picture by John Singleton Copley in the Tate Gallery. The Norman chronicler Wace, who wrote the 'Roman de Rou' (i.e. Rollo), was a native of Jersey. The senior seigneurs are those of de Carteret and Lemprière. Mr. Justice du Parcq and C.T. Ie Quesne. K.C., Dr. Marett, Rector of Exeter College, Oxford, Lord Portsea, and Lord Trent are proud to call themselves Jerseymen, as were Lord St. Helier, Mr. Justice Bailhache, and General Pipon. Sir John Everett Millais and W. W. Ouless, the Royal Academicians, were also born in the island.

The announcement that the Channel Islands had been demilitarized was finally received by Berlin, which meant that there would be no more bombing raids. What it also meant was that the path was now clear for an unopposed German occupation of the Channel Islands.

123

10

'Marching against England'
German Invasion Plans

At 15.00 hours on Thursday, 19 June 1940, a wireless signal was sent from Berlin which stated 'The capture of the British Channel Islands is necessary and urgent'. It was followed a short time later by a detailed directive from Admiral Otto Schniewind, Chief of the Naval Operations Staff, to the *Marinebefehlshaber Nordfrankreich* (effectively the 'Flag Officer Commanding, Northern France', who was *Vizeadmiral Eugen Lindau*), and other Operational Commands' – which included the following:

> The expeditious occupation of the three large British Channel Islands, Alderney, Guernsey and Jersey, and the French Island of Ushant [near Brest] is essential.
>
> The British Channel Islands in enemy hands constitutes a forward enemy observation position right in our own flank, to the detriment of our own naval and air operations in the centre and west of the Channel. The Island of Ushant is highly important as a navigational point for shipping and for aircraft.
>
> As far as is known the old defence installations on the Channel Islands have not been extended.
>
> On the island of Jersey there is an old casemate fort for the defence of the harbour of St Helier, and this is alleged to have 7 guns of questionable value all pointing towards the south.
>
> Little is known of the defences of the harbour of St Peter Port on Guernsey. But their value is questionable.
>
> Nothing is known about the defence installations on Alderney, but in 1939 mention was made of the importance of the island as a base for anti-submarine vessels and motor-boats. Should the Alderney harbour of St Anne have been used for this purpose then auxiliary defences can be expected.

On all three islands there are airfields which were used in peacetime. On Alderney the airfield is supposed to have been taken over by the R.A.F. and extended ...

The occupation of the Channel Islands and Ushant should, from a practical point of view, be carried out simultaneously by units of naval assault parties already in northern France. Army and air support will be arranged in co-operation with the local commanders of these armed services. The troops should be transported to the islands on coastal vessels or tugs seized in the area in question. Light weapons appear to be necessary in order to facilitate the formation of a bridge-head and for defence against attacks by enemy aircraft. In any case, *Luftwaffe* support for the landing appears essential ...

Should Naval Group Command West consider it necessary, additional staff can be recruited for the preparation and execution of the operation.[1]

Historian and author George Forty has described the plans that the Germans drew up for the invasion of the Channel Islands:

The original proposal had called for a force of some six battalions to be used – three for Jersey, two for Guernsey and one for Alderney. They would be lightly equipped because difficulties were foreseen in manhandling any heavy weapons or equipment from ship to shore and then getting if off the beaches.

The assault force would also contain a suitable naval ground element, a *Marinestosstruppabteilung* (Naval assault detachment – the *Kriegsmarine* equivalent of the Royal Marines) and two engineer companies. Due to the shortage of suitable amphibious craft, the assault would have to take place over two days – Alderney and Guernsey being the objectives for Day 1, then Jersey on Day 2. The amphibious landings would be preceded by naval operations to clear gaps through the sea minefields and 'softening-up' air raids on land targets, whilst the actual assault would be supported by Ju 87 Stuka dive-bombers which had wrecked such havoc during the Blitzkrieg in France. The *Luftwaffe* would also clearly play a major role, protecting the convoys, whist the *Kriegsmarine*'s main task would be to prevent interference from the Royal Navy.

After hearing the results of the [air] raids on the 28th and the lack of reaction from the Islands' defences, it was agreed that the assault force should be scaled down to just one battalion for Guernsey, one for Jersey and a single infantry company for Alderney. The troops would come mainly from 216. ID, which was now stationed in the Cherbourg area, supported by *Kriegsmarine Abteilung 'Gotenhafen'* (Naval Assault Group 'Gotenhafen') …[2]

Despite the seemingly well devised plans for the operation, it is interesting to note just how ill-informed the Germans were about the Islands, for example in their belief that Alderney airfield had been used by the RAF and that the harbour was used as an anti-submarine base, as neither was the case. Some of the latest information obtained by the Germans was, in fact, from a traveller to the Islands before the war. In attempt to rectify the situation, the *Luftwaffe* had been ordered to conduct aerial reconnaissance flights over the Islands.

Naturally the appearance of these enemy flights were worthy of mention by Guernseyman Kenneth Lewis in his diary. Summarising events between 23 and 26 June 1940, he wrote:

Life of the people was still somewhat unsettled owing to the evacuation, but gradually it was settling down. On several occasions aeroplanes were spotted flying at a great height over the Island which was quite alarming to many people as the sounds of the engines did not seem to coincide with those of the British planes we had formerly heard, and owing to the great height the markings on the planes could not be seen.

The following day, Lewis recorded the following, though he also incorrectly identified the exact type of aircraft involved:

At about ten o'clock in the morning a plane was seen flying at a great altitude over the Island and continually circling over the town. At about 11.30 it was seen from our office windows to be coming lower but it was still at too great a distance to be distinguished; suddenly at 11.55 the sound of the engines grew clearer and on rushing to the windows I spotted the plane coming up over the harbour at a height of about 100ft and, as it flew low over the Royal Court, I saw quite clearly the black and white cross on the wings which immediately told me that it was a German plane, and later investigation it proved to be a Dornier 215 bomber commonly known as the Flying Pencil.[3]

One of those who was soon to have a major role in the occupation of the Channel Islands was *Major* Albrecht Lanz, the Commanding Officer of II./Infantry Regiment 396 (II./IR 396), which, in turn, was part of the

216th Infantry Division. The division had been created on 26 August 1939 by reorganizing several Army Reserve and border defence units from Lower Saxony. With a then total strength of approximately 17,200 men, the division, the Commanding Officer of which was *Generalleutnant* Hermann Böttcher, was deployed in the west of Germany and not involved in the invasion of Poland.

By the end of June 1940, the 216th Infantry Division, including Lanz, was in Cherbourg having swept across France as part of the Blitzkrieg. 'After all,' he later recalled, 'what is the road there for – marching – and how we marched. Day after day in the sun and dust. Forty-five miles was our longest day's march. After forced marching from Lys in Belgium, via Caen, we reached the Channel in the Cherbourg neighbourhood.' It is clear that Lanz had no complaints about his arrival at what he described as 'the end of the continent':

> We were enchanted by a glorious view of the longed-for sea. Now we could be sure that the marching was nearly over. Our battalion was allotted the Western Section of Cherbourg, over to the well-known lobster port of Goury, and in the South down to the Cap de Flamanville.
>
> The companies lay spread out far from each other in this lovely district with its steep coast, falling in picturesque shapes to the sea, and its shimmering white bays, where the water, crystal-clear and the snow-white sand invited us to bathe. Every Company Commander was King in his own Kingdom.
>
> As the well-to-do inhabitants everywhere had fled, quartering caused no great difficulty. In a very short time men and horses were provided for in the best of style, and the allotted task – securing the coast – surveyed in all directions and carried out with soldierly thoroughness.[4]

It was not long, probably a matter of hours rather than days, before Lanz had his first sighting of the Channel Islands, the question of which he then brought up during a conversation with one *Kapitänleutnant* Theodor Koch, who, having been the last Captain of the great ocean liner SS *Hamburg*, was the commanding officer of *Stoßtrupp Abteilung*, or Naval Assault Group, *Gotenhafen*:[5]

> From my No.3 Company's position, on the Nez de Jobourg, Islands can be seen. I said in the course of the conversation [with Koch], 'I have found out that it is Alderney'. With the ordinary six-fold glasses

one can see every little detail on the Island. 'It is apparently uninhabited, English territory, though many assert that it is French. It would be a great thing for us to land over there.'

Koch was fired with the idea and said he too had often thought, why should we not cross over and occupy these beautiful Channel Islands – even those lying South of Alderney, Guernsey and Jersey. The great snag though, he said, in carrying out such an undertaking was the lack at the moment of proper shipping space. With this unsatisfied desire in our breasts we parted, not dreaming that the occupation would come about sooner than we thought.

As was typical of the time, events moved fast. As Lanz would soon discover, the German planners had already been busy on the matter of the Channel Islands. His account continues:

Two days later, on 1 July, the sun, as on the day before, streamed from a brilliant blue sky and bathed the glorious landscape in a magic light. On the spacious glass verandah of our HQ at Urville, surrounded by a well-tended garden, with exquisite subtropical plants, were gathered the officers of my staff, sitting comfortably at breakfast.

Suddenly the clatter of a motor-cycle shatters the glorious calm of the morning. In comes, hurried and excited, a DR [Despatch Rider] with the order, 'Sir, you are to report immediately in Cherbourg to the Admiral Commanding North France'.

I didn't believe my ears and thought 'what's all this about "Admiral Commanding", we're not the Navy, after all'. I said to the DR 'you must have come to the wrong address, what should I have to do with the Admiral Commanding North France'?

Then his sunburnt face lit up, and he said, his eyes afire, 'We're attacking England, sir, the Islands. A rifle company, a troop of heavy machine guns, and, if possible, infantry guns of the battalion are to be warned immediately to report to the airport at Cherbourg.'

To the DR, I said 'I'll go at once', and rapidly gave the necessary orders. Within two minutes I was sitting with my Adjutant in the car, tearing to the Naval HQ in Cherbourg. There I met the Ic (equivalent to 'Intelligence' Translator) of our Division, Capt Willers, who had been ordered there as Liaison Officer. He introduced me to the Admiral Commanding North France, Vice-Admiral Lindau.

Immediately with the map before us, the situation was discussed. On the day before, i.e. 30 June, German Air Reconnaissance personnel had landed on Guernsey, to reconnoitre, and encountered no

128

opposition at the airfield. Thereupon the High Command had decided to take the Channel Islands by surprise from the air, using the Naval assault detachment *Gotenhafen*, and units of the Division established round Cherbourg. An exquisite thrill, that it was precisely my battalion that lay nearest to hand.

At the conference it became clear that there was no reliable information available. According to one report, battery positions had been recognised on Guernsey. The day before, a British minesweeper was said to have put in to the Island. According to other reports, the Island was clear of the enemy …

In higher Staff circles, opinions were varied. One considered a whole regiment was necessary, another a few platoons. Eventually one Rifle Coy, reinforced with heavy MGs and baggage, and the Naval assault detachment *Gotenhafen* were set the task of landing in Guernsey by air. [The] preparation and execution of the plan were entrusted to me.

One of Lanz's most immediate concerns was to establish exactly what resources might be available to him and his units for the invasion. He soon had his answers:

Nine Ju 52 transport machines were available for this purpose, and were expected to arrive from Paris at the Cherbourg-West airfield about 09.30 hrs. As this operation was principally a Naval action, Admiral Linda proposed to put the Naval assault detachment *Gotenhafen* in the first Jus.

Directly the Conference was over we went out to the airfield at which in the meantime the Naval assault detachment *Gotenhafen* had already arrived. The allotted groups of my battalion rolled up, at about the same time, to the Naval Barracks, where No.1 Coy, whose positions were near the airfield, was billeted. 'Don't let too many people be seen on the airfield' was the order, for only two days before a British 'plane had disposed of the Admiral Commanding's car, which was on the airfield, diving three times in broad daylight.

Quickly various questions were discussed between the Admiral's Chief of Staff and *Oberleutnant* Rettighaus, OC Naval assault detachment *Gotenhafen*, and dispositions and loading were decided. Rifles and heavy weapons separated, and an Officer was entrusted with the supervision of the operation after our departure.

Understandably there was much interest being shown in the activities at Cherbourg-West airfield, so much so, remembered Lanz, that 'meanwhile a crowd of high-ranking officers had arrived'. These included, 'the CO of my Regiment and his Adjutant, who had only just before learnt that his first battalion was about to set out against England, [and] The Chief of Staff of V. *Fliegerkorps*, *Oberstleutnant* [Hermann] Plocher, who wished to come with us':

> One aircraft after another landed, but no sign of our Jus for which we were so longingly waiting. Meanwhile the order was given to warn the rest of the Battalion, who were to follow up after the first landing.
>
> At about 12.00 hrs, another Ju landed, out of which climbed the General Commanding *Luftflotte* 3, *General der Flieger* [Hugo] Sperrle, who personally took a hand in things. Meanwhile, a report came in that the 9 Ju[52]s ordered, on the way from Mannheim, had encountered thick ground mist in Paris, and therefore had to land at various outlying fields in order to fill up, so that the formation had been broken up.
>
> In order at last to get a clear picture of the situation on Guernsey, General Sperrle ordered an Me 110 to reconnoitre over Guernsey and make an immediate report. After about an hour he returned and reported: Guernsey airfield occupied by German Recce personnel – what the outlook was on the rest of the Island he could not say.

Impatiently, Lanz and the others at Cherbourg-West could only sit and wait until all the Junkers Ju 52s had finally arrived. Then,

> At 13.30 hrs, the first of the long-awaited Ju[52]s landed, for the time being unfortunately only two.
>
> Still another half hour passed. We could stay no longer, so we decided, after discussing it with Lt-Col Plocher, to set off with these two machines, and get the business started at last.
>
> Plocher announced his intention of joining us with his machine and a Radio-Ju. Quickly two platoons of the Naval assault detachment *Gotenhafen* were loaded into the two Junkers; already the engines were roaring.
>
> With many good wishes from all those left behind, who envied us our glorious task, we rolled forward to the taking off point. With a drone of engines one Ju followed the other across the field.
>
> Soon the ground vanished beneath our feet. A few seconds later the machines turned out to sea in a great loop and arranged themselves in ordered formation. Turning to the land again we

crossed Cap de Flamanville and out to the open sea, heading towards the Islands.

The distance from Cherbourg to Guernsey, as the crow flies, is barely forty miles. Consequently, the flight time for the Junkers Ju 52 crews was not long. That said, the risk of encountering patrolling RAF aircraft was, as Lanz went on to note, very real:

> We had scarcely left the Mainland when there was a slight jolt to the stomach, and the Ju[52]s dived down towards the foaming waves for we could only fly between 25 and 50 yards above the wave-crests in order to keep out of sight of British fighters and remain hidden. Evenly the engines droned their former song, already in the distance the first contours of the longed-for Island began to show themselves.
>
> Then someone began to sing and in a moment the whole of the occupants of the aircraft joined in. With steady voice and shining eyes the battle song resounded through the aircraft: *Denn wir fahren gegen Engeland* – 'For we're marching against England'. Now, at last, we really were.

11

'The first landing on English soil'

The Germans Arrive on Guernsey

As his Junkers Ju 52 droned its way across the English Channel, *Major* Albrecht Lanz found the time to consider the situation that he found himself in. It was, he declared, 'an unforgettable moment'. That said, there was still much trepidation about the reception that the invaders were going to receive. 'We still did not know what to expect, battle or peace,' mused Lanz.

Detailed information or intelligence was all but non-existent, though, as they had learnt before take-off from Cherbourg-West, Lanz and his small force were not the first Germans to arrive on Guernsey.

As a result of the *Luftwaffe*'s earlier reconnaissance flights the German high command concluded that the Channel Islands had at least been partly evacuated of civilians and military. Although the anti-aircraft defences were light, it seemed certain according to the information available to the Commanding Admiral that the Islands were likely to be defended by armed forces, and that artillery and mines could be expected.

In fact the only resistance that the German aircraft encountered on their 'armed reconnaissance' was light anti-aircraft fire at St. Peter Port. This, as it happened, came from the only weapon in the harbour area, a twin Lewis machine-gun mounted on the Southern Railway mail steamer *Isle of Sark*, which was about to set sail from St Peter Port harbour on passage from Guernsey to Southampton. However, it was enough to delude the Germans into thinking that there was a military presence on the Islands and that something more than a raiding force would be necessary to effect a successful occupation.

To this end, on Sunday, 30 June, the *Kriegsmarine*'s Naval Commander Northern France, held a conference in Paris to discuss what should be done. During the course of this conference it was at last learnt that the Channel Islands had been de-militarised. Some hours after the air raids on 28 June, the BBC had belatedly made the appropriate announcement, but this was missed by the German monitoring service and it was left to the American Embassy in Paris to pass on an official message. Plans were then laid for a swift implementation of what had been code-named Operation *Grüne Pfeile* ('Green Arrow'), the main occupation of the Channel Islands.

It can be imagined that the entire operation was intended to have been a grand propaganda exercise for the benefit of German newsreels. *Luftflotte* 3 promised to have ten Junkers Ju 52 transport aircraft as well as fighter, bomber, and reconnaissance units on stand-by at Cherbourg, while Army Group B ordered *X Armeekorps* to have units ready to support the operation. Naval Assault Group *Gotenhafen* prepared to board the craft from which they would storm ashore to capture their first piece of British soil as a rehearsal for the later invasion of mainland Britain.

All these grandiose schemes, however, came to nothing as they were pre-empted by a couple of bold and resourceful air crews of *Fernaufklärungsgruppe* 3.(F)/123 (Long Range Reconnaissance Group 123).

The Island's Attorney General, Ambrose Sherwill, recalled the moment when, at around midday on 30 June 1940, two German aircraft appeared over what had been until just a few days previously, RAF Guernsey:

> One landed while the other remained in the air. A *Luftwaffe* officer found the airport terminal building deserted and broke open a door. He left in a great hurry as British planes approached and left his revolver behind. It was brought to me and, that night, I handed it over to the officer commanding the German force which had later landed.[1]

Just who the German airman was who left his revolver in the terminal build has not been established. However, *Oberfeldwebel* Roman Gastager, a Dornier Do 17 crewman from *Fernaufklärungsgruppe* 3.(F)/123, later described how he was the first enemy serviceman to set foot on the Channel Islands:

> On the 30th June 1940 at 12:53 I started on my first enemy flight. It was to be an exceptional event for Germany and especially for me. In a Do 17D (4U-FL) and with *Leutnant* Hauber as pilot, we took off with a view to occupying the first English island.

Together with two other planes we headed for Guernsey. We had no idea whether the English [sic] were still there or whether they had already retreated.

We flew straight to the airfield and were relieved to see cows grazing there as that meant there were no mines. We flew at low altitude to disperse the cows and was the first plane to land. We rolled towards the hangars. I jumped out, released the safety catch of my machine gun and held it in position. The others remained in the aircraft. Luckily the airfield appeared to be deserted and we notified the two planes above. The second machine landed and the third provided protection from the air.

No sooner had the second aircraft landed, than three Bristol Blenheim bombers appeared out of nowhere. The alarm was raised and we once again took off. Our watchdog in the sky immediately chased the bombers and was able to shoot two of them down. The third quickly took to its heels and with that, our orders had been fulfilled successfully. We returned to Buc and fetched crews with our Ju 52.

After our first reconnaissance mission we flew straight back to Guernsey with the squadron and occupied the island with our Ground Personnel, while the 2nd Squadron headed for Jersey. I was happy and at the same time proud to have been the first German soldier to have set foot on English [sic] soil during the war.

The inhabitants of the island didn't offer any resistance. They were visibly relieved that we had carried out the occupation without a single shot being fired. It would have been much worse for them if the navy had been used to take care of things.

Everything continued in the town as if nothing had happened. The police controlled the traffic and greeted every soldier in a friendly manner. Only the post office workers continued communicating with England until one of us cut the connection.[2]

The claims of having shot down two of the aircraft were wishful thinking at best, as none were engaged by the German aircraft – it was the British who engaged them. Having left behind a number of personnel to 'wait for the army to take over', once airborne again, Gastager and his colleagues returned to their base at Buc, which was fifteen miles south-west of Paris. Dr Alistair Rose was one of those on the Island who witnessed that first, fleeing arrival of the Germans:

On Sunday 30th June at about 11.00am, I had an extraordinary experience. I was driving in my wife's small open car from the

134

hospital towards Bailiff's Cross, when I heard the sound of an aircraft very low, and quite close. Suddenly above the trees on my right a plane appeared at a height of only a couple of hundred feet or so. It was coming towards me, but suddenly it banked and swept round in an arc. As the wing lifted I was aware of a large black cross on the underside. Of course, I had taken it for a British plane until this moment, and my heart nearly stopped beating! I was out of the car in a second, only delaying long enough to switch off the engine, and dived head foremost into a clump of bushes.

From here I warily peeped out to take stock of what was happening. I thought that I had had a lucky escape for with our recent experience of the raid, I felt sure that the plane was merely looking for a target to practice on, and what a lovely target I would have made! I still expected to see the car go up in smoke at any time, and I remember thinking how fed up Jean would be to see the end of her little car.

Now I saw that there were five planes, and I could easily recognise them as Dornier 'Flying Pencils'. One was flying at a higher altitude than the others and appeared to be keeping watch, and the lower four were circling round and round the airport. They would come right up to where I was, then bank and go off in the opposite direction again, and as soon as one plane had turned and was flying off, the next was coming up, so I had very little chance to make a get-away. Then I heard planes behind me, and to my astonishment I saw three British Blenheims flying in a tight circle a mile or so away, obviously watching Jerry but making no attempt to have a scrap with him at the moment.

I did not know how long this circus was likely to go on, but I at any rate was getting tired of crouching under a bush, so I decided to make a bolt for it. At the psychological moment, I dashed out and hastily backed the car into a gateway, where I hid until I could make off. I got back to town safely, and just in time to see one of the Dorniers roar over the town and make off towards the French coast, with two of the British planes in hot pursuit. Afterwards people could be found who said they heard firing over the Platte Fougere lighthouse, and that the German plane had been shot down into the sea.

It appears that one of the Dorniers actually made a landing at the airport, and that they had been circling to scare the cows, which had been grazing on the runway. The airmen had no doubt suspected a trap for they left so hurriedly that one of them departed without his automatic pistol [sic], which was found in the control room. In the evening they arrived for good, and the superintendent of the Police was ordered to go out to the airfield to escort them into town. I remember we were all sitting round the dinner table at Dr. Gibson's when Dr. Sutcliffe arrived and indicated by the thumbs-down sign that our worst fears were now confirmed. Dr. Sutcliffe then asked Dr. Gibson if he considered himself one of Guernsey's leading citizens. In answer to a vigorous reply in the affirmative, Dr. Sutcliffe said, 'Well, goodbye old boy. You must be prepared to be shot as a hostage!'

Gastager and his colleagues landed at 16.15 hours, back at Buc, to a rapturous reception. An official acknowledgement of his unit's achievements was not long in coming, as Gastager recalled:

That night we heard a special announcement on the radio that *Luftwaffe* squadrons had occupied the English Channel Islands, thereby making the first landing on English soil. Göring came to congratulate 'his' squadron personally for the surprise coup, which we had carried out under the command of *Staffelkapitän* Liebe-Piderit. Göring told me that if I took part in a few more enemy flights I would be awarded the Iron Cross.[3]

Albert Peter Lamy MBE, BEM, QPM, had a most distinguished career in the Guernsey Police. Having joined the Guernsey force on 30 July 1928, by the outbreak of the Second World War Lamy had attained the rank of Clerk Sergeant and served as the Secretary to the Island Police Committee from 14 August 1939. He later noted how the Blenheims recalled by Rose had not been sent to intercept the German aircraft, or indeed defend the Channel Islands:

On the Sunday morning an RAF launch escorted by three Blenheims came to Guernsey with the intention of picking up some GPO personnel. The Officer in charge of the launch came to the Police Station and while he was there the air raid siren sounded.

I was talking to him at the time and he remarked that the wardens were getting jumpy and mistaking his Blenheim escort. I took him to the window and pointed out a large green-grey aircraft carrying a black cross and I asked him whether he identified his Blenheim. You can well imagine his reply. He went off post-haste and we knew later that he did return to England.[4]

The Star's journalist Frank Falla remembers how he had become accustomed to the reconnaissance flights of the German aircraft – that was until Sunday, 30 June 1940:

Outwardly all was calm, but there was this uncomfortable feeling of uneasy peace – the lull before the storm. At that time my mother and I were living with friends at the western extremity of the island. Normally a peaceful place with only the noises of nature, sea and birds, the tranquillity was shattered when a Dornier 'Flying Pencil' flew low over the coast – so low that I felt the heat from its exhausts and saw the unmistakable German plane markings. There must have been quite a few Nazi planes in the vicinity for they seemed to be taking it in turns to do low-flying recce flights. Eventually they moved on, but at seven o'clock in the evening the flying circus started its tricks again.

The earlier, morning flying, had ended when one of the planes landed on the grass airfield, despite the presence of the cows from Alderney which had been put to graze there until homes could be found for them. No doubt this pilot had had a look round the place while his colleagues kept a weather-eye open for any possible British opposition, but after a chat with some of the German women domestic workers resident in the island, who probably gave him the lie of the land, the airman soon decided he'd better be airborne. Whether he paid dearly for his short visit to Guernsey we shall never know.

Once he was airborne with his team-mates they all scurried off towards France as fast as their Dorniers and Messerschmitts would carry them …

In the evening the irregular moan of the German planes continued for some time. Then, all of a sudden, one became aware that this seemingly endless noise had been replaced by a creepy, eerie silence. The drone of the German planes had not faded off into the distance as before – it had stopped with dramatic suddenness. We were left to imagine the worst; had the Nazis landed on Guernsey? As the silence engulfed us, I thought to myself: This is it. Goodbye freedom.[5]

It was perhaps unsurprising that as Falla left home to head into St Peter Port, and the offices of *The Star* for a 'normal night duty', he was in 'a distinctly apprehensive mood'.

I got out my bike and started on my way, but I'd not gone very far along the coast road when my worst fears were confirmed. I stopped, and stood staring along the road ahead of me. I found I was gazing at the first member of Hitler's army I had ever seen in real life: the green uniform, queer-shaped helmet, the jackboots, the gas-mask in tin and rifle at the ready. A Nazi soldier standing here in Guernsey, on British territory!

I wasn't quite sure what to do. Should I just cycle on past him as if nothing had happened? I went on staring for what seemed minutes, but he didn't bat an eyelid, and when I didn't move he waved me on my way with a rather imperious arm-gesture.

As I rode the eight-mile journey into town I saw more German soldiers. There was no doubt about it – the island had been occupied.[6]

On that fateful Sunday evening Bill Green had made his way to his cousin who lived the top of the Water Lanes at Moulin Huet, St Martin:

While there, we heard the sound of planes; looking up we saw two Dorniers with big black crosses on them, flying low over the house. They were obviously preparing to land at our La Villiaze Airport. After I had taken Mabs home, I drove around the back of the Airport and sure enough there were two or three German troop carriers parked adjacent to the terminal building. I knew then that we were occupied.

His mind racing, and upset with himself for not having been able to see his English-born wife and his mother safely evacuated, Bill made his way back to his house:

Slowly and wearily I returned home, not knowing what the future held. How would the German Army of occupation treat us, would we be allowed to lead normal lives, would we still be able to live in our home? Would our womenfolk be safe? Would there be enough food, would we go hungry? Would I be able to earn a living, would I be forced to work for the Germans? Would we be deported? What facilities would be available for the birth of our baby? All these questions and many, many, more ran through my mind, none of which I could answer …

So we went to bed. I recall lying there, thinking of all the opportunities we had missed to leave the island, thinking of all the problems that could face us, wondering whether we would live to see the end of the war.[7]

Albert Lamy was ideally placed to witness the momentous events of June and July 1940, such as the arrival of the first German aircraft:

Three large German aircraft landed on the Guernsey airport. That information reached the Police Station by telephone. At the Police Station there was a letter which had been handed in a few days earlier for my Chief [Inspector William Sculpher] to hand to the Officer Commanding German troops in Guernsey.

You can well imagine our feelings on first seeing such an address. However, it was there for delivery and we were told German aircraft were on the aerodrome. So, with my Chief and a couple of other Police officers, we set out for the Airport.

On the way we were stopped and told that three Blenheims had appeared on the scene and the three German aircraft had taken off and got away. However, we continued to the Airport and saw the marks of their landing wheels across the grass. They had broken into the Terminal Building and we were then under the impression they had left booby traps with the intention of blowing up the place. We searched and found nothing.

It was a peculiar feeling at the Airport – a place usually so full of noise and bustle was then as quiet as a grave, with only sufficient wind to rattle the hangar door and these noises did not help our peace of mind. However, we found nothing and returned to the Police Station.

As we have already seen, later that evening the *Luftwaffe* was soon back on the scene. Shortly after the *Luftwaffe* airmen had taken control of the airport at Guernsey, Inspector Sculpher of the Island's Police arrived and handed over a letter addressed to 'the Officer Commanding the German Troops in Guernsey'. It was signed by the Bailiff, Mr (later Sir) Victor Gosselin Carey.

The document explained that Guernsey had been declared an 'Open Island' by His Majesty's Government and that there were no armed forces of any description. Following this the *Luftwaffe* officer in command, *Major* Hessel, was driven to St. Peter Port to meet the Bailiff and took military command of the Island. How the note was delivered was described by Lamy:

At about 8 o'clock the same evening the sirens again sounded and five large German aircraft circled the Island finally landing on the Airport. This time they came to stay.

I did not make the journey that evening but Mr Sculpher, my Chief, did with other Police Officers. As they approached the road leading to the Airport they were held up by armed German sentries,

139

who accompanied them the remainder of the distance, riding on the running board.

When they reached the Terminal Building they were immediately told to get out of the motor car and stand up against a pile of sandbags and surrounded by soldiers with machine guns. The note was then delivered and German troops, by means of commandeered cars, came to the Town area. They immediately set up their Headquarters at an hotel and asked to see the leading officials of the Island.[8]

Following the initial arrival, and then departure, of the first *Luftwaffe* personnel at the airfield, Ambrose Sherwill decided to remain at home so that he could be near to the telephone. It rang, noted Sherwill, at about 19.00 hours, the caller being Pierre de Putron, the head of the Island's Air Raid Precautions:

> [He called] me up to say that several German troop carriers were flying down our West Coast. This time there was no firing and no bombs were dropped. So quickly was the invasion of Guernsey conducted that many people, not living near the airport, were unaware that the island had been occupied until their daily paper arrived the next day and they read the first set of German orders.[9]

It was not long before the Attorney General experienced his first encounter with one of the initial German invaders:

> About half an hour later, a young German *Luftwaffe* officer, still in flying kit and driven by our Police Sergeant Harper, arrived at my house. He spoke English. Now, because of the bombing on the Friday, my wife and I had put our two small boys to sleep in the hall of our house. We imagined that the arches were of solid granite ...
>
> I went out by the side door and intercepted him and said: 'Will you please come in by the side door?' Instantly suspicious, he said: 'And why?' I told him our young children were asleep in the front hall and he said, 'I would not dream of disturbing your children'.[10]

Having dealt with basic formalities, the German airman asked Sherwill to accompany him to the Royal Hotel, one of the principal hotels in St Peter Port. 'His demeanour', recalled Sherwill, 'had greatly reassured me and I was not in the least alarmed as to what might happen in the near future'.

At the hotel, Sherwill encountered other members of the Island's government, but had no idea who had assembled them. The group was

140

waiting for the arrival of the Bailiff, who, for his part, had been devolved the powers normally bestowed on the Lieutenant Governor who had been evacuated. Sherwill was despatched with a German officer to collect Carey.

On his return, Sherwill found himself witnessing the occupiers' first steps towards a functioning military administration. After discussion surrounding the stocks of weapons held on Guernsey (just twelve service rifles, but no bayonets or ammunition), as well about the quantity of aviation fuel (70,000 gallons, with 'had been doctored with tar, sugar etc'), the German commander instructed those present to construct his the first proclamation for the Islanders, as Sherwill recalled:

> He spoke some English and understood more. Finally he, verbally, issued a series of orders in German. They were interpreted to me by Mr. Isler, a German speaking Swiss national. The German officer had obviously been briefed. I put various questions for the purposes of clarification. My only contribution was to obtain the concession about the consumption of spirits that the order did not apply to stocks in private houses.
>
> He then said: 'Put all that into good English'. I then went into a huddle with Mr. Isler and, so far as I can now remember, Louis Guillemettte went away and typed out copies and arranged for their delivery to the Editors of our newspapers.[11]

One of the editors Sherwill referred to was that of *The Star*, the paper for which Frank Falla wrote. Having reached the paper's offices, and endured his first encounter with the new arrivals, Frank found himself contemplating the future with his colleagues, including his editor, Bill Taylor:

> [Bill stated that] 'the Nazis are down at the Royal Hotel now with guards mounted outside, waiting for the heads of our government to accept the dictated terms of occupation. I've been warned that within the next hour or so I'll have to go there and take down these conditions for publication in tomorrow's paper.'
>
> Sure enough, after we'd chatted and exchanged our most pessimistic fears as to what would happen to us and to the people of Guernsey, the call came that the Editor of *The Star* was to be ready in about ten minutes when a car would come and collect him.
>
> In under ten minutes a car hooter sounded in the street and Bill walked down the stairs and into the police car which was to take him

to the confrontation of local dignitaries and civil servants with the Nazis.

For the next two hours we waited for Bill's return. It was no good our getting the linotype operators into action or asking the stonehands to start dropping type into the forme. We just didn't know if we'd have a paper at all the next day, and if we did have one no one had a clue as to what we would be allowed to print in it.

Eventually Bill returned to the office. He had had a couple of whiskies and we could smell them. I could have done with a couple of brandies myself, but I couldn't get them, for this was a Sunday, the one day in the week when pubs are closed all day.

He turned the leaves of his notebook and showed me the shorthand notes which he had to translate into the front-page news for every islander to read the following day: Monday, 1st July 1940.

The Nazis, he said, had asked to see the most recent issues of the two local newspapers and after studying these for quite a time, told Bill: 'Mr Taylor. You will print our instructions to the people of Guernsey on the front page of tomorrow's issue in large print like this (a Nazi finger pointed to the story of the German bombing raid on the harbour) and you will deliver copies of the paper free to the people.'

Once he had transcribed his notes Bill came in to tell us that the rest of the paper, apart from the Nazi front-page orders, could be filled by us, but we had to be very careful that there was nothing in it offensive to the Third Reich! More, they wanted to see the final proof before we went to press.

We had no difficulty in filling our three pages of the paper, and had the circumstances been different we would have had a good laugh with the compositors as we dropped into the forme the advertisement for the Regal Cinema which boldly told everyone they were screening Tommy Trinder in *Laugh It Off*. Also in that epic issue, under the heading 'The Royal Hotel', this advertisement was reprinted: 'The Manager will be pleased to make special all-inclusive terms for residence with full board. Also special weekly terms for non-residents for meals. For particulars, apply to the Manager or phone 300'. Had anyone done this they would probably have been answered by a guttural German voice forcefully discouraging reservations.

It was a strange experience having to produce a newspaper and then give it away. Naturally that free issue was a 'sell-out', figuratively speaking, and there weren't enough copies to go round. Whether the people wanted it or not, they had to read the conditions laid down by the Nazis.[12]

Miss A. Le M. Mainé, the member of the Trinity First Aid Depot who had witnessed the bombing of St Peter Port on 28 June, and who worked tirelessly in its aftermath, also recalled the German arrival:

On Sunday, June 30th, several German 'planes landed bringing Senior Officers who officially took over the occupation of the Island. Everything went off without further incidents, and as we had no guns or means of defending ourselves that brutal air raid was unnecessary, and the Germans could have walked in without any opposition. Be it said to their credit that the German officers expressed regret at the injuries caused by the raid, and a young airman, named Roberts, brother of the above two sisters who were fatally injured, was demobilized and allowed to return home.

It may be here stated that since the departure of the RAF the Air Port had been used by farmers for grazing and when the Germans landed a man was milking his cows. He was naturally rather scared when he saw them, but they shook hands and told him not to run away, that they were not going to hurt him. They then asked him who was going to win the war. 'Why the British, of course!' They said: 'We shall see.'[13]

For the Germans, however, there was little doubt just who was the victor on 30 June 1940. At least one part of the British Isles had been captured, as this subsequently decoded 'Most Secret' message made clear:

Reported at 0030 1 July that Guernsey had been occupied. 2(F) 123 was starting as early as possible on 1 July for Jersey and Alderney to drop summons to surrender by 0700 (German time?), 2 July.[14]

The issuing of a German communiqué regarding the occupation of Guernsey was reported around the world, even in the United Kingdom:

There was much blowing of trumpets by the Germans over their first capture of British territory. The announcement was made in the shape of a special communiqué of the German High Command, broadcast after the rendering of the Nazi battle song 'We are off to fight against England,' and it read as follows:

'On June 30 the British island of Guernsey was captured by a daring coup de main by detachments of the German Air Force. In an air fight a German reconnaissance aeroplane shot down two Bristol Blenheim bombers.'[15]

Under the title 'Invasion of Channel Islands', *The Sydney Morning Herald* carried the following news piece in its edition of Tuesday, 2 July 1940:

> It was officially announced in Berlin this evening [1 July] that Guernsey had been partly occupied on Sunday … Earlier, it was announced in London that communication between England and the Channel Islands had been suspended. The partial occupation of Guernsey was described by the German Official News Agency as 'a surprise air force attack in which two British bombers were shot down.' … The heightened activities of both the German Air Force and the RAF in the last two days suggested that some invasion move was imminent.

Interestingly, whilst Gastager states he was the first German to step foot on Guernsey during the invasion, according to many accounts that honour was officially credited to *Hauptmann* Reinhard Liebe-Piderit, the Commanding Officer of *Fernaufklärungsgruppe* 3.(F)/123.[16]

Inspector Sculpher was also required to carry out one of the first post-occupation instructions issued by the Gemans, as Bill Green recalls:

> Many of the cattle rescued from Alderney during the days following the evacuation of that island, were put out to graze on our airport runway. When the first Germans arrived by troopcarrier they had difficulty in landing because of the danger created by the presence of the cattle. One of the first orders they issued, required the clearance of the runway, so that further troopcarriers could land.
>
> The Island Police were given the task of organising the removal of the cattle. P.C. Fred Short, who was on night duty, was instructed by Inspector Sculpher, to go to the airport, do whatever was necessary, and to assist the Germans in any way he could. He organised a number of farmers to help remove the cattle and they arrived at the Airport at dawn, around 5 a.m. Fred and the farmers were debating whether they should drive the cattle across the Route des Landes and into a field on the other side, when three Junkers troop-carriers landed, miraculously missing all the grazing animals.[17]

With the wandering cattle dealt with, once the three Ju 52s had come to a halt, Police Constable Fred Short had another task to deal with, as Bill Green's account reveals:

> They disgorged their cargo of fully armed German troops, together with a number of motorcycles and sidecars. The Jerries without

144

transport immediately commandeered all the farmers' cars and motorcycles. None of the Germans spoke English, but Fred clearly understood what they wanted when they kept repeating, 'Benzin, Benzin'. He led them, on his police motorcycle, out of the airport and down the road passed the Happy Landings Hotel to Snell's petrol pump at Le Bourg. He broke open the door and started to turn the pump handle, but the tank was dry.

Not knowing quite what to do, he was reminded by a colleague that the force had 'acquired' a supply of petrol from a damaged R.A.F. Spitfire. When the island had been demilitarized, and the R.A.F. evacuated, the police had been put in charge of the airport. It had been guarded by Special Constables. A Spitfire which had crashed landed and was damaged beyond repair, had been left in a hanger.[18]

Regular Police Officers on the night shift had discovered that the wings of the aircraft were still filled with fuel. They unofficially collected twenty, 5 gallon cans of high octane petrol, and secreted them in a store next to the Police Garage in Lefebvre Street. Fred Short decided that there was no alternative but to lead the Germans to that supply of petrol. He led the 'convoy' of German Military motorcycles, with their mounted machine guns, the commandeered farmers' cars and motorcycles into St Peter Port, and stopped outside the Police Station.

Fred and the Germans had arrived just as the change over from night shift to early shift was taking place. A Nazi Major, motioned all the police to line up against the wall. Fred told me that he and his colleagues did so, only very reluctantly, as they were confronted by fully armed German combat troops. They began to wonder whether they were going to be mown down in cold blood. Instead the Major produced a camera and took a photograph of our Policemen, lined up outside the Guernsey police station.

The Germans then drove into the Police yard in Lefebvre Street, at the end of Court Row, seized the entire stock of petrol cans, and proceeded to fill their vehicles with the high octane fuel. It was perhaps fortunate that the aviation fuel was suitable for the vehicles, otherwise the Germans may have thought that Fred Short had committed an act of sabotage.[19]

In his memoirs, Bill also details the circumstances surrounding what he describes as 'probably the first casualty of the occupation':

[It] occurred on the evening the Germans landed in the island. Charlie Froome was on duty at the St John's Ambulance station when an islander, Harry Ingrouille, came in and asked for a wound in his arm to be dressed. Charlie inspected the wound and asked, 'Where the hell did you get that from?' 'Never you mind,' replied Harry. 'Come on, that's a bullet wound, where did you get that from?'

Apparently when the Germans arrived at the airport, Harry had been at the top of the Petit Bot valley. He saw them coming, got scared and ran down the valley. The Germans saw him running away and shot him.[20]

School teacher P. Girard recalled what he described as the 'next memorable event' after the German air raid of 28 June, this being the arrival of the first German troops:

I remember sitting in my chair in the dining room at home and idly leaning backwards to look out of the window as an aeroplane passed overhead. I expected to see the usual British markings but to my horror I saw the enormous wing of a huge German transport aircraft adorned with big black crosses.

Other planes eventually passed over and when the nurse who had been looking after my wife and daughter returned from St. Peter Port we eagerly questioned her about her experiences and she told us that she had seen a number of lorry loads of German soldiers coming down the Grange. The soldiers had waved at her and with shame, she admitted that she had been so frightened that she had waved back.[21]

Though the original plan to capture the Channel Islands had been formulated by the *Kriegsmarine*, now that the *Luftwaffe* had landed on Guernsey a fully-fledged amphibious assault was no longer justified. The *Wehrmacht* therefore ordered a change of plan.

Under this rapidly improvised scheme it was decided to use Junkers Ju 52 13m transport aircraft to airlift naval assault troops, an infantry company and a number of light anti-aircraft guns to Guernsey the following morning, 1 July 1940. However, as we have already seen, bad weather delayed these aircraft from reaching Cherbourg for the planned departure at 09.30 hours; it was not until the afternoon that some machines became available and the airlift commenced.[22]

At about 14.45 hours the first of these transports landed at Guernsey. Amongst those on board was *Major* Dr. Albrecht Lanz, the Military Commandant designate of the Island. About the same time, *Oberstleutnant* Hermann Plocher also landed in his personal Ju 52. Lanz later recalled his arrival:

146

When we approached the coast our Ju climbed and soon we were circling over Guernsey. Quickly the experienced eye of the pilot picked out the airfield, one more loop and already the machine was on the runway, and halted in front of the airport building. I and my Adjutant were the first to jump out of the 'plane – I didn't want anyone to take that pleasure from me.[23]

As Lanz set about rapidly giving orders to each of the platoons that had just flown in, he was approached by the officer in charge of the German contingent already on Guernsey:

At the outer corners of the airfield were German Recce [reconnaissance] machines. From the airport the OC Recce Group 123 *Major* Hessel came towards us, smiling.

He had already landed with his men the evening before, and welcomed us heartily. He told us that everything was quiet on the Island, both here at the airfield and down in the town; we could count on there being no opposition from the enemy, and everything was under control. I rapidly put Hessel in the picture regarding the conduct of the operation, and I in turn was informed of conditions on the Island.

At the same time, *Major* Hessel advised Lanz that he had commissioned the manufacture of a German war flag from a local business in St Peter Port.[24]

At around 15.00 hours the flag was delivered to the airport and, with due ceremony, hoisted on the terminal building's signal mast. Lanz was amongst the witnesses to this historic moment:

A few minutes after 15.00 hrs the first German War Flag, sewn with English hands, was hauled up the mast of the airport building to float over British territory. The beautiful Isle of Guernsey was thereby visibly taken under German over-lordship. A few days later I got the bill from the shop, so that *Major* Hessel might frame this unique document and hang it with this Imperial War Flag in the Mess of his Recce Squadron.

As the minutes ticked by, a constant stream of German reinforcements, as well as other senior officers, continued to be airlifted in:

One Ju after another now landed on the airfield. At 16.00 hrs Admiral Lindau and General Bottcher, our Divisional Commander, arrived in a Ju in order to be present in person at this operation. Major Hessel handed over the command on the Island, which he had held since the previous evening to me, for he himself wished to get back to the Mainland that evening with his squadron.

With the small flag-raising ceremony at the airport completed, Lanz now had a far more pressing matter to deal with – the formal processes to be completed with the Island's authorities. He was, therefore, to be driven to St. Peter Port to meet the Bailiff and other States dignitaries and officially take command of Guernsey:

> There were crowds of cars in front of the airport. We took one quickly, a policeman sat at the wheel and down we went to Town, St. Peter Port, about 5 miles away, through narrow roads, mostly with fences, hedges and walls on either side, continually bending; devilish difficult to find one's bearings here. Several times thought an approaching wagon was going to crash into us, but that was a typical case of false impression, for here they drive on the left, one must get used to that first, and anyway these fellows drive like the devil.
>
> The Royal Hotel at the harbour, hitherto Maj Hessel's HQ, was surrounded by hundreds of people curious to see what was going on. The first necessary Regulations had already been announced and published in the evening paper. Now it remained to find the British Governor, known here as the 'Bailiff' to inform him of the transfer of command.
>
> In the car with the policeman at the wheel off we went again at a rapid speed through narrow roads, round many corners, past interminable glasshouses, until our car turned into a park surrounding the house of the Bailiff, who is responsible directly to the British Crown. We had brought an interpreter with us. A short ring at the bell, and the door was opened.
>
> Now came a moment that I shall never in my life forget. Easily the proudest of this war.

Major Lanz would later recall the moment that he, *Major* Hessel and the interpreter were all ushered into Victor Carey's office:

> Maj Hessel and I entered the large richly furnished living room …
> The old gentleman of 68, in a dark suit, was standing in the background of the room. In a few words the interpreter explained that Maj Hessel had handed over the command to me and that we had

come, Maj Hessel to take his leave, and I to meet him in person. With his arms folded, the old gentleman bowed deeply before the representatives of the German Army – the first time in the history of England that a Governor and the direct representative of his Britannic Majesty has ever bowed to the German Army.

He thanked us particularly and repeatedly for the correct behaviour of the German troops and promised to make all necessary arrangements for our wishes and regulations to be carried out in the smallest detail. Everything we needed was at our disposal.

There were some Islanders whose enquiring nature got the better of them. As Bill Green noted on the morning after the Germans had landed, 'I was desperate to know what was going on':

As the local Press would not be published until later in the day, my inquisitiveness took me down into St Peter Port and to the Royal Hotel, which the Germans had temporarily made their Headquarters and from which the Swastika now fluttered. There, I saw local people handing in guns. Apparently an order had gone out, requiring everyone to surrender them immediately. German soldiers were making a stack of the weapons outside the Hotel. These Germans, in their soon to become all too familiar field grey uniforms, were the first I had seen.

For Bill Green and his wife one of their next meetings with the invaders took on a somewhat comical scenario, as he later recalled:

Whilst I had seen German soldiers in town, the first time Mabs and I saw Germans near Seaplane bungalow, our home, was when two tall young blond Hitler youth types, stopped us in our road and asked; 'Vitch vay London?'

'Across the sea,' Mabs replied. The answer clearly annoyed them, so Mabs, pointing westward repeated; 'Over there, across the sea.'

Eventually they indicated that they understood what she was saying and by their expressions, were not very happy. They were obviously under the impression that they had landed in England and we were delighted to have disillusioned them![25]

Though he had not yet encountered one of the invaders, Guerseyman Kenneth Lewis was made aware of their arrival, by his father, on the evening of 30 June:

British aircraft could be seen flying over the Island during the morning, but high above these we spotted a German 'plane however no action was taken. At about 1.10 p.m. the 'plane came lower and we saw clearly the black cross with the white facings on the wings, and we heard the Air-Raid warning sound.

We at once rushed to our shelter and were accompanied by neighbours. Dad who was on duty came down to tell us that German planes had landed on the Airport, however much to our delight they took off again as British Aircraft had been sighted. We went to Chapel that evening quite relived.

In the evening we decided that it would be best not to go for a walk and it so happened that we were not quite home when the throb of aircraft engines could again be heard and the Siren again sounded. We once again rushed to our shelter which this time held 16 people. Again Dad came down with the news that the plane had landed and that this time they stayed. This was at 7.50 p.m. and from that time we considered ourselves under German occupation.

That evening people went to bed with heavy hearts.[26]

Similar sentiments were expressed by one of Guernsey's clergymen, the Reverend Sidney Beaugie, a Methodist Minister:

On Sunday evening Guernsey was occupied by the German Forces … There was no opposition. No one who experienced it will ever forget the feeling of depression with which we awoke … Our beloved Islands in the hands of the enemy, dreading what the future might hold, conscious of our complete isolation, we realised with sinking hearts that life would be totally different, but how different none could guess.[27]

12

'Strike the flag'

The Germans Arrive on Jersey

With the occupation of Guernsey progressing well, and having met the Bailiff and other States dignitaries to begin the process of officially taking command of the Island, the Military Commandant designate, *Major* Lanz, returned to the airport. 'There was,' he wrote, 'still a point that we were not satisfied with. There lay about sixteen miles to the south, the Isle of Jersey, almost twice as big. That we also wished to have.'

Earlier, in the small hours of 1 July, three copies of an ultimatum signed by *General* Richtofen, the *Luftwaffe* commander in Normandy, had been dropped on Jersey. Each copy had been dropped in a stout canvas bag to which were attached a number of long red streamers. One of the bags fell at the airport, this being taken to the Island's Bailiff, Alexander Coutanche, by the airfield's controller Charles Roche, whilst other snagged some railings near St Mark's Church in St Helier.

One problem immediately presented itself to the Island's authorities – that was that the ultimatum was in German. 'We could at first find nobody capable of translating it,' remembered Coutanche:

> It evidently contained instructions and we were able to make out, by certain words, that unpleasant things would happen if they were not complied with. It was obviously imperative to know quickly what the instructions were.[1]

Jersey's Attorney-General, C.W. Duret Aubin, set out to have the document translated. His first port of call was Father Rey of the Jesuit Order of St. Helier. Though Rey did not speak German, he succeeded in getting hold of an Alsatian priest. The translation was soon in Coutanche's hands. Amongst the German ultimatum's many stipulations were the following:

151

> I intend to neutralize military establishments in Jersey by occupation
> … As evidence that this island will surrender the military and other
> establishments without resistance and without destroying them, a
> large white cross is to be shown as follows from 7.0 a.m., July 2nd,
> 1940 – a) In the centre of the airport in the east of the island; b) on the
> highest point of the fortification of the port; and c) on the square to the
> north of the inner basin of the harbour. Moreover all fortifications,
> buildings, establishments and houses are to show a white flag.

To reinforce the message, Richtofen added that, 'If these signs of
peaceful surrender are not observed by 7.00 a.m., July 2nd, heavy
bombardment will take place: a) Against all military objects; b) Against
all establishments and objects useful for defence.' He went to add the
following orders: 'The signs of surrender must remain up to the time of
the occupation of the Island by German troops; Representatives of the
Authorities must stay at the airport until the occupation; All radio traffic
and other communications with Authorities outside the Island will be
considered hostile actions and will be followed by bombardment.'

In conclusion, Richtofen confirmed that 'every hostile action against
representatives will be followed by bombardment', though 'in case of
the peaceful surrender, the lives, property and liberty of the peaceful
inhabitants are solemnly guaranteed'.[2]

However, for the Germans newly-arrived on Guernsey, the situation
on Jersey remained uncertain. Indeed, still on Guernsey, Lanz noted that
'no one knew whether any of our Recce troops had landed over there'.
In fact, they had.

Sonderführer Hans Auerbach later penned the following account of
the initial landings in Jersey for German consumption. Though
entertaining, it is clearly inaccurate in many of its details. It was entitled
'How a Young Lieutenant took the Island of Jersey':

> From Normandy, from Cape Carteret or Cape de la Hogue [also Cap
> de la Hague], the Channel Islands appear grey shadows between the
> horizon and the sea, shadows which in hazy weather disappear. What
> do they conceal? The telescopes of Coast Guards were continually
> fixed upon them, as this was England [*sic*]; this was the last bastion
> turned towards Europe after she had been driven from the Continent.
> Headquarters were, therefore, very much interested in the Islands, as
> they greatly desired to know what was happening in them. Rumour
> had it that they had been completely evacuated. Reconnaissance
> undertook to discover the true state of affairs.

On June 30th, Lieutenant Kern flew over the Islands for that purpose. He saw Guernsey with its glass-houses; he saw apparently inhospitable Alderney, the small Island of Sark, and then he turned to the largest Island of Jersey. He flew over the beaches and harbours, over small estates and villages until he reached St. Helier. The streets of the town were almost deserted. The Island seemed dead. Finally, after close investigation people were discernible. They emerged cautiously from the air raid shelters and gazed curiously upward. There was, therefore, still life on Jersey. The most important fact was that it could be reported to the General that there was no sign of defence.

On the second flight, the machine met three 'planes of similar type from the sister squadron. They were flying towards Guernsey and, as was later known, that morning they occupied the Island.

In the meantime, the English must have smelt a rat for they sent two Blenheims over the Channel. They met three Dornier Fighters near Guernsey, and Lieutenant Forster was able to shoot them both down with one reconnaissance 'plane.

As a result of the information obtained, the General decided to call upon Jersey to surrender. It was two o'clock in the morning when the summons, signed by the General, reached the squadron. There were three summonses each for Jersey and Guernsey all in the same terms. As it was a letter of parley, the usual coloured pouch could not be used; pouches were, therefore, cut from bed-linen belonging to the Captain of the French squadron whose deserted quarters had been taken over by the German squadron. It was still dark when the machine started for Jersey.

The Island was reached in the early hours. Once more a German 'plane was droning over Jersey. Only a few islanders were up, but the pouch containing the summons to surrender which had been dropped was soon found and taken to the Authorities. Later, it was recounted in the Island how surprised the dreamy town of St. Helier was to receive such an early visit.

After dropping the summons the 'plane returned, and the General awaited signs of surrender. It can be imagined how tense the German airmen were during the period of waiting. The General had stipulated that, as a sign of surrender, white flags should be flown. There could be no peace of mind until the undertaking had been carried to a successful conclusion.

Wild rumours were running through the services. According to these an English cruiser was supposed to have made its appearance in the vicinity of Jersey. In order to clear up this point, Lieutenant Kern was sent back to the Islands. He arrived without being attacked, and could see nothing of any active defence. The Island lay there as peacefully as on the previous day. Then, as the machine flew over the beaches and gardens and town, an idea came to the Lieutenant. He saw life going on peacefully below him; he saw the beautiful Island and he had been ordered to bring back accurate information. As he flew towards the Airport and saw the beautifully situated landing ground with its elegant white buildings, he made his decision.

He would take Jersey.

The 'plane banked over the flying field. He gave the order to land. What were the sensations of the crew? If the field were mined, then it would be all over. If there were means of defence, it would not be much better for them. But if things went smoothly, and no one doubted that they would, then they would be the first Germans to set foot on British soil. Lonely the machine rolled over the ground. The Lieutenant strode towards the Administration Building, followed by the 'plane which was to secure the way into the unknown – with its machine gun ready.

Nothing happened. Finally, from the Airport Building, emerged an excited man who, to the astonishment of the newcomers, spoke German. He took the Lieutenant to the telephone and got in touch with the Bailiff.

Yes, the Bailiff had received the summons to surrender.

Why were the white flags not flying?

Because the Bailiff had to wait for the decision of the States, and the States had in the meantime agreed to unconditional surrender.

The Bailiff requested that the General should be informed to that effect. Lieutenant Kern informed the Bailiff that the Island was under German occupation.[3]

The surrender summons dropped on Jersey that Hans Auerbach refers to was that signed by General Richtofen and described at the start of this chapter.

At the time unaware of the presence of German personnel on Jersey, back on Guernsey *Oberstleutnant* Hermann Plocher ordered a fighter aircraft to fly there and reconnoitre. This maybe the aircraft that Charles Roche telephoned the Island's Bailiff, Alexander Coutanche, about on the afternoon of 1 July. Coutanche was in his office when the telephone rang. He later gave this description of the conversation that ensued:

Charles said 'A German plane landed a few minutes ago and taxied up to the apron. I went out and spoke to the pilot. He said that he was aware of the orders instructing Jersey to display the white flag as a sign of surrender, and that he could see that white flags were being shown all over the Island. Might he take it that the Island was going to be surrendered without any fuss? If so, he would go back and tell his chiefs. I told him that he was correct and he has flown off.'[4]

Coutanche immediately assured Roche that his actions had been completely correct. Indeed, as he pointed out to the airport controller, 'My orders are to surrender as soon as anybody capable of accepting the surrender comes along'. That moment, however, was still to come, as the *Luftwaffe* pilot did not loiter, quickly taking off for France to report on his encounter.

In view of what he subsequently learnt, Plocher ordered his personal Junkers Ju 52 to immediately fly him to Jersey. He was accompanied by Lanz who took with him the newly-made German flag which he had begged from Major Hessel pledging his own head as security.

Upon their arrival on Jersey the party was met by *Hauptmann* von Obernitz of *Aufklärungsgruppe* 123 (Reconnaissance Group 123) who reported that he and his men had landed there at about noon and that all was quiet. Lanz later recalled the short flight from Guernsey:

Off we went and even flew over alone, to complete the formal surrender. *Oberstleutnant* Plocher's 'plane again rolled across the airfield with us on board. Out we went over the blue sea, [and] again the machine dived almost to the wave crests.

Twenty minutes later we were circling over the airfield on Jersey. The landing was smooth. As we rolled across the field to the airport building Capt von Obernitz came smiling towards us and reported that he had landed with his men on the Island at noon that day and taken possession of it. Asked if he had spoken to the officer of the fighter 'plane that was there half an hour before, he replied that he had not seen any fighter recently. Where the latter actually landed remained an unsolved mystery.[5]

It was whilst Plocher's aircraft was heading towards Jersey that Coutanche decided to deal with a matter that he personally considered of great importance – the nature of which he detailed in his memoirs:

The Union Jack was still flying at Fort Regent ... I had told the people that, while the Union Jack continued to fly at the Fort, it meant that I was still able to afford them a measure of protection. I promised them, on these occasions, that as soon as circumstances made it impossible for me to give them protection any longer, the flag at the Fort would be lowered but that it would never be lowered by any other hand than my own.[6]

With Roche's news still ringing in his ears, Coutanche was driven up to the imposing nineteenth-century fort on Mont de la Ville overlooking St Helier. 'I think that it is perhaps time to strike the flag at the Fort,' he had remarked. Coutanche had only just arrived when a telephone call was received in the signalman's hut. His secretary, Ralph Mollet, had an important message:

I went in [the hut] and Mollet said 'The Germans have landed at the airport. They want you to go out and meet them.'
'Tell them that I am on my way.' With those words I lowered the flag which would not be hoisted again for another five long years.

Mirroring the scenes that had been played out at the airfield on Guernsey only hours earlier, the Germans immediately set out stabilising their presence on Jersey. Lanz's description of the dramatic events of 1 July 1940, continues:

Cherbourg was informed quickly through the wireless at the airport, and presently, after a short time the first Ju [52]s came directly from Cherbourg carrying my No.1 Coy ... As soon as the first company had landed the last of its men, a regulation Flag parade was laid on.
On the right flank was *Oberstleutnant* Plocher with all the other officers present, then a section of the *Luftwaffe*, consisting of the crews of the Obernitz Squadron, then the men of the Naval assault detachment *Gotenhafen*, and finishing with the whole of No.1 Coy.
Kapitänleutnant Koch, who, naturally was with us, had the allotted task of hoisting, with his own hands, the German Imperial War Flag high above the roof of the airport building. I myself gave the orders.
With arms at the slope and eyes right, over the airfield rang the command 'Hoist Flag!' Slowly, and ceremonially, over this British territory also, for the first time in history rose the German Imperial War Flag high upon the mast. Now Jersey too was under German over-lordship.

Meanwhile, and as requested, Coutanche had travelled the short distance from Fort Regent across to Jersey's airfield, where he found that Duret Aubin was already present:

> When we arrived at the airport in my car, flying my flag, we found about half a dozen German officers waiting for us. They had a civilian with them to act as interpreter. I imagine that he was a German waiter from one of the hotels.

Coutanche recalled that the first thing that the German officer in charge, presumably Lanz, did was to say to him, 'You realise that you are occupied?' The only response the Bailiff could muster was a simple 'Yes'. For his part, Lanz also had a number of administrative duties to dispense with:

> I appointed the OC No.1 Coy, *Hauptmann* Gusseck Island Commander of Jersey. After giving brief instructions about the most important measures to be put into immediate operation, and a few tactical instructions for the garrisoning of the Island, back we went over the sea to Guernsey, where I intended to make my stay, for although this Island is the smaller, it is on the other hand of more tactical importance.

In a 'mood of deep depression', Coutanche, having asked Duret Aubin to deal with some of the matters arising from the German proclamation – namely the billeting of the invaders and handing over control of the telephone and communication systems on the Island – decided to return home. It was there, a short while later, that the Bailiff had his first encounter with *Hauptmann* Erich Gusseck.

Having spent some time in his garden, as Coutanche's evening meal was drawing to a close his houseman, Coleman, who was looking out of the window, suddenly remarked, 'Sir, the drive is full of Jerries. What do we do?' To this, Coutanche replied, 'There is only one thing to do and that is to open the door and let them in'.[7]

Gusseck and his entourage were shown into the drawing room. Still wearing his gardening clothes, complete with torn trousers, Coutanche went to greet them. As he walked in, Duret Aubin, marshalling his most commanding tone, announced 'His Excellency, the Governor'.

Standing near the fireplace, Gusseck stepped forward to introduce himself. As Coutanche himself later remembered, the German commander was somewhat taken aback at the Bailiff's dress:

His method of expressing some surprise at my appearance was to put a monocle into his right eye, the better to take me in. In those days I used on occasion to wear a monocle myself and it so happened that it was in the pocket of my jacket now. I was, therefore, able to repay the compliment and I did so. We took good stock of each other.[8]

This 'comic-book confrontation' – as it was described by the author Barry Turner – was brought to an end by one of Gusseck's subordinates, who handed him a document which was then given to an interpreter to read out. 'It was the same proclamation as that which had already been read to me at the airport,' remarked Coutanche, who added that 'While this was taking place I could see through the window that Duret Aubin had retired to the dining-room and was fortifying himself with a glass of my port'!'[9]

After a brief discussion, Gusseck took his leave, having agreed that he would meet with Coutanche at the latter's office in the Town Hall the following morning. The formalities of occupation were complete.

For virtually every islander, the surrender was a bitter pill to swallow. One author recalls that the whole of King Street in St Helier had been 'a mass of white flags'. Margaret Vaudin expresses her memory of the scene they represented thus:

> I shall never forget the sight of those white flags hanging from every house. It was both sickening and demoralising, and I never felt more depressed in my life.[10]

Donald Journeaux read the notice that had been placed in the Jersey *Evening Post* on 1 July and had, unwilling, been obliged to comply with the German demand that the Island should surrender:

> Like many others, Irene and I suffered greatly that evening. We felt humiliated at having to hang out a white flag. Nothing could be more abhorrent to us, but we knew that it had to be done. Everyone had to comply as you could not put others at risk by ignoring such an order. With a feeling of hopelessness I found an old torn cloth (I could make that small gesture of defiance), attached it to a stake and fixed it to the chimney pot.
>
> After a sleepless night, we went over to Irene's parents' home. The gardener had put up their white flag – and so they had not even been obliged to see it, thereby at least saving them some trauma.

Everything seemed strange. We felt so agitated. Something needed to be done, but we did not know what. How could we possibly make any plans?

Everything everywhere was confusion.[11]

Despite Journeaux's view that confusion had reigned, according to one account the German invasion was 'carried out efficiently and without disorder':

The first many people knew of it was the sight of German troops on motor cycles and in cars making for St Helier, and the posting of guards at the Post Office, Telephone Exchange and other buildings in the town. Billeting of the troops was speedily carried out, various hotels being taken over for the purpose, and, thanks to the appeal made by the Bailiff and loyally observed by the population, there was no disorder of any kind.[12]

In the hours that followed, there were others across Jersey who experienced their first meeting with a member of the occupying German forces. Francis Le Sueur was one of them:

My first encounter with the occupation forces was on a rather comical note. Shortly after their arrival on the island I was standing at the junction of Conway Street and the Esplanade, waiting for someone, when I spotted a couple of young Nazi sailors, full of the joys of life. They were fiddling about with a motor-cycle, which they probably found abandoned, with petrol in the tank. It was a powerful model and the sailors did not seem over conversant with it.

In the end, they managed to start the engine and then wheeled it into the middle of the road. Then one of them seated himself in the saddle, while the other sat on the pillion seat. The former started revving up the engine and at the same time fiddling about with the clutch and the gears. The one behind was holding on to him fairly firmly but in the end relaxed his hold, as he obviously did not expect his pal to shoot off without any warning.

I felt sure that something or the other was about to happen, so I stayed put to see the result. The first sailor continued to rev up the engine in short bursts giving it more and more gas. At the same time he continued to play around with the gears, a dangerous procedure for a novice, which he undoubtedly was.

The inevitable soon happened. The bike without any warning suddenly shot forward, like a shot out of a gun. The second sailor, previously on the pillion, now found himself still in a sitting position but this time on thin air. He landed on the asphalt with a jolt that must have jarred every bone in his body.

The whole incident was so comical that I could not help bursting out laughing. It seemed to be straight out of a comic film. The young Nazi, who must have been in pain, nevertheless, picked himself up and came over to where I was standing. He more or less pushed his fist under my nose, at the same time muttering threats in German. I decided that discretion was the better part of valour, and having had my share of fun, at the expense of the Third Reich, I pushed off without saying a word.[13]

As well as remembering how his mother had 'hung a sheet out of the window', Brian Ahier Read, also recalled his first encounter with the enemy:

I remember walking to the centre of the town to visit my friend Ronald but when I got to the house I found the curtains drawn and nobody in. A woman in the house opposite opened her window and shouted, 'They've all gone. They've evacuated.'

I ran back towards my home but as I passed a large hotel (called the Ommaroo) a taxi pulled up and three German soldiers carrying rifles and other kit got out and went into the hotel! It was the first time I had ever seen a German soldier.

Curious to see what would happen, I waited on the pavement on the opposite side of the hotel. More taxis came along. They had come from the airport. More soldiers went in to the hotel. None of them spoke to me.

I went home, telling my mother very proudly that I had seen German soldiers. But she remained indoors, saying that she did not want to see any.[14]

A short while later, Brian's father arrived home from work – he was an employee at the Post Office. He was, Brian noted, 'in a bad mood':

'We're all German now,' he said. 'Goodness knows what's going to happen to us. They've cut all the lines to England.'

He told my mother and me that three German officers had come in to the Post Office during the afternoon and had gone to the room where he worked with the teleprinters (machines used to send telegrams). 'They were very polite and shook hands with us when they came in,' he told my mother. 'But we had to do what they said as they were all carrying guns.'

My father had been told that he must disconnect all the machines. At the same time all the telephone lines to England in the telephone exchange were cut.[15]

The troops seen by Brian Read were small in number, though reinforcements were continually pouring in. A young serviceman at the time, Dr. Ulrich Kaser later recalled the arrival of his unit, I./Flak-Regiment 9 *Legion Condor*, which was equipped with four 88mm Flak 18s and a pair of 20mm Flak 30 anti-aircraft guns – though he did not reach Jersey on the first day of operations:

On the 30th June 1940, the 1st Battalion had been positioned in and around the Cherbourg area. These had been deployed; 1st battery, one kilometre north west of Henneville, 2nd battery, at Fort du Roule, Cherbourg, the 3rd battery, three kilometres east of Brettville, whilst both the 4th and 5th batteries were located at the fort and airfield at Querqueville.

On the 3rd July, the 5th battery was flown in Junkers 52 transport aircraft to Guernsey and Jersey, with six 20mm Flak 30 being sent to each island. Once on the islands the weapons were then transported with requisitioned vehicles, and placed to repulse any attempted landings from the sea, and to help secure the airfields.[16]

The deployment of *Legion Condor*, or a similar unit, did not go unnoticed by the British security services. A decoded Enigma transcript dated 2 July 1940, states that,

A section of Flak 5/9 by orders of the German Naval Command has been transported by air to JERSEY (1/7). Flak 1/9 reported ready for action (1/7). Both belong to Flakbrigade Frantz.

Of interest here is the discrepancy in dates compared to Kaser's recollections. It may be assumed, therefore, that the intercept was actually a movement order and not a notification of final deployment.[17]

Back on Jersey there remained one further act to finalise the process of occupation. John Blampied was outside the Town Hall when the Jersey flag was lowered to be replaced by the German one:

A few hours after that we heard the sound of marching and there were the Germans. They congregated at the Cenotaph ... It was scary because we were looking at a modern army, we'd never seen this in our lives ... Even the older people, those who'd fought in the First World War, were a bit confused because our boys, the regiments that had been here, they all had First World War guns.[18]

No one really knew what to expect that first day of the German occupation. How would the invaders behave? Similarly, how would the Islanders react?

For some, the initial response to the news that the enemy had landed was one of fear. One family in St Helier, for example, had expected the German troops to immediately begin searching houses, seizing whatever took their fancy. As a result, they felt compelled to hide their stocks of food and drink:

We had a trap door in the roof of our scullery, so I stood on the top of the step ladders while the rest of the family passed me all the food they could find. Once the food was up there the trap door was so narrow and it was such a business to get at it that we thought twice about bringing it out. Later it was quite exciting bringing the food out bit by bit – 'ooh look at this' we used to say – and in fact what we had hidden lasted most of the first year. The drink we buried in the yard and we used to dig up a bottle of whisky for special occasions such as Christmas.[19]

In reality, the invasion of the Channel Islands was rather benign and, aside from the small ceremonies at the two main airports, almost entirely free of great drama. Indeed, to some Islanders their first encounter with the enemy was marked by surprise:

The first intimation I had of what was going on was when I was returning home, coming along near Rouge Bouillon. I was just driving the car normally when to my astonishment about 40 or 50 German soldiers suddenly appeared on bicycles – riding on the wrong side of the road! So I pulled to one side and looked at these chaps going by and thought, 'What on earth's going on here? Where have they sprung from?[20]

His duty done on Jersey that fateful day, 1 July 1940, *Major* Lanz boarded a Junkers Ju 52 for the short journey back to Guernsey. It was, he later wrote,

An unforgettable flight in the glorious evening sunshine, under a cloudless sky, the deep blue sea beneath us, and on the horizon glowing red the jagged cliffs of the rocky Guernsey coast. And above all the proud consciousness on this historic day of having taken the Channel Islands into German possession.

But there was little time to savour the pleasure of this impression, for we had hardly landed again in Guernsey before we went down to the Town, to the Royal Hotel, still surrounded with crowds of people. Innumerable urgent necessities and personal wishes were to be dealt with.

The hotel itself was almost without windows, which had almost all been shattered by a German bombing attack on the harbour three days before. Far into the night there was coming and going and it was long past midnight before the day's work was done and this first great day drew to its close. [21]

13

'Breeches, jackboots and forage caps'

The Occupation of Sark and Other Islands

With the Swastika having been raised over Guernsey, German attention naturally turned to the other occupied islands in the archipelago – of which there were six more in total (including Alderney). 'There were still Islands in my sphere of command that were waiting to be officially taken over,' noted *Major* Lanz.

It seems that at the same time that the invaders were dealing with Jersey, they had also been eyeing the virtually abandoned Alderney. The following is the text of an intercepted and decoded message that had been sent by *Luftflotte* 3 at 15.15 hours on 1 July 1940:

> Flieger Korps VIII: 2 Do.17 of 2.(F) 123 (take off 04.00hrs) for Alderney and Jersey, to drop messages onto the airfields there with the request that the islands by 2 July 40 07.00hrs, are handed over unconditionally. About 11.00hrs repeated flight, close by, it became apparent that Alderney was uninhabited, the airfield blocked with wire obstacles and was not approachable. In Jersey, the Governor handed over the island unconditionally. Fl. Korps VIII has sent strong reinforcements with Junker transports for island of Jersey.[1]

According to another decoded message that had been intercepted later the same day, again after being sent by *Luftflotte* 3, but this time at 21.20 hours, the news that Alderney was reported to have been 'uninhabited' appears to be swiftly acted upon:

> To 2a): 16.00 - 17.00hrs a small unit occupies Island of Alderney. Operation was executed by use of 3 Storche a/c.[2]

Mirroring events on Guernsey, and virtually simultaneously on Jersey,

164

the first enemy arrivals on Alderney, almost certainly *Luftwaffe* personnel, were quickly bolstered by additional resources:

> [They were] reinforced at once by seaborne force from Cherbourg. It was not, at first, an impressive garrison, only eighty men all told, commanded by Sergeant Major Schmidt. On the other hand, since there were only seven inhabitants, all of whom kept strictly recluse, and since all the animals were dead or gone (except for an increasing plague of rabbits, as was reported in the autumn), there was little for the garrison to do. The German Customs Officers who had hopefully been included in their number found small scope, in the way of contraband, to engage their vigilance, as they moodily surveyed the empty sea and sky, and listened to the everlasting wind.[3]

Major Lanz was amongst the early German visitors to Alderney. 'Acting on the orders of the GOC,' he explained, 'I explored the island':

> After many twists and turns Lt Rudolf who was himself flying the machine made a good landing on the airfield at Alderney. I found there a few members of *Flieger Korps* VIII fetching food. The island had been evacuated by the civilian population and many cattle had died for want of water. The last Guernsey people who fetched part of the cattle to Guernsey, made use of the opportunity to loot the shops. After a brief examination and report the order came to [fully] occupy Alderney also. One half of the occupying force went the same day by air in two Jus [Junkers Ju 52 transports]; the other half was sent over by boat.[4]

There were, of course, other islands to be occupied, perhaps the most important of which was Sark, whose turn came on 3 July 1940. Herm, however, was all but bypassed by the Germans during Operation *Green Arrow*, despite being just three miles off the east coast of Guernsey.

It was not until 20 July, that Herm was finally seized, a small garrison (of just nine men according to one account) being landed, although by then there was only one or two individuals on the Island to greet them. One person was Frank Dickson, who, by rights, should not have been there. The author Martin J. Le Page explains how 'Mr. Kemp, caretaker of Herm for Sir Percival Perry, approached him [Frank] to look after the island for a few days, whilst he went to the mainland':

> The trouble was that Mr. Kemp never came back. Whether he was prevented from doing so, or not, will probably never be known, but

that left Frank stuck on Herm. He watched the raid on the harbour with considerable apprehension, believing, from what he could see, that it was the town itself that was being bombed. It was not until the following Tuesday that he found out what was going on, when a boatload of Germans arrived and took possession of the island in the name of the Third Reich.[5]

Intriguingly, one of the occupiers' first acts on Herm was to shoot a propaganda film, *The Invasion of the Isle of Wight*.[6]

As with Herm, the small island of Jethou, which, the property of the British Crown and is leased to a tenant, is immediately to the south of the former, was all but unoccupied when the Germans finally arrived. Only Mr. and Mrs. MacDonald, the tenant's retainers, were still living on the Island. *Major* Lanz recalled:

Meanwhile the two little Islands lying between Guernsey and Sark, namely Herm and Jethou, were taken over and searched. The only life we found there was countless rabbits and various pheasants, the only ones that exist in this neighbourhood.

With a surface area of about seventy-four acres, the tiny island of Brecqhou (also spelt Brechou) is considered to be part of Sark and, in turn, the Bailiwick of Guernsey. Located just west of Sark, the first Germans are believed to have arrived there following the occupation of Sark.

The Island's tenant, Captain Thomas Arthur Clarke, had departed on 20 June 1940. He left behind five of his staff, four of whom were Irish nationals (and thereby neutral persons). The fifth resident, the cook, was 41-year-old Ernie le Bourg from Alderney.[7] There was little immediate effect following the German arrival, this tiny population being allowed to remain until April 1941.[8]

Returning to Sark, on hearing news of the British Government's announcement, on 19 June, that the Lieutenant-Governors of Jersey and Guernsey were likely to be recalled, Dame Sibyl Hathaway, the hereditary feudal ruler of the Island of Sark, travelled over to Guernsey for the day to learn for herself what plans had been put in place either to defend the Islands or to evacuate the population. She was appalled with what she saw:

The High Street was packed with winding queues of people waiting to draw money from the banks, and their strained faces showed how

166

anxious they were to get away. The States offices were in a state of utter confusion and the only man who appeared cool, calm and collected was the Bailiff's secretary. Having seen what I came to see I boarded the afternoon boat back to Sark and during the crossing made up my mind how best I could protect my own people.[9]

Though part of the Bailiwick of Guernsey, Sark, with a population of just a few hundred and little more than two square miles in extent, has always been fiercely independent. It could be certain that Dame Sibyl's people would react quite differently from many of those on the other islands. Sibyl Hathaway herself was determined that no-one would drive her from her ancestral home, La Seigneurie. As it transpired, most, if not all, of the 471 Sarkese opted to remain on the Island. This was due, in no small measure to Dame Sibyl, as Ambrose Sherwill explained:

In Sark, under the leadership of La Dame, calm reigned. We had offered them a ship to bring away those wishing to leave. Our offer was declined. Scarcely anyone left or sought to leave. Such is the effect of leadership.[10]

It is believed that some seasonal staff and a number of visitors did leave Sark in May and June 1940. Indeed, the number of passengers landed at both Weymouth and Portsmouth during the time of the crisis, who are recorded as being from Sark, amounts to 129. Further to this a yacht left Sark whilst the Dame was in Guernsey in early June carrying some twelve Islanders/visitors, including the resident doctor, Doctor Fisher. It is known that Fisher remained in touch with a neighbour once he reached the UK and that he asked for the house and contents to be looked after in his absence. It would appear that Dame Hathaway was not amused at Fisher's departure, it being mentioned in a letter which she subsequently wrote to the Home Office:

No Sark native has left. Much panic was caused by the sudden news of evacuation. Guernsey authorities did not inform Sark till 7 p.m. on 19th that any children for evacuation should be registered by 7.30 am on the 20th and our medical officer behaved disgracefully and bolted, leaving no medical man for the island at all and making more panic.[11]

Despite such incidents, it remained relatively tranquil on Sark until the *Luftwaffe* air raids on the 28th, which Dame Sibyl recalled in her autobiography:

It was a perfect summer day and Sark was utterly peaceful under a cloudless blue sky until, at six o'clock in the evening, we heard the intermittent drone of German aircraft and went out into the garden to watch three aeroplanes flying low over the island on their way to Guernsey. A few minutes later we heard the ominous explosion of bombs which were being dropped on St Peter's Port; but we were too far away to hear the machine-guns which fired on civilians in the streets, haymakers in the fields and an ambulance carrying wounded to the hospital ...

Within half an hour the planes flew back over the sea to Sark, swooped down and machine-gunned our small fishing boats around the coast. As luck would have it their aim was faulty and no hit was scored either on the fishermen or their boats.

With the departure of the German aircraft the Island settled back into its normal routine. There was nothing to do, Dame Sibyl explained, except to keep calm and wait for the next development. That development came a week later, when on 3 July, the Dame was informed that a boat was heading towards the Island.

From the top of La Seigneurie, she saw that it was the Guernsey lifeboat that was crossing the waters of the Great Russel. She guessed that it carried German emissaries. Dame Hathaway immediately telephoned Mr William Carré, the Sénéschal (or Judge), asking him to go and meet the Germans at the harbour to conduct them up the hill to La Seigneurie. She then went to the Island's school to reassure the children and some of the mothers who were waiting there. This is because tales of brutal beatings and rape by the ill-disciplined German soldiers, sparked by French refugees, had been circulating in Sark.

After putting the minds of the women at rest, the Dame returned to La Seigneurie to discuss with her husband, the Seigneur, the most dignified way in which to receive the invaders.

'We wanted to show the Germans that we were rulers.' Dame Hathaway told one of the Islanders. 'We scored a point,' she mused, after all, 'it was we who were receiving the Germans. They were not receiving us!' The Dame continued to consider how best to receive the new arrivals:

'Let's take a leaf out of Mussolini's book,' I suggested. 'We'll put two chairs behind the desk at the far end of the drawing-room. It is a long room and they'll have to walk the whole length of it, which will give us a certain advantage,' adding, 'Besides, they'll have to walk up those few stairs from the hall and then turn right before they are announced, and that will also help us to look more impressive'.

Dame Hathaway was determined to impress the enemy by her dignity and her total lack of submission. She had instructed her maid to show no sign of surprise or panic when the enemy arrived and to conduct them to her drawing room as if it was an everyday occurrence – an event of no special significance whatsoever.

Meanwhile, the Seigneur, adopting the same unruffled manner as his wife, finished the gardening job he was doing and went for a drink at the Bel Air Hotel. He was in no hurry as, judging by the tide, the lifeboat would not reach Creux Harbour much before noon. At the Bel Air it was agreed that no horse carriage would be available to convey the Germans up the harbour hill. One of the local fisherman remarked, 'Let's make the blighters walk!'[9]

Sufficiently prepared, William Carré walked to the harbour to carry out a task never before performed by a Sénéschal in the Island's long history – that of meeting an invader with orders to offer no resistance.

One of the officers on the boat was *Major* Lanz. He later wrote that after two hours of being tossed around in the little craft, he arrived at what he regarded as the tiniest harbour in the world:

> I made the first journey to Sark in a suitable motor boat that had meanwhile been made seaworthy. After a journey of nearly two hours on a rather rough sea, which tossed us about violently, we reached the tiniest harbour in the world ...
>
> There was no sign of life, except that we were awaited by the Sénéschal of the Island, a kind of major-domo, at the same time the chief police official. He conducted us through a long tunnel in the cliffs up the steep road to the 'Seigneurie' the seat of the ruler. Here also it seemed as if everyone was dead. Only when we turned round to notice curious eyes peeping out of the houses.[12]

Those inquisitive observers, peering out from behind twitching curtains, later allowed the historian Michael Marshall to provide this account of the German officers' journey after they had been greeted by the Sénéschal:

> This was the moment. William Carré could be seen leading two German officers in field-grey across the Seigneurie courtyard to the main entrance. The three men walked in stony silence. It was a hot

noon-tide. They were all perspiring after the trudge up Harbour Hill. A cuckoo was calling from the copse in L'Ecluse valley and the nettles were covered with golden dust … Opening the door, the maid announced in a calm voice: 'Major Doktor Albrecht Lanz and Dr. Maass'. Both officers raised their arms high in Nazi salute, but they did not utter the words 'Heil Hitler'.[13]

Robert Hathaway stood by his wife's side inside La Seigneurie as they waited for the enemy to arrive. They heard the crunch of boots on the gravel and, a few moments, later William Carré walked into view leading two Germans (a third, *Leutnant* Müller, remained at the harbour with the lifeboat).

Opening the door, the maid announced in a calm voice: 'Major Doktor Albrecht Lanz and Dr Maass.' Dame Hathaway did not offer her hand to the Germans.[14] Dame Hathaway later described her 'visitors':

> They both wore the drab green uniform of German officers, service dress jacket, breeches, jackboots and forage caps. Both gave the Nazi salute as they entered the room. I fully expected to hear 'Heil Hitler', but I must say here and now that it was never once said it in my presence during the five years of Occupation.
>
> Lanz, the Commandant, was a small, alert, quick-spoken officer, with dark hair and dark eyes. In civilian life he had been a Doctor of both law and philosophy, and I believe he came from a family of agricultural machinery manufacturers in Stuttgart. Maass was a Naval surgeon who spoke perfect English and had studied tropical diseases for eight years in Liverpool.[15]

Lanz would later write warmly of the manner in which he and Maass were greeted at La Seigneurie, that the pair had been 'politely and formally received'. He went on to add:

> I officially took the Island and its ruler under German over-lordship and ordered that the same new arrangements as on the other Islands should apply to Sark. The Dame explained that a large proportion of the Sark people are descendants of the Vikings who came from the far North …
>
> According to the ancient law, the 'Dame de Sercq' has the power of life and death over her subjects. She is married for the second time to an American named Hathaway, and has five grown-up children by her first marriage. There is even a prison there, a small square thick-

170

walled room with a vaulted roof. Even this has its own charm, for since it was built 50 years ago, no one has ever been shut up there. According to that the Sark people seem to be very well behaved. They live by tilling the land, fishing, and tourists in the summer. There is not a single inhabitant serving in this war in the British Army.[16]

Dr Lanz duly produced a large sheet of white cardboard on which was printed in both German and English: 'The Orders of the Commandant of the German Forces in the Channel Islands.' These orders were that all weapons were to be surrendered at once, the sale of alcoholic drinks was to cease and that all public houses were to be closed until further notice. No boat or vessel was to leave the harbour without permission of the military authorities. Finally, the use of motor cars for private use was forbidden.

Dame Hathaway replied in fluent German (she had worked as a librarian for the YMCA in Cologne), 'We have no motor vehicles on Sark', adding that she would have the orders displayed for the Islanders to read. She also recalled:

When I had read the notice I turned to Lanz and said in German, 'Please sit down. I will see that these orders are obeyed.' Both men seemed astonished that I could speak the language and Maass said, 'So you can talk German.'

'Badly, but well enough to understand it and to make myself understood.'

Then he gave me a wonderful opportunity by remarking, 'You do not appear to be the least afraid.' Looking as innocent as possible asked in a surprised voice, 'Is there any reason why I should be afraid of German officers?' This question had an immediate effect. They assured me that I was indeed right in my assumption. Their manners suddenly became most affable and Lanz went so far as to say that if ever I found any difficulties I was to communicate directly with the Commandant of the Channel Islands in Guernsey.[17]

The Dame pointed out to the Germans that Sark was a self-governing territory just as any other British Dominion. Lanz was therefore in some doubt whether or not Germany was actually at war with Sark and later had to send a letter to the German Foreign Office for confirmation.

It was Sybil Hathaway's duty to welcome official visitors and so she duly invited Lanz and Maass to stay for lunch, as Lanz noted after describing the Ancient Rights on Sark:

171

At important ceremonies in London, like the Coronation, the Dame de Sercq, by reason of an Ancient Right, sits at the King's right hand, before the crowned heads that are present as guests.

She speaks German and knows Germany from having often travelled there. Her second daughter spent a year, fifteen years ago, in Schweidnitz with the family of a German Officer.

Sometime later I heard from a third person that, on account of her marriage, she is no longer entitled to call herself Dame de Sercq, as, she still does, because all the rights are transferred by the marriage to her husband, who thereby becomes Seigneur de Sercq, and the real ruler. As he is easy going he lets his better half have her own way, for on Sark, clearly, 'La Dame' very energetically wears the breeches. After settling our official business, we were invited to a good lunch.

The following day ten German infantrymen, led by a Sergeant Hans Hamm, came ashore on Sark – a moment described by Michael Marshall:

Shouting raucously at his ten infantrymen, [Hamm] came ashore, marched up Harbour Hill and installed his contingent in the comfortable Bel Air Hotel. Soon they commandeered a flagpole which they fastened to the railings outside the hotel. The swastika was run-up.[18]

Author Richard Le Tissier states that 'the eleven-man garrison [then] maintained a two-man guard at Creux Harbour and a two-man patrol at night around the Island to enforce the curfew and black-out regulations. The troops were polite and well-behaved and some spoke quite good English. They found Sark's small shops well-stocked at this time and were soon sending home butter and other goods that were unobtainable in Germany. Very soon the off-duty soldiers adopted the Mermaid Tavern as their local and the ban on spirits did not last very long.'[19] Sark resident Julia Tremayne wrote the following comments in a letter on 3 July 1940:

Everybody says they seem very nice and if we keep to all the rules laid down, things will go on much as usual. No one must be out after 11pm, no spirits sold in hotels, only beer, all guns to be given up, the national anthem is not to be sung. We can go to church or chapel. German money is to be used, and worst of all the swastika is flying over the Bel Air. Who would have thought we would have lived to see that in this beautiful little Island that I have loved for nearly forty years and you have all known since you were babies.[20]

The following day Tremayne wrote that on Sark 'all goes according to plan, and apart from being cut off we are quite happy'. In her next letter, dated 5 July, she added:

I expect the German troops are revelling in the luxury – plenty of good Sark butter, home-killed meat, home-made bread, gallons of milk and the shops well-stocked.

Such sentiments aside, the significance of the date of the arrival of Hamm's unit was not lost on Robert Hathaway. As an American citizen it was a bitter day – the fourth of July, the United States' Independence Day. It was, he remarked, 'A hell of a day to surrender one's independence and one I'll never forget.'[21]

As experienced by each of the Channel Islands, for the Sarkese this was the start of almost five years under the German jackboot.

14

'A heavy yoke'

Reactions to the Occupation of the Islands

Ambrose Sherwill made an address to 'the people of the United Kingdom and, in particular, to those who left Guernsey and Alderney during the evacuation', to make them aware of the situation in the Islands now that they were under German rule. The address ran as follows:

> I imagine that many of you must be greatly worried as to how we are getting on. Well, let me tell you. Some will fear, I imagine, that speaking from a transcript thrust into my hand by a German officer.
>
> The actual case is very different. The Lieutenant-Governor and Bailiff, Mr Victor Carey, and every other island official has been and is being treated with every consideration and with the greatest courtesy by the German Military Authorities. The Island Government is functioning. Churches and Chapels are open for public worship. Banks, shops and places of entertainment are open as usual.[1]

K.M. Bachmann wrote letters from Guernsey to her mother who was one of those that had been evacuated to the UK. The following is taken from her first letter:

> This German Occupation is a heavy yoke for our British shoulders and we find it hard to accept. A lot of traditional grit, humour and dignity will be needed if we are to surmount it. I feel at times that this incredible situation cannot be. But there is no ignoring the metallic ring of jackboots in our little cobbled Town, Swastikas floating in the breeze over all the main buildings, the clipped, full-throated singing of their marching troops, the heel-clicking and arm-raising; and, above all, the shattering din of the German Band, a vigorous reminder of our change of fortune. If our little High Street were Whitehall, and

174

Guernsey the Heart of the Empire, they could not look more triumphant.[2]

Churchill, who had authorised the demilitarisation of the Channel Islands, typically then reacted in the opposite direction, as revealed in a memorandum to General Ismay, his Chief of Staff:

> If it be true that a few hundred German troops have landed on Jersey or Guernsey, plans should be studied to land secretly by night on the Islands and kill or capture the invaders. This is exactly one of the exploits for which the Commandos would be suited. There ought to be no difficulty in getting the necessary information from the inhabitants and from those evacuated. The only possible reinforcements which could reach the enemy during the fighting would be by aircraft carriers, and here would be a good opportunity for the Air Force fighting machines.[3]

On 2 July 1940, barely hours after the German occupation of the Channel Islands had begun, the War Cabinet, having considered Churchill's views, drew the following conclusion during a meeting held at Richmond Terrace in London:

> The Prime Minister said that the German occupation of the Islands gave us an excellent opportunity for a cutting out expedition by General Bourne's organisation.
>
> The War Cabeint [sic]:- Agreed that instructions should be issued to General Bourne to take action against the German forces in the Channel Islands as soon as possible.[4]

At this stage, however, the possibility of taking offensive action against the German forces on the Channel Islands was the last thing on most people's mind. Letters appear to have poured into the offices of *The Times*, the subject of the invasion of the Channel Islands creating a large pile in the Editor's in-tray. Two of these were published in the newspaper on 5 July. The first of these was written by C. de Sausmarez of Sunninghill in Surrey, who was originally from Guernsey:

> On Saturday, June 29, after hearing of the bombing of Guernsey I was fortunate in getting through to my sister on the telephone, and it was a relief to hear the cheerful assurance that she and my brother and his wife were 'all right.' I did not then think that the Germans would

consider it worth their while to occupy the Channel Islands, but Monday night's news showed that I was wrong.

So far as Guernsey is concerned, I feel sure that the people with the coolest heads and the largest hearts have remained behind. They have, I know, a good leader in the Bailiff, Victor Carey. If they adopt an attitude of passive obedience, as I feel they will, I can only hope that the enemy will treat them with some consideration. This, I am told, was the case with those of the Czechs who did not actively resist their invasion. Of course the helplessness of our fellow islanders and the indignity of being in the power of the Germans make their situation deplorable. There is, so far as I know, no neutral Consul in Guernsey with whom the British Government can get in touch, but perhaps news will be forthcoming through the Ministry of Information or some other source.

The second letter to the Editor published in *The Times* that day was from Eric Shepherd of London who wrote on 3 July 1940:

Sir, - May an Englishman closely connected by marriage with the Channel Islands express the deep grief and sympathy which he is sure is felt by other Englishmen for the most unmerited fate which has fallen upon the islands? Their occupation by the Germans was announced in a sentence, without comment, by the Ministry of Information in the evening broadcast of July 1. Many besides myself will feel that something more than a bald official sentence was due to a thousand years of loyal devotion to the English Crown. And this English allegiance of the islands has been of free choice. Their position on the map and their ancient Norman speech might have indicated France, but the islands chose England. They bred a race of indomitable seamen for England, including one of Nelson's admirals; and their war effort in the late War was, in proportion, unexcelled.

Wishful thinking would have us believe that the 'bulk' of the population has been able to leave the islands. It is true that most of the children were sent, and the young men loyally sped to their duty in England. But for the rest, time was very short, counsels were contradictory, and means of transport limited. It was obviously impossible for ancient and deep-rooted communities to pull up their stakes and flit overnight like a caravan of gipsies. So, as announced in a sentence, very many of the Channel Islanders have fallen into German hands, and very many people here in England, including many members of his Majesty's Forces, are left in the most painful uncertainty. Can anything be done to relieve this uncertainty?

The letters just kept on coming, such was the strength of feeling throughout the British population as a whole. An example of this can be seen in a letter sent to *The Times* by a Mr Cyril Winton of Winchester, on 4 July 1940:

> The demilitarization and the German occupation of the Channel Islands have come as a sudden and terrible blow to a small but most loyal community. These beautiful and interesting islands are the oldest possessions of the Crown. Their natives are hard-working, frugal, shrewd, and independent; with a passionate pride in the history and traditions of their islands, combined with a deep loyalty to the Crown. This loyalty has been proved by the large number of men from them who voluntarily joined the fighting Forces both in this and in the last War. Demilitarization was followed by the voluntary evacuation of thousands of the islanders.
>
> This has been a terrible uprooting, as many had never previously been out of the islands, they and their forefathers for centuries have tenanted and cultivated the small farms and holdings into which the islands are divided. Many have left behind literally all their possessions: families have been broken up, and parents separated from their children. I hope that in whatever part of Great Britain these islanders find themselves they will be treated and welcomed not as alien refugees but as our loyal fellow citizens upon whom the calamities of invasion and exile have unexpectedly fallen. Alderney alone has been completely evacuated. In the others the majority of the people still remain. At the best they will have a hard and trying time: they will be cut off from communication with the mainland. Food problems are bound to be severe, and there are certain to be numerous and irksome restrictions.
>
> But this is not the first time these islands have been invaded and occupied. Always at the end they have recovered their independence under the Crown. In these days of bitter humiliation once again the tenacity of the character of the islanders will show itself in the confidence and resolution in which they will look forward to the hour of their deliverance.

From some quarters, however, there was some praise of the manner in which the German units had carried out the occupation of the Islands.

On 9 July 1940, *The Evening Post*, which was already under the control of German censors, carried the following:

> The German forces have been in occupation for just over a week, and it is but fitting that we should record the fact that the courtesy and consideration of the officers which was a feature of the actual taking over of the island has been continued, and the behaviour of the men has throughout been exemplary.
>
> The fortunes of war have decreed that Jersey, one of the oldest parts of the British Empire, and one whose loyalty has been unquestioned, should be occupied by German armed forces. We feel sure that the islanders, while abating no whit in their loyalty, will, nevertheless, wish to pay this tribute to the officers and men of the German Reich now in control of the island.

On the same day that the above appeared in *The Evening Post*, Robert Ranulph Marett, then at Exeter College, also wrote to the Editor of *The Times*:

> Sir, I have no right to speak for the authorities of the Channel Islands. As, however, they cannot make their voices heard at this unhappy moment, may I, as a Jerseyman who holds his land by homage directly from his Majesty the King, be allowed to thank him on behalf of all islanders for his gracious and heartening words to us in our sore trouble? We are proud to think that our Islands are the oldest possession of the Crown, and to a man or woman we can be counted on as loyal to the death.

In the days after their fall, Lord Portsea, ever the spokesman and representative of the Channel Islanders, participated in a debate in the House of Lords on the fate of the Channel Islands. The following account details some of what was said:

> The noble lord … said that the islands had up to this always defended themselves. They had believed that they were safe, and they had sent their young men to the war as they did in 1914. This morning they had been much relieved by the gracious words of the King, and had derived much comfort from them and from the promises he had given. But they asked how, if no one could defend the islands, could the Germans hold them?

It was a difficult question to answer. Guernsey was farther away from the French coast than Hythe or Dover. One of the reasons given for the evacuation was that it was only a few miles from France. That did not quite satisfy the islanders, one of whom had given £125,000 of his own money to the British Government. They had given their all in blood and treasure. The islanders soon found that demilitarization was a near relation to abandonment and the breaking of ties which were 800 years old.[5]

Similar sentiments were expressed by Lord Mottistone, who said 'that the sooner the Government made it clear that this mysterious happening – the surrender without a shot of possessions over which the British flag had flown for 800 years – was unique and that nothing like it would ever happen again the better'.

The debate then moved on, some of the speakers having set out to call 'attention to the financial position of persons evacuated from Jersey and Guernsey whose money and bonds were deposited in the banks of those islands and transferred to the head offices of those banks in London, but who were at present unable to draw on those moneys'. Some of the evacuees had found themselves destitute

> People went to the local branches of the five great London banks which accepted their bonds and money, [stated Lord Portsea] telling them that they would be safer deposited in London. Now they could not draw them out; the reason given was that the territory from which they came was in the hands of the enemy. What were those poor people to do? They were penniless in the midst of plenty. It seemed reasonable to think that something should be done for those people who had trusted this great nation, and that they would be helped to get at any rate a percentage of the money which they had trusted to the London banks and to the honour of England.

The recently-appointed Lord Chancellor, 1st Viscount Simon, duly responded to Lord Portsea, as the account in *The Times* of 10 July 1940, went on to reveal:

> The joint stock banks in this country were treating the deposits which were made in the Channel Island branches, and which belonged to persons who had come here from the Channel Islands, as accounts which were transferred to this country. Although an islander might

have banked in a branch in Jersey, if he came here the bank would do its best to see to it that he was treated as having an account here, with the result that evacuated depositors should have little difficulty in being able to draw their money. In the case of a credit balance it would be necessary to satisfy the bank that the person staking the claim was a person entitled to the money.

Where securities were deposited for safe keeping and the local branch had been able to bring them away – and that was so in many cases – there should be no difficulty in the true owners of these securities making good their claims. The main thing was that the banks in this country which had branches in the Channel Islands were prepared to treat refugees from the islands who had come over here as their customers in this country. Such difficulties as remained must be met as best they could in view of the necessity of proof and the like.

Similar arrangements were being made to enable depositors in Jersey and Guernsey savings banks who were in this country to draw upon their deposit accounts so long as they had brought with them their pass-books or other evidence of title. This applied both to Trustee Savings Banks and accounts in the Post Office Savings Banks. An Order in Council would be made tomorrow which would clear up this position so far as Jersey and Guernsey Trustee Savings Banks were concerned. The proposed regulation would enable the Trustee Savings Banks in this country to conduct business in effect as agents for the Channel Island banks. No special arrangements were necessary in the case of the Post Office Savings Banks depositors.

The Lord Chancellor seemingly spoke as well of his own personal feelings regarding the German occupation of the Islands, and the effect on both the evacuees and those who had opted to remain:

He shared most completely the feeling of concern and distress that this withdrawal should have been necessary. After all the islands were not only possessions of the British Crown but they were older than the Battle of Hastings itself; 1066 and all that came after the time when these islands first became attached to the ancestors of the British Crown.

Throughout that time the islanders had shown themselves not only industrious but very brave and chivalrous folk. (Hear, hear.) The Bailiffs of Jersey and Guernsey were continuing to carry on in the islands, to the best of their powers, the civil administration for which they were responsible, and that was a splendid tribute to the courage of these distressed people. (Hear, hear.)

He humbly echoed the words of his Majesty and he trusted that the day was not far distant when by prevailing in our purpose – as we were determined to do, come what might – we might have among our triumphs the supreme satisfaction of seeing these good people returned to their homes.

15

'It's the finish for all of us'

Escape From the Enemy

The hurried, and entirely unsatisfactory, evacuation had finished with details being presented to the War Cabinet held at 10 Downing Street, on Tuesday, 2 July 1940, at 12.00 hours:

> The War Cabinet was informed that out of a total of 92,000 inhabitants in the Channel Islands, between 21,000 and 22,000 had been evacuated under official arrangements. The number who had left under private arrangements was not known. The highest proportion of those evacuated had been from Guernsey. An appeal had just been received in the Admiralty for ships to take off more of the population of the Islands. This would, of course, be very difficult now that the Germans were in occupation.
>
> The Islands were of no military value to the Germans, who could operate aircraft equally well from the French coast. The occupation had been carried out in order that they could say that they were occupying British soil.[1]

In fact, an approximate total of 17,000 people had evacuated from Guernsey, 129 from Sark (believed to be seasonal workers), 6,600 from Jersey and 1,400 from Alderney. Most of the vessels involved sailed to the nearest British port, Weymouth. The latter was put under considerable strain with, at the peak of the evacuations, fifty-eight ships having berthed in just three days and 25,484 evacuees passing through the port's small terminal building. By comparison, Southampton handled only 2,400 evacuees from the Channel Islands.[2]

As the figures for these two UK ports exceed the approximate totals of evacuees from the Channel Islands, they are believed to include other displaced persons from Europe. These individuals may well have travelled on ships that sailed from French ports to the UK via the

Channel Islands, where they remained on board before finally disembarking in Britain.

It is worthy of mention that it would appear that nobody was charged for their passage on any of the official evacuation ships.[3] At the same time, those vessels that were sent by the British government were considered to be 'On His Majesty's Service' which meant that crew members were paid for every day's service.

Following the end of the official evacuation and the fact that it would no longer be possible for ships to be sent to the Islands to take any more people to the mainland, it did not stop some people trying to escape. Such a journey was a considerable endeavour; Start Point, the nearest part of the English coastline, was sixty-two nautical miles distant as the crow flies, but the actual distance covered would have been much greater because of the combined effect of the wind and of strong tidal currents.

Despite the dangers involved, a total of seventy-eight bold adventurers escaped from Guernsey during the years of the Occupation (two Guernseymen also left via Alderney). Of these, about three-quarters slipped away during the first two days of the occupation.

The first boat to leave from Guernsey following the German invasion was *Dauntless* which left Perelle Bay, on the west coast, under power at 01.00 hours on 1 July 1940. The seven people aboard were Mr and Mrs J. Savident, their three sons, John, Cyril and Joe, and Herbert Pike and his daughter. After sixteen hours at sea they reached the English coast at Budleigh Salterton in Devon.[4]

The second and third boats to anticipate the German orders announced on 1 July (which included one stating that all local shipping, particularly small boats, must not be moved from their moorings without the permission of the military authorities) made their way out of St. Peter Port Harbour close together at 02.30 hours on the 1st.

One of the pair was the yacht *Dodo II* which embarked under sail crewed by Mr. James G. Wheadon and Mr. Reginald Fryer. On leaving the harbour she set off to the north and arrived at Plymouth later that same day. The other vessel was the motor yacht *Florida III* which took the alternative route along the south coast of Guernsey to avoid the German shipping lane to Cherbourg, before turning north-west towards the British coast. Carrying a party of twelve, *Florida III* reached Falmouth in Cornwall in the good time of sixteen hours.[5]

There was a fourth vessel that left on 1 July – the cabin cruiser *Mayflower*. She was a substantial boat, being an ex-naval pinnace 42 feet long with a 12-foot beam and was well known as a committee boat and contestant in pre-war Island regattas.

183

Mayflower's owner, Clifford J. Falla, had narrowly escaped injury in the bombing of White Rock having left his lorry laden with tomatoes at the harbour only a few minutes before the German bombers arrived. He determined to get away from Guernsey if ever the Germans landed, and on the Sunday evening, the day of the occupation, he took with him two other men and, having rounded the north of the Island, temporarily placed her on an outer mooring in Grand Havre Bay.

The men then returned home at 05.00 hours on the Monday morning. Falla let it be known that anyone willing to take the chance was welcome to join him in escaping to Britain. Within a few hours he received about sixty inquiries. In the event a total of twenty-eight people left on *Mayflower* when she set off from Grand Havre at 23.00 hours on the Monday evening, the 2nd.[6]

After an uneventful crossing they made landfall at Start Point in Devon. Falla and his companions were able to give the naval authorities at Dartmouth a first-hand account of the damage caused by the air-raid of 28 June and of the Germans' activities to date, together with a copy of *The Star* newspaper of 1 July in which the first orders of the German Commandant had been published. This was in turn featured in the *Daily Mirror* on the following day. In common with other refugees from the Islands, Falla's party was fed, given ration books and identity cards and, where necessary, issued with train warrants to enable them to reach their chosen destinations and to find jobs or to join the Services for the duration of the war.

A similar journey was described by one man, following his family's arrival in England, to Laurence Wilkinson, a reporter for the *Daily Express*, soon after he landed:

> The last of the troops and guns were leaving the harbour as the first of the stream of civilians boarded the ships awaiting them. There were thousands – men, women and children – carrying every ounce they could.
>
> Things were quiet for a day or two after they had gone, but everywhere I met people who had tried to get away from the island, only to find there was no more ship accommodation. The mail boats were crammed.
>
> Then on Friday [28 June] the German 'planes came over, bombing and machine-gunning, killing and wounding civilians indiscriminately. We didn't have a chance. There wasn't a gun, not even a revolver, left in the island. I was in the car on the coast road when two bombers came

roaring low at us from the direction of the harbour. I flung myself down by the sea wall. The bullets spattered all around me.

On Saturday morning they came over again, but did no damage. On Sunday they came skimming over the housetops – huge Heinkels – singly, at intervals of half an hour.

At 5 a.m. I was awakened by the roar of a dive bomber. He swooped very low and dropped something on to a roof. Someone climbed up and found it was a German flag. Attached to it was an ultimatum from the general commanding the Nazi air force in Normandy. It was taken to the Bailiff, Mr. Alex Coutanche, who ordered it to be printed and posted up all over the island. By the evening there were white flags showing from the houses all over the island. The Germans were already in the streets. They had arrived at 5 p.m.

By that time I had made plans for escape, though I had little hope of their succeeding. I tried to buy a passage to England in a motor-boat. The owner wanted £50, then backed out at the last moment, after I had made all preparations to leave.

Then I met the captain of a Dutch cargo vessel which had come to collect potatoes. In the air raid of Friday his cook had been injured, and the skipper had taken him to hospital. In his absence, the crew had gone off with the ship, leaving the captain stranded.

Another man pointed out a motor-boat left by an Englishman who had gone in the general evacuation. We decided to take it to England and hand it over to its owner.

We got two loaves, a large jar of water, and a chart of the Channel. Then we hid inside the boat, and waited for darkness and high water. A man on the quay begged a passage. I knew it lessened our chances, but we agreed to take him. I told him to come back later, and not to breathe a word to a soul.

A woman of about fifty drove up in a car and begged a passage. I said she could come. She turned to a man lounging on the quay and said, 'Do you want my car? You can have it.'"

The man said, 'What's the use of a car? I can't even drive.' But he said he would have it, as it was free.

The woman told me she had just seen the Germans in the town. She said they were lined up, heavily armed, with motor-cycles, with which they had landed from 'planes.

I gave orders, 'No smoking, no talking, no moving about. If you don't obey these instructions it's the finish for all of us.'

Twilight was coming on when I heard voices. I crept to the hatch and peeped out. I saw between fifty and eighty Germans soldiers swinging along shouting the Horst Wessel song. They marched past within ten or fifteen yards of us, and went up to the fort. After that I saw motor-cyclists patrolling. Otherwise there was not a soul to be seen.

As the minutes ticked by, the tide gradually came in. As the small boat started to float, the moment of departure rapidly neared:

We put up the sails, but there was not a breath of wind. We got hold of a rope tied farther along the quay-side, and tried to haul ourselves out. It took us almost an hour to travel fifty feet. We thought we should be caught in the middle of the harbour. We dared not start the engines.

We had just got through the harbour mouth when we started the engines. We took a circuitous, amateurish route. North-west of the Guernsey the engines seized-up for lack of oil. We heard scores of 'planes and expected them to spot us at any moment. We heard the sound of explosions from the island.

We thanked heaven for a mist which came up at that moment. But we had to have oil. I searched our provisions and found 3lbs of butter. We melted it on the exhaust pipe and poured it into the sump. The engine ran the whole day until eight o'clock that night on Jersey butter.

We were within twelve mile so of the English coast when darkness fell. There was a big swell and our engines failed. The German bombers dropped flares. Searchlights swept the sky, then coastal guns blazed into action.

At daybreak a cutter spotted us and towed us in, more dead than alive. Someone made us coffee. Everybody shook hands, thanked everybody else, and then drifted away – perhaps never to meet again.[7]

Another reference to an escape from Guernsey is to be found in an account published in the *Daily Sketch* of Friday, 6 September 1940. In accordance with wartime security regulations no details are given as to times, places and persons involved. It was stated that a twenty-foot auxiliary cutter had arrived at a small fishing cove on the south-west coast of England. Two Guernseymen were aboard, a father and son, who lived near the airport and ran a large farm and also had an interest in hotels.

In making their escape they had gone over the cliffs (possibly at Saints Bay or Le Gouffre) and had swum out to a boat anchored off some rocks. Petrol was scarce but they had managed to obtain some, along with some paraffin. The boat was rowed for half a mile before the engine was started; when the fuel ran out they continued the journey under sail. Whilst no date is given for their escape, it is almost certainly in the early days of the Occupation. The full facts of this story, however, remain a mystery.

A similar experience to those recounted above was endured by three Frenchmen, Henri Letrourneur, Andre Courval and Clement Milet, who also escaped in the immediate aftermath of the Occupation, this time from Jersey. The trio later gave information that led to this account being recorded:

> They escaped from CARTERET [France] to Jersey on 29th June 1940 in a fishing boat. The Germans began to occupy Jersey the following day, and they thereupon started to plan their escape to England.
>
> They discovered that the 'Suzanne' lying at Rozel, was relatively poorly guarded by the Germans and they decided to make their escape in her. Parts of the magneto had been removed and there were only 4 gallons of petrol aboard. With assistance of Mr. RICHARDSON, Advocate, of St. Helier, they obtained the necessary parts for the magneto and about 30 gallons of petrol.
>
> They escaped undetected by the Germans. They were at sea about 35 hours, having had a great deal of engine trouble.
>
> They brought with them a map of Jersey, upon which they had marked with ammunition dumps, gun emplacements, W/T posts, barracks, and the German GHQ. They also brought a number of letters from people in Jersey, who helped them to escape, addressed to relatives in this country.[8]

During their debriefing, Letrourneur, Courval and Milet provided 'the following information about conditions on the island', all of which was, despite its dubious veracity, dutifully recorded in the subsequent report. Some of the statements they were reported as having made included:

> Morale of German soldiers not very high. They are unenthusiastic and listless.
>
> The day following the aerial battles in which 140 German planes were destroyed, 6 German pilot officers committed suicide rather than take the air.

Civilians as a whole well treated by the Germans, who are trying hard to make friends with them, with little success.

Two-thirds of all foodstuffs requisitioned and sent to France.

Aerodrome of St Pierre extensively used by German bombers, fighters and troop carriers. The planes are parked in wheat fields surrounding the aerodrome and the wheat is used for camouflaging them. Planes to and from France never rise more than about 100 ft above the water.

Very few restrictions on activities of civilians; they may listen to the BBC news in English or French. There is a curfew at 2300 hrs.

A group of ex-service men on the island is planning to blow up the aerodrome.[9]

Individuals such as these were the brave, and lucky, few. For the many who were unable to seize the opportunity and slip away in the days after the arrival of the Germans, ahead lay several years of isolation and deprivation.

16

'Flushed with victory'

The First Days of German Occupation

On Monday, 1 July 1940, the occupation of the Channel Islands by German forces was officially announced to the United Kingdom and the rest of the world through the Ministry of Information. This was reported in *The Times* the following day:

> As has already been announced, the Channel Islands have been demilitarized. It is now learned that enemy landings have since been made in Jersey and Guernsey.
>
> Telegraphic and telephonic communications have been cut, and no further information is at present available. The German battle songs, beginning with the *Engellanidlied* ('For we're off to fight against England') were again turned on last night, after the broadcasting of a special communiqué of the German High Command announcing the capture of the demilitarized islands of Guernsey and Jersey. The communiqué read:- On June 30 the British island of Guernsey was captured in a daring *coup de main* by detachments (*Teilen*) of the German Air Force. In an air fight a German reconnaissance aeroplane shot down two Bristol Blenheim bombers. On July 1, the island of Jersey was occupied by surprise in the same manner.

No sooner had they established their headquarters on the main islands, the German garrison, such as it was in the very early days of the Occupation, began to stamp their authority on the Channel Islanders. On Guernsey, Police Sergeant Albert Lamy saw first-hand some of the early steps the invaders took, starting on the day after their arrival:

> All [British] Service personnel left in Guernsey were instructed to report to the Police Station in the morning. They did so and were marched to the Royal Hotel and were interned at Castle Cornet,

189

Guernsey for some weeks, and received extremely good treatment, being allowed out on their own at certain hours etc. but in course of time they were removed to a Prisoner of War Camp in Germany.[1]

There were some actions that required Lamy's immediate attention, a number of which related to those German nationals who had been on Guernsey:

Before the War we had a small German Colony in Guernsey connected with a firm manufacturing Mohair rugs and one of the principals was a leader in the German Labour Front movement. They were all interned. All Nationals were interned in Guernsey at the outbreak of War, but at the time of the evacuation all the internees were released, with the exception of this small German group, who were sent to England and interned.

We had collected quite a large amount of information concerning these and this was contained in files in the Police Office. My first duty on the 1st of July was to burn these files in case they fell into enemy hands, and it was a good job I did so, for one of the first demands of the Germans was the whereabouts of this particular Colony, and any files which we might have had on them. Aliens being my particular duty at the time they came to me for their information.

I told the Germans that the files had accompanied the internees when they left the Island and stuck to that story throughout. On numerous occasions they came to me and each time with the same request.

The early German arrivals on Guernsey were quickly bolstered by a rapidly-swelling garrison, as Lamy recounted in his post-war lecture:

The first days following the 1st of July a very large number of troops were brought in by air – Junkers transports were used for this purpose and there was a continuous stream of aircraft all day long and well into the night bringing in men and equipment. Troops at this time were all in first-class condition, flushed with victory. They bought up as many suit lengths as they could and stated they would be taking them to London to be made up in Saville Row. At that time they gave a date for London as the 15th of August. However they were disappointed.

The set-up at this time was purely military with just a few semi-civilian officers in the personnel, all of whom spoke perfect English.

190

Police were allowed to go about more or less normally, and they did not at first post sentries, except at their various headquarters. During the night a body of men patrolled in an omnibus, but apart from that little other activity was noticed.[2]

At about the same time that Lamy was busy destroying some of the Police files on 1 July, the new German *Kommandantur* on Guernsey – *Major* Lanz – issued his first proclamation – these being the orders referred to by Ambrose Sherwill. Published in special editions of the *Star* and the *Guernsey Evening Press*, each of which carried on their front pages a signed statement from the Bailiff, Mr Victor Carey, that, 'The public are notified that no resistance whatever is to be offered', the directive stated:

All inhabitants must be indoors by 11 p.m. and must not leave their homes before 6 a.m.

We will respect the population in Guernsey, but, SHOULD ANYONE ATTEMPT TO CAUSE THE LEAST TROUBLE SERIOUS MEASURES WILL BE TAKEN AND THE TOWN WILL BE BOMBED!

All orders given by the military authority are to be strictly obeyed,

All spirits must be locked up immediately, and no spirits may be supplied, obtained or consumed henceforth. This prohibition does not apply to stocks in private houses.

No person shall enter the aerodrome.

All rifles, airguns, pistols, revolvers, daggers, sporting guns and all other weapons whatsoever, except souvenirs, must, together with all ammunition, be delivered at the Royal Hotel by 12 noon to-day, July 1.

All British sailors, airmen and soldiers on leave in this island must report to the police station at 9 a.m., to-day and must then report to the Royal Hotel.

No boat or vessel of any description, including any fishing boat, shall leave the harbours or any other place where the same is moored, without an order from the military authority, to be obtained at the Royal Hotel. All boats arriving from Jersey, from Sark or from Herm, or elsewhere, must remain in harbour until permitted by the military authority to leave. The crews will remain on board. The master will report to the harbourmaster, St Peter Port, and will obey his instructions.

The sale of motor spirit is prohibited, except for use on essential services, such as doctors' vehicles, the delivery of foodstuffs, and sanitary services where such vehicles are in possession of a permit from the military authority to obtain supplies. These vehicles must be brought to the Royal Hotel by 12 noon to-day to receive the necessary permission.

The use of cars for private purposes is forbidden.

The black-out regulations already in force must be observed as before.

Banks and shops will open as usual.[3]

On Guernsey these orders were accompanied by the threat that St Peter Port would be bombed if there were any signs of trouble. This was, mused Lamy, 'a true case of the mailed fist inside the velvet glove'. A resident of Guernsey, Miss A. Le M. Mainé recalled the first German proclamation:

> Monday, July 1st 1940 is, I believe, the only day in the history of Guernsey when the local newspapers have been issued to the public free of charge. By 7 a.m. all householders and received their 'Press' or 'Star' whichever they were in the habit of taking. A glance at the front page told us why. There was a long list of orders issued by the Commandant of the German Forces of Occupation.
>
> Amongst others was the imposition of curfew from 11 p.m. to 6 a.m. I suppose most right-minded people are indoors between those hours on normal nights, but being a 'free' people we dislike to be ordered in by 11 p.m. All weapons had to be given up, so there was no chance of defending ourselves and we had therefore to submit quietly, otherwise we were told that if there was any trouble the town would be bombed. Well, we had already had an unpleasant experience in that way and were not anxious for another. We were also forbidden to listen to the British National Anthem, except on the radio.[4]

Almost identical instructions were issued and published on Jersey on 1 July 1940. That day, with his paper carrying a 'translation of a communication addressed to the Governor of the Isle of Jersey,' the *Evening Post*'s editor also published this appeal under the title 'Keep Calm':

> We urge our readers to study most carefully the proclamation from the Commander of the German Air Forces to the authorities of Jersey which we publish in another column. The island is called upon to

surrender peacefully, and this morning the States took the necessary steps to comply with the order. The proclamation sets out the methods which have to be adopted to denote the island's surrender, and one of these is the display of white flags from public buildings and all houses. We enjoin the inhabitants to remain calm and to follow implicitly whatever instructions they may receive. If this is done we believe there is no need for undue alarm for, as will be observed from the terms of the proclamation, the lives, properties and liberties of the inhabitants are solemnly guaranteed by the Commander of the German Air Forces in Normandie.

After what the Reverend Ord on Guernsey had described in his diary as a 'broken night' – after all, he added, 'the strain of past weeks and the uncertainties of the morrow combined to prevent sleep' – he was awoken on the morning of 1 July 1940, by 'a German 'plane … on its way to the airport'. The rest of Ord's day was spent sampling a new life under enemy occupation, his views of the German personnel being committed to paper:

Most of the firms advertising speak of 'business as usual' but on a cash basis only, customers taking their purchases with them. A confectioner informs us: 'You can still obtain your usual supply of high quality cakes at reasonable prices,' but from what we have already seen, the locusts will soon force him to change his tune.

After the privations involved in 'Guns before butter' the Island must be a paradise to the invaders. A coal merchant, with what looks like second sight, tells us that 'we shall need fuel more than ever' now. The paper includes burial notices of nearly a score of raid victims. The first inquest has been held on an Occupation suicide – the first, doubtless, of many.

A lady offers temporary shelter to birds belonging to evacuees. Fresh owners are found. Her original stock is reduced to around 50. There is a waiting list of over 500 applicants.

All day men have been cycling in with firearms. Back from his Bank for lunch my neighbour told me he had the new Kommondant to see him and to change Marks into our currency. 'He couldn't have been more courteous.' So that's their line! We must wait until the garrison increases and they start exchanging Marks in big quantities and raid our shops.

All day long 'planes and troop carriers have been coming over from France, flying very low with deafening din to impress us. As we went down the Grange to Town, car after car went by packed with officers and NCOs. The men were fetched in local buses as they arrived and stared open-mouthed at the well-dressed civilians, the clear, freshly-painted houses and at the shops with their windows invitingly full of good things.

At an open window of the telephone department of the GPO sat a soldier on guard eating as if for a wager. Below in the street a bus was disgorging soldiery armed to the teeth. It was instructive to see Germans eating butter in half-pound packets without bread as they went about the streets. Every strongpoint had been occupied immediately – particularly the cafés and confectionery shops! Germans are everywhere, eating, eating, eating. They prove their prowess as trenchermen, ordering omelettes made with eight eggs. From time to time they go out into the street to be sick and then valiantly resume their place at the festive board unless ousted by others.

A rather doleful lady observed to G: 'They say they are behaving with unexpected courtesy, but one dreads the Gestapo' – a thought better left unexpressed. On our way home G remarked that it seemed strange to feel more secure tonight. At least we shall not be blasted off the face of the earth as seemed all but certain on Friday night.[5]

The following day, the 2nd, was a busy one for *Major* Lanz. He was also forced to learn quickly, particularly when it came to the Channel Islands' unique situation:

The whole of the next day was filled up with conferences on every possible subject, in particular with Mr. Sherwill, the Attorney General of the Island, who did all the executive business for the Bailiff. The Bailiff himself, because of his age, is very forgetful, so that he does not take a very active part in affairs, but confines himself to representation.

Now we had slowly to find our bearings, for the relationships that we found were most extraordinary. The inhabitants of this Island do not consider themselves to be English in the ordinary sense although they are loyal subjects of his Britannic Majesty and component parts of the British Empire. It is not, for example, England, they say that conquered the Island, but we, the descendants of the Normans that, under William the Conqueror, conquered England in 1066. From this arise the ancient privileges that exist in the Islands. The King of England reigns in these Islands not in his capacity of His Majesty the King of Britons, but in his capacity of Duke of Normandy. This is shown also in their ancient independent Laws.

194

Thus, it comes about, that both Islands, Guernsey and Jersey, have their own Parliaments, elected by the people. The Parliaments in their turn elect the ministers in Jersey, in Guernsey these are called 'Officiers der Roi', the 'King's Officers'.

At the head of each Island is a Governor, called the Bailiff, directly appointed for life by the King of England [sic] in his capacity of Duke of Normandy. Beside him stood a Military Governor, who, however, left the field in good time, taking all his effects with him. On both Islands there is a Parliamentary Building. Parliament is summoned as circumstances demand. Through this institution the whole work of Government is carried out. The Legal System is also quite different from the English one. On the Islands the old Norman Law is current. Everyone who wishes to become an advocate or lawyer studies, not at an English University, but at the French University of Caen, where ancient Norman Law is taught.[6]

Continuing his account, Lanz then decided to provide 'a short outline of the attitude of the population when we came':

It is incredible for us, for we have no idea how British propaganda works and how it is accepted. The Attorney General, Mr Sherwill himself, responsible leader of the destinies of the Isle of Guernsey, a man with grown-up children, who has himself often been in Germany, and his wife likewise, and so knows Germany, explained to us that even he had eventually fallen under the influence of British propaganda and was convinced that if we came (in his actual words) 'the Island would be overrun by a horde of wild cannibals', the opinion was widely held that, as had been asserted in 1914, we would cut off the children's hands and violate women and girls.

Therefore, in the first days we were here, apart from the curious crowds in front of the Royal Hotel, scarcely a single person was to be seen on the streets. The feminine sex held themselves very timidly back. Before our arrival they had shot their dogs by the hundred, so that the Barbarians could not torture them to death and even eat them. The Veterinary Surgeon, who had, when weapons were surrendered, to give up also his humane killer, appealed to retain this and 500 cartridges, giving as his reason that people would still come in hundreds begging him to shoot their dogs.

Mr. Sherwill's wife told us herself that her 11-year-old son was very eager to see a German soldier. When they met one, and the mother pointed out the German soldier to her son, he was hugely disappointed, and said 'Why, Mummy, they're only men, exactly like us'. Another woman wrote a heart rending letter with the request that her 7-year-old daughter and 5-year-old son should be allowed to see and speak to the Commandant, because the children had not been able to sleep for weeks and were in a dreadful state of nerves. This all goes to show how English [sic] propaganda had not even stopped short at the souls of little children, and had poisoned even the tiniest of them.

All the Islanders therefore were faced with a situation that was incomprehensible to them, so that they did not at first emerge from their incredulous bewilderment. Wonderingly, they recognised the extraordinary correctness and discipline of the German troops, their politeness, and readiness to help.

At first therefore one heard only a gratefully bewildered 'I thank you'. Soon it was asserted 'Yes, you are special troops chosen out of the whole German Army to occupy these Islands. The others that follow you will be very different.' It was not easy to talk them out of such stupid ideas. 'Do you get lessons in politeness in your training,' we were asked, 'for otherwise it could not be possible that all German soldiers should be so uniformly polite and obliging.'

It was not only Lanz who encountered the Islanders' references to barbaric behaviour. Writing in 1940, the German War Correspondent Kurt G. Stolzenberg claimed that the Vice-Bailiff on Guernsey had stated, 'We really did believe that a horde of wild cannibals would fall upon us!' In the same article, Stolzenberg wrote the following:

At first the island's inhabitants were practically invisible. If a German soldier wandered by, he faced anxious looking eyes who followed his path. Soon, however, the blond Hannoverians won the respect and trust of people, who expressed their sentiments in interesting ways. An English lady wrote the German commander to request that her anxious children might meet German soldiers to see that they were not cannibals. This was the first letter that *Major* Lanz received in his new office.[7]

The differences between Islanders and occupiers were bound to be revealed in a myriad of ways, some, as Lanz recalled, in the very first hours of the Occupation:

On the first evening there was a slight friction at the Royal Hotel, as the Management could not understand that German Officers should

196

eat in the same Dining Room and sleep under the same roof as their men. We quickly and thoroughly put the German point of view before them. From this one can see that there is nothing they are afraid of so much as Socialism.

There can be little doubt that ahead of him Lanz faced a somewhat herculean task in stamping German rule on the Islands:

And now we had to tackle all the problems that demanded quick solution. Basic decisions were necessary in questions of Traffic, Administration, Food, Justice, Finance, Fishing, and many aspects of public life, quite apart from the urgent military problems. The heads of the respective departments were called together, all questions discussed in detail and then decided on the spot.

Instead of trains and trams, which do not exist on the Island, there are a relatively large number of cars, on Guernsey alone there are over 5,000. These were immediately taken off the road; only those who had to transport essential commodities got a permit, and had to stick on the windscreen a coloured licence quickly printed for the purpose. In place of 5,000 scarcely 300 were allowed. Similar undertakings were divided up into small districts that could only be served from neighbouring ones, and so save petrol.

The bus service was suspended. Soon the more business-like brought out of the stables their horses, some of them foaled in the reign of Charles the Mouldy, and soon there was a horse-bus traffic going with the most amusing vehicles. One must know how to help oneself.

Street signs in German for the most important roads followed. On both Islands German time was introduced the second night. The Government continued to exercise its functions in full. The Island police were brought under the German Commandant. By public notices the population was enjoined to carry on their work normally, all banks, businesses and industries to reopen, and to carry on in a quiet, orderly and disciplined way, then the property and lives of the inhabitants would be guaranteed.

The question of food was particularly difficult, for Guernsey is a 'Tomato-Island'. In hundreds of hothouses all over the Island there was fruit, especially tomatoes, growing, that reached the peak of the harvest in July. We had to bear in mind that the harvest at its peak exceeds 1,000 tons of tomatoes per week. However, much as we should have liked to supply the troops on the mainland we had not the necessary shipping space.

So I ordered that half the plants should be immediately lifted so as to make room for other vegetables to supplement the food of the inhabitants in the future. The necessary measures for seizing all stocks of food (including luxuries) were put into operation so that the exact quantity could be ascertained and an estimate made of how long they would last. The sale of spirits of all kinds in public houses as well as in shops and clubs was prohibited. A week later a second meatless day was fixed for both Islands and meat-cards introduced by which a shilling's worth per head per week could be bought. Everything necessary for the introduction of a complete system of registration was set in motion, especially an exact Census, as, through the flight of about half the Island to England, there were no general statistics available.

As Lanz had already pointed out, the Channel Island's relationship with the rest of the British Isles also extended to the legal system. Needless to say, this required some immediate thought on the part of Lanz and his officials:

It was permitted that all existing laws should remain in full force as far as they were not contrary to the interests of the German Empire and its Forces, and the civil courts were allowed to carry on their functions as hitherto. In order to give new ordinances and laws, and the civil courts due legal authority, it was agreed that in future the signature of the Commandant was to have the same legal and legislature validity as that of the King of England had hitherto held. In cases of Breach of Public Order the German Commander retained the right of disposal in all cases, whether judged by a Civil Court or the German Military Courts.

I was requested to make an Order that the official language of administration, which had hitherto always been French, should in future be English, on the ground that only a small section of the population understood French, whereas everybody knew English. Upon my asking why the official language was French, the answer was that it dated back to Norman times and was obsolete practice. To my further question, why if such a necessity existed, the alteration had not been made before, the reply was that the agreement of the King of England had been necessary, and that besides the problem, as an Ancient Right, was a very difficult one. Upon this I decided 'the German Forces have no interest whatever in altering ancient customs of this kind. It will remain as it has been hitherto.' Who knows how

198

such an alteration, if one had ordered it, might at some time, in some way or other, have been used against us.

The military and civil authorities were also faced with the pressing problem of the Islands' finances – almost mirroring discussions that were about to held in the UK regarding the plight of the evacuees:

> The momentary problem too, is not altogether easy [continued Lanz]. On both Islands there live a great many pensioners, chiefly former British Colonial Officers, who have settled in these Islands with their sub-tropical climate, upon their retirement. For the time being an exchange rate of 5 RM to the £ was settled, while a definitive settlement was reserved for further discussion. As all remittances from England had ceased a credit system was permitted, so that in future everyone should have money enough to live on, and something over, if only on a smaller scale.

In his propaganda report, which had the title 'The First Attack on England', Kurt Stolzenberg highlighted some of the other issues or directives that the Germans dealt with in the first days of occupation:

> Someone else wanted to know what would happen with church services. The German commander put no barriers in the way of religion. He prohibited only the former insults against the German leadership.
>
> The question of weapons was readily resolved as well. Sark could keep its ancient cannons, dating back to Queen Elizabeth. The court seneschal retained the ability to deal with the plague of rabbits.
>
> Aside from these rather amusing matters, there were more serious economic problems. The export of granite, livestock, flowers, tomatoes, Guernsey apples, apple wine tea, porcelain and Jersey potatoes stopped. The supply of the islands would have to become difficult within three months, particularly on Guernsey, whose artistic landscape was filled with greenhouses growing tomatoes. The guests in the fashionable hotels got tomatoes for breakfast and dinner. The German commander ordered that half of the land should be planted in other necessary vegetables, e.g. potatoes. One directive quickly followed another …
>
> The sale of alcoholic beverages was halted. The population learned that order and discipline were the best guarantee for their lives and property. These small islands of 117 and 78 square

kilometres had little to say about the great events of our day. However, the fact that German soldiers have raised the German flag on territory that was traditionally English is of great significance: London is in difficulty.[8]

Throughout the early days of July 1940 a deluge of additional orders and instructions flowed from the *Kommandantur* on Guernsey – after all, wrote Lanz, 'there were hundreds of other questions to order and regulate'. Amongst these was the declaration issued on 5 July that, owing to a glut due to exports having stopped, farmers were instructed to feed surplus tomatoes to cattle,[9] whilst, the following day, meat, butter, bacon, ham and sugar were rationed. The exchange was altered on 9 July, 1 Reichsmark now fixed at 2/6d. That same day the sale of rationed goods to German personnel was forbidden, whilst, on the 10th, all trees, except fruit trees, were requisitioned.

Then, added Lanz, 'permits to be out at night for doctors, ARP, etc., for entering the docks and the Forts, had to be issued. Blackout regulations made, regulations given for holding Church Services, Public meetings, visits to the cinema, listening to the wireless, prohibition of altering prices in public life, immediate surrender of weapons, and a thousand other things.'

According to Lanz, the introduction of the blackout regulations provided a 'little incident [which] shows how the population worked with us':

A night patrol discovered that some Islanders had not blacked out according to orders. I therefore had a warning put in the newspaper, saying that if in future the Blackout Orders were not fully carried out I should be compelled to punish offenders severely.

In the same newspaper, inside, I found a long article, which we had known nothing about, saying that it was a lasting disgrace to the Island that the German Commandant who had treated the people in so generous and correct a way, should have found it necessary to put such a warning in the paper. It went on to say that if there were still people who could not see for themselves that such Orders must be strictly carried out, then not only must their neighbours keep an eye on them, but also they would find themselves blacked out by the States and for so long that they would learn once for all to carry out the Orders given.

When, a few days later some reports came in of insufficient blackout, there was found among them even the ARP chief of the Island. He was fined and warned in friendly fashion, that he would

200

be locked up next time. Since then there have been no more complaints of inadequate blackout.

'Thus the first days were quite filled up with work,' concluded Lanz. It was work 'in which we were helped by the MO [Medical Officer] of the Naval assault detachment *Gotenhafen*, Dr. Maass, a man who spent more than seven years in Africa and Abyssinia, and made an exemplary interpreter. Instead of his medical work, he took over the office of official interpreter, and departmental chief for all questions of administration and Public relations.'

One of the very first steps taken by the occupiers had been to change the rules of the road, as Frank Hubert, who had only just obtained his driver's licence, discovered:

> Little did I realise that very soon after I got my licence I would find myself having to learn to drive again, on the right hand side of the road, as instructed by the Germans. It was not long before I caught my first sight of a German soldier. He was walking along the top of Smith Street. I don't know what I was expecting but I remember thinking that he looked quite human really.[10]

Learning to drive on the opposite side of the road may well have been the least of the issues facing motorists on the Channel Islands following the occupation. Far more pressing, continued Miss A. Le M. Mainé, was the question of fuel supplies:

> Well, there we were, under German domination, like so many other countries, and all communication with England was cut off. No more telephone, no telegrams, no letters and no English newspapers. We still had our wireless set, however, for which we were duly thankful.
> That Sunday was the last time civilians were allowed to use their cars without special permission. A few people whose work demanded it were given special permits for a limited amount of petrol, otherwise only Germans were seen driving in cars, and these were requisitioned from private citizens, always of course selecting the best.[11]

Lanz's counterpart on Jersey was *Hauptmann* Erich Gussek who set up his headquarters in St. Helier's Town Hall where he combined his military duties with the administration of civil affairs. Also one of the first German soldiers to arrive in Jersey, Werner Grosskopf recalled how pleased he was when he realised where he was going:

I did not know I was going to the islands. We got a top secret order and we wondered if we were going to invade England. We had been trained for weeks on the Normandy beaches. We weren't told where we were going until we were on the ships.

It was a wonderful day when we sailed – a blue sky – and there was real enthusiasm on the ship. The harbour front of St Helier with the white villas and houses and the blue sky above and the blue sea below looked wonderful. When we landed I thought back to my time as an exchange pupil in England in 1929 when learnt about English life. We were in a country where milk and honey were flowing day and night. We were all on top of the world at that moment. We felt like holiday-makers.[12]

Dr Alistair Rose, as a key medical person, had remained behind on Guernsey to tend to the needs of the Islanders as there could be no certainty that the Germans would provide the medical services the community would need:

On 1st July the first orders from the German Command appeared in the local paper, and there was the expected threat of reprisals for any trouble at all caused by the civilian population; in this case the town would be bombed, it said. Later we were to hear much of the threat of 'fusillation'. We were highly amused to think that we would not merely be shot, but fusillated!

Otherwise, the orders imposed a curfew, brought in prohibition, ordered the handing over of all weapons, the immobilisation of any British troops and of all boats, and the commandeering of all petrol. That was the start and it was mild compared with what was to come.[13]

That same day, 1 July, the first full day of Occupation, Alf Le Poidevin, a lorry driver for the firm W. Head and Son in Guernsey, was back at work with the few drivers that had survived the raid of the 28th, wondering what would happen next now that the Germans were in charge:

The late George Head who had taken over the firm was trembling as he spoke to the drivers. 'They had phoned from the Royal Hotel saying we want five lorries at the Hotel now or we are coming to fetch them and the drivers!' George Head then said, 'I am not telling you to go, I am in the same boat as you.'[14]

The men conferred and, although understandably hesitant to do anything the Germans wanted, the drivers decided to go.

Many people recorded their first sighting of the Germans. One of those who did was Bill Gillingham who worked at La Riches Bridge Cash Stores:

> On Sunday morning I was in the yard at Le Hamel Farm when we heard the sound of motorcycles and sure enough, two German motorcycles and sidecars (driver, pillion passenger and also one in a sidecar with rifle at the ready) passed the farm and drove straight up to the 'Mill', an old mill on high ground which overlooked quite an area of the north west coast of the Island. ... From now on, we went about our daily lives as best we could.[15]

Though the occupation by the Germans had taken place in relative calm, not everyone was able to restrain their emotions, as this report in the *Jersey Post* on Friday, 5 July 1940, reveals:

> James Colgan (30) Ireland, was charged by the Constable of St. Helier, with having on Wednesday, July 3rd, 1940, about 11 p.m., at [the café at] No. 18, Seaton Place, assaulted Fritz Scholle, a soldier of the German forces in occupation of the island by striking him in the face with his fist ...
>
> Colgan and the soldier were in the café and the civilian had for some reason unknown, struck the soldier ... When questioned Colgan stated that he had no recollection of the affair and had been drinking.

Colgan was subsequently found guilty of the offences he had been charged with and was duly sentenced to one month with hard labour.

Frank Collenette recalled how worried he was in those first few days of the Occupation. His first concern, as it was for many others, was 'respect'. How much respect would the Germans show the islanders, and how much should the islanders pay to the Germans. Soon, though, more practical concerns took precedence:

> Every day, big carrier planes arrived, taking away what they could lay their hands on. But the worst was food. So that we got to learn that instead of two years stores in hand, it had dwindled down to six months. We then knew that our glasshouses would have to be turned into vegetable gardens if we were to survive.[16]

For his part, Lanz appears to have been quite content with the way in which the invasion and occupation of the Channel Islands had proceeded:

> Thus everything fell quickly into its place, both Army and Administration took pains to work together and meet each other half way. The mass of the population gratefully recognised the correctness, generosity, and obligingness of the occupying troops.
>
> From the many letters that went abroad and so were subject to censorship one could make a very interesting cross-section of existing opinion. A point often repeated was put well by one writer: the German Commandant did more in 48 hours than the States in 48 years![17]

Donald Journeaux owned a small farm with a lovely old house, one horse, one cow a tractor and a lorry. He also employed one person. Donald grew mainly potato and tomato crops, for export. Farms such as his would prove to be, quite literally, life-savers in the years to come, but that was in the future:

> The occupation of the Island was carried out efficiently and in an orderly fashion. Shortly after the order to display white flags, which had been given by the Commander of the German Air Force in Normandy, German troops landed at Jersey Airport. Guards were at once posted at the Post Office and Telephone Exchange, and soldiers were billeted in hotels.
>
> Very soon it became known that money would be devalued. Local people and even the German troops were descending on the shops and I decided I should have to join them and bring in some of the many things we should require. Tea, coffee, tins of meat, sugar, rice, candles and matches, medicines … what did we need? It was so difficult to make up one's mind. We had nothing to go by and felt as though we had been thrown in at the deep end.
>
> The town was packed with people and soldiers. The soldiers looked happy, no doubt because they were, for a time at least, away from the fighting. The sensation of strangeness continued. I felt as though I were in a comic opera!
>
> Time, of course, would change that.[18]

References and Notes

Chapter 1. 'We knew our turn was coming'

1. Ralph Durand, *Guernsey Under German Rule* (The Guernsey Society, London, 1946), p.7. A note at the beginning of this publication, dated March 1946, states that, 'The Council of the Guernsey Society deeply regret that Ralph Durand died before it was possible for him to read the proofs of this book. Malnutrition during the German occupation had seriously weakened him and it was only with a great effort that he was able to complete the last chapters and revise the whole manuscript before sending it to the printers in November. He died on December 22nd, 1945.'
2. Leslie E. Roussel, *Evacuation* (New Horizon, Bognor Regis, 1980), pp.2-3.
3. Ralph Durand, *op. cit.*, p.8.
4. 'A Startling Experience for Both Sides, Alderney and Guernsey 1940', the unpublished personal recollections of E.V. Clayton.
5. Gillian Mawson, *Guernsey Evacuees* (History Press, Stroud, 2012), p.15.
6. R.C.F. Maugham, *Jersey Under the Jackboot* (Coronet Books, 1992), p.12.
7. Quoted in Brian Aheir Read, *No Cause for Panic* (Seaflower Books, Jersey, 1995), p.9.
8. Ralph Durand, *op. cit.*, p.9.
9. R.C.F. Maugham, *op. cit.*

Chapter 2. 'No strategic use'

1. William M. Bell, *Guernsey Green* (The Guernsey Press Co. Ltd, Guernsey, 1992), p.84. William Bell, also known as Bill Bell, has told Bill Green's story.
2. Manuscript of Charles Roche, quoted in Charles Cruickshank, *The German Occupation of the Channel Islands, The Official History of the Occupation Years* (The Guernsey Press Co. Ltd., Guernsey, 1991), p.62.
3. The National Archives (TNA), CAB/65/7/57.
4. TNA, CAB/66/8/27.
5. TNA, CAB/65/7/57.
6. TNA, CAB/65/7/58.
7. TNA, CAB/66/8/38.
8. Personal diary of A.C. Robins, in the archives of the Channel Islands Occupation Society.

9. Ralph Durand, *op. cit.*, p.9.

10. *Ibid.*

11. TNA, CAB/65/7/67.

12. William M. Bell, *op. cit.*, pp.89-90.

13. R.C.F. Maugham, *op. cit.*, pp.21-2; Cruickshank, *op. cit.*, p.32.

14. Frank Falla, *The Silent War, The Inside Story of the Channel Islands Under the Nazi Jackboot* (Burbridge, Guernsey, 1981), p.13.

15. *Ibid*, pp.12-3. In his memoirs, Frank Falla goes on to consider one possible ramification of the decision by Guernsey's leaders to not release the King's letter publically: 'Might it have been knowledge in official circles in England that the authorities in Guernsey had failed to comply with the request that the King's message be conveyed to the people of Guernsey, that prompted the first RAF leaflet raid on Guernsey on 24th September 1940? There were two separate operations by RAF planes that day and the first pamphlet they dropped was headed, "News from England". It read: "The Queen and I desire to convey to you our heartfelt sympathy in the trials which you are now enduring. We earnestly pray for your liberation, knowing that it will surely come."'

16. Following the liberation of Guernsey on 9 May 1945, all of the German guns from the occupation were removed and scrapped or dumped at sea. The two 13.5cm Kanone 09 guns remained buried and all but forgotten for the next thirty-eight years until the author's grandfather, Arthur Oswald Hamon, who was at the time Chairman of the Ancient Monuments Committee, approached States member Roger Berry with the proposal that the guns should be dug up and restored. This suggestion duly became a subject of the November 1978 States meeting. The States approved the recovery and granted a budget of £2,000 to excavate and restore them. It was decided to replace both guns in the gardens, one at either end. Work was soon underway, the task being completed in December 1978. Exposed to the elements, both artillery pieces were quickly painted with Croda Triple Coat grey paint. This was done not to conform to any military colour scheme but purely as this was the same paint that was used during the maintenance of the cranes in St Peter Port. The guns still retain that colour scheme today. Still on display beside Victoria Tower, the artillery pieces in Guernsey are believed to be two of just three 13.5cm Kannon 09 guns, from an original production run of just 190 of the type, that have survived worldwide. For more information, see *Britain at War Magazine*, Issue 70, February 2013.

17. Frank Falla, pp.15-6.

18. Peter and Mary Birchenall, *Occupation Nurse* (Woodfield, Bognor Regis, 2001), p.31.

Chapter 3. 'Vague, unspecified dangers'

1. Quoted in Madeleine Bunting, *The Model Occupation, the Channel Islands under German Rule, 1940-1946* (Harper/Collins, London, 1995), p.23.

2. Ralph Durand, *Guernsey Under German Rule* (The Guernsey Society, London, 1946), pp.10-1.

3. The diary of Reverend Robert Douglas Ord, in the archive of the Channel Islands

Occupation Society.

4. William M. Bell, *op. cit.*, pp.86-7.
5. Tony C. Bourgourd, *Stolen Childhood* (self-published, Guernsey, 2002), pp.18-22.
6. Malcolm Woodland, BBC's People's War Archive, Article ID A3992349.
7. Jill Harris, BBC WW2 People's War Archive, Article ID 01/A38447601.
8. Imperial War Museum, Department of Documents, Accession No.12219.
9. 'My Occupation Memories', a personal account by Roy Burton in the archives of the Channel Island Occupation Society.
10. Dr Alistair Rose, 'Impressions of the Occupation of Guernsey' in the *Channel Islands Occupation Review*, No.28, 2001, pp.6-28.
11. *Ibid.*
12. Frank Stroobant, *One Man's War, The Dramatic True Story of Life in the Channel Islands Under the Jackboot of German Occupation* (Burbridge, Guernsey, 1992), p.14.
13. Minutes of a Guernsey Education Meeting Council held on 28 June 1940, p.2, quoted in Mawson, p.18.
14. Ambrose Sherwill, *A Fair and Honest Book* (Lulu, 2006), pp.80-1.
15. Leslie E. Roussel, *op. cit.*, pp.3-5.
16. Imperial War Museum, Department of Documents, Mr and Mrs G. Attenborough typed diary, Accession No.11646.
17. William M. Bell, *op. cit.*, p.87.
18. Frank Stroobant, *op. cit.*, p.16.
19. Imperial War Museum, private papers of Mrs E.M. Simon, 13251.
20. Imperial War Museum, private papers of P. Girard, 10992.
21. Alan Wood and Mary Seaton Wood, *Islands in Danger: The Fantastic Story of the German Occupation of the Channel Islands 1940-1945* (Four Square, London, 1967), p.31.
22. Barry Turner, *Outpost of Occupation, How the Channel Islands Survived Nazi Rule 1940-1945* (Aurum Press, London, 2010), pp.15-6.
23. The diary of Reverend Robert Douglas Ord in the archive of the Channel Islands Occupation Society.
24. *Ibid.*
25. Madeleine Bunting, *op. cit.*, p.19.
26. Quoted in Brian Ahier Read, *No Cause for Panic, Channel Island Refugees 1940-45* (Seaflower Books, St Helier, 1995), pp.25-6.
27. Hamel, E., Imperial War Museum, Department of Documents, Accession No.12219.
28. 'Occupying My Mind 1940-1945', the unpublished personal memoirs of Frank Hubert.
29. *Ibid.*

Chapter 4. 'Women and children first'

1. Imperial War Museum, private papers of R.E.H. Fletcher, 2986.
2. Quoted in Charles Cruickshank, *op. cit.*, p.44.
3. Brian Ahier Read, *op. cit.*, p.11.
4. *Ibid.*
5. Madeleine Bunting, *op. cit.*, p.24.

6. Donald P. Journeaux, *Raise the White Flag: A Life in Occupied Jersey* (Ashford, Buchan & Enright, Leatherhead, 1995), pp.1-2.
7. Imperial War Museum, private papers of R.E.H. Fletcher, 2986.
8. Anon, *Hitler's British Islands: The Channel Islands Occupation Experience by the People Who Lived Through It* (Channel Island Publishing, Jersey, undated), p.45.
9. Betty Harvey, BBC WW2 People's War Archive, Article ID 01/A2871939.
10. Quoted in Brian Ahier Read, *op. cit.*, pp.23-4.
11. *Evening Press*, 26 June 1940.

Chapter 5. 'Snatched out of the grip of the Boche'
1. *Evening Times*, Glasgow, 11 April 2014.
2. Quoted in Michael St. J. Packe and Maurice Dreyfus, *The Alderney Story 1939-1949* (The Alderney Society and Museum, Alderney, 1971), pp.26-7.
3. Island Archives: File No.1/3/1. Alderney – Agriculture.
4. Madeleine Bunting, *op. cit.*, p.34.
5. Michael St. J. Packe and Maurice Dreyfus, *op. cit.*, p.28.
6. Miriam M. Mahy, *There is an Occupation* (The Guernsey Press, 1993), quoted in Barry Turner, *op. cit.*, p.19. The work of the St John's Ambulance throughout the difficult days of June and July 1940 was acknowledged by the Bailiff of Guernsey, Victor G. Carey, who offered the following Vote of Thanks later in the year: 'I now desire to bring to your notice the unselfish and valuable services which have also been rendered to the Island for some time past by the members of the Medical and Nursing professions, both at the Emergency Hospital and at the other Nursing Institutions, as well as by the members of the St. John Ambulance Brigade, with which I am intimately associated. All have worked unceasingly and most devotedly, and have given their services without any thought of remuneration whatsoever, and I feel that the least we can do is to pass a resolution conveying to them our sincere and grateful thanks for all their self-sacrificing work on behalf of the community. I, therefore, submit to you the following proposition which I feel confident you will pass with unanimity.'
7. Brian Aheir Read, *op. cit.*, pp.10-20.
8. Ralph Durand, *op. cit.*, p.23.
9. 'A Story of Survival', published in the *Guernsey Press*, 7 August 2006. Maria Blatchford points out that, 'the next day, a Saturday, she [*Courier*] sailed for the UK in company with the *Joybell III*, another local passenger vessel. It was in 1947 that the *Courier* returned to local waters, but her owners found her too expensive to run and, in 1951, she was broken up in the Netherlands.'
10. Imperial War Museum, private papers of P. Girard, 10992.

Chapter 6. 'Unnecessarily hasty action'
1. *The Methodist Recorder*, 4 July 1940.
2. As well as evacuation by sea, a small number of people left the islands by air. Though the seriousness of the war situation had led to the suspension of all of the scheduled passenger flights to and from the Channel Islands on 15 June 1940, and the passenger aircraft transferred to the mainland, Jersey and Guernsey

Airways, then based at Exeter, operated special evacuation services. By this route a total of 319 people left the islands in unarmed de Havilland DH 86s.
3. Hansard, vol 116 cc754-73.
4. Brian Ahier Read, *op. cit.*, p.13.
5. Hansard, vol. 363 cc1349-70.
6. House of Lords Debate, 9 July 1940.

Chapter 7. 'The blackest day Guernsey had ever seen'
1. In one of the last *KG.55* raids against the United Kingdom, in the early hours of Thursday, 8 May 1941, Flight Lieutenant E. Deansley and Sergeant W.J. Scott of 256 Squadron, flying a Defiant night fighter, intercepted a Heinkel He 111P-4 at 01.20 hours. In the ensuing combat, the German bomber, coded G1+KL, was shot down and crashed. Such was the force of the impact that little more than a smoking crater remained to be seen at Hazel Grove in Stockport. However, the four-man crew had managed to bale out and was taken prisoner. The pilot, subsequently promoted after his participation in the bombing raid of 28 June 1940, was *Oberleutnant* A. Knorringer.
2. Imperial War Museum, Department of Documents, Accession No.11109.
3. *King-Hall Newsletter*, 2 August 1940.
4. Quoted in Roy McLoughlin, *Living With the Enemy* (Starlight Publishing, Jersey, 1995). pp.20-1.
5. Ambrose Sherwill, *op. cit.*, p.95.
6. Malcolm Woodland, BBC's People's War Archive, Article ID A3992349.
7. Personal 'War Diary' of Kenneth Lewis, in the archives of the Channel Islands Occupation Society.
8. Peter and Mary Birchenall, *op. cit.*, pp.34-5.
9. William M. Bell, *op. cit.*, pp.89-90.
10. Molly Bihet, *A Time for Memories* (privately published, St Peter Port, 2005). p.26.
11. 'Occupying My Mind 1940-1945', the unpublished personal memoirs of Frank Hubert.
12. William M. Bell, *op. cit.*, p.94.
13. Ralph Durand, *op. cit.*, p.22.
14. Malcolm Woodland, *op. cit.*
15. P. Girard, *op. cit.*
16. Frank Hubert, *op. cit.* In his account, Hubert went on to note how his service in the demolition squad was cut short: 'There was not enough support to maintain a demolition squad as a separate branch of the Auxiliary Fire Service, so I joined the firefighting team. We had to learn the location of all fire hydrants, jump some 20 feet off the drying tower, on to a blanket held by other firemen and go on several practice runs. I was appointed No.1 driver and I remember the thrill and excitement on those dummy runs ... the speed, the bells ringing out loud, the people rushing out of my way and the hair standing up on the back of my neck! Despite the training I underwent and all the air raids the Island suffered, not once was there a need for the Auxiliary firemen to be called out, to tend a serious fire, the regular teams were able to cope. In a way that was a good thing, but it was frustrating for us.'

17. A record of those Guernsey Fire Brigade personnel in attendance at White Rock following the air raid on 28 June 1940 has survived. From the Regular Brigade were the Chief Officer, W.D. Oliver, and the following Firemen: H. Mudge, W. Mudge, Adolph Le Prevost, A. Hamon, Archie Le Prevost, Arthur Le Prevost, A.J. Edmonds, B.E. Mauger, R. Gardiner, F. Donnelly, C. Harding, and J. Daly. The following Auxiliary Fire Service Firemen were present: F.R. Giles, P.J. Carre, G.W. Knight, H. Langlois, H.J. Lavenne, H.G. Stonelake, E.W.H. Vaudin, W.S. Udle, W.H. Martin, S.C. Smith, H.G. Bienvenu, W.H. Lawrence, W. Le Cras, G.O. Taylor, G.W. Burrows, W.H. Gillingham, R. Fryer, and R. Green. The Patrol Firemen on scene were G. Staples, P.C. Malzard, W. Le Page, A. Zabiela, R. Elliston, H. Pomeroy, T. Le Sauvage, H.C. Mudge, W.G. Guilbert, and A. Mellish. The Watch Room and ARP staff were B. De Guerin, A. Piprell, W.G. Luscombe, and F.W. Hubert.
18. Dr Alistair Rose, *op. cit.*
19. *Ibid.*
20. Imperial War Museum, Department of Documents, Accession No.11109.
21. Frank Falla, *op. cit.*, p.15.
22. *Ibid.*
23. 'My Occupation Memories', a personal account by Roy Burton in the archives of the Channel Island Occupation Society. After the *Luftwaffe*'s attacks Roy's school was closed. 'After the bombing raid we were off school for three months,' he recalls, 'until Mr Peter Girard, School Master from the College, went around the Island on horseback asking people with children if they would send them to school if it was started again. And that is how school under the Occupation was re-started in September 1940.'

Chapter 8. 'A terrifying experience'
1. J.P. Sinel, *German Occupation of Jersey: A Diary of Events from June 1940 to June 1945* (Jersey, 1945), p.12.
2. Imperial War Museum, private papers of R.E.H. Fletcher, Accession No.2986.
3. Roy McLoughlin, *op. cit.*, p.21.
4. TNA, London, HW 5/2.
5. National Archives and Records Administration (NARA), Washington D.C., T311/231 frame 1208.
6. NARA, Washington D.C., T311/231 frame 1206. The historian and author Pierre Renier has provided the following description of the events surrounding the Channel Islands in relation to intercepted German messages and signals: 'In the Channel Island Occupation Review 1986, pages 56 to 64, Michael Ginns wrote about "The Channel Islands and the Ultra Secret", stating then that all the Enigma decoded material alone would fill a book, [nearly] all of which covered the war from 1941 onwards. Since that initial release of material in the 1980's, in more recent years much has become available, together with the records of the units involved in its interception. Importantly though, much is of *Heer* (German army), and *Luftwaffe* (German Air Force or GAF) messages, and covers the earlier campaigns in Western Europe, providing a fresh insight into military events of June and July 1940. Intercepted by the listening posts of the Y Service, it was indeed one of the greatest secrets of World War Two.

'This GAF Enigma material is examined in conjunction with rare examples of surviving *Luftwaffe* messages. Prior to the cessation of hostilities in Europe, May 1945, *Reichsmarschall* Hermann Goring (Commander in Chief of the GAF) ordered the thorough destruction of all unit records. Consequently GAF documents are immensely scarce, and when seen against the mass of material available for the *Heer* and *Kriegsmarine* (where in many cases only material from the last months of the war is absent), his orders were carried out to the letter. Ironically these GAF messages from *Luftflotte* 3 (3rd Air Fleet) were found amongst records of *Heeresgruppe* B (Army Group B), whose zone of operations encompassed the Channel Islands.

'Each message, providing up to date information on events at the front, was sent by the Führungsabteilung Ic (HQ Operations Intelligence Officer) of Lfl.3 to a number of recipients; Lw. Filhningsstab Ic or Oberkommando der Luftwaffe (OKL) Ic (Air Force High Command), Kurfürst, and finally Asien Ic. OKL was the subordinated HQ to the OKW or Oberkommando der Wehrmacht (German High Command), being Adolf Hitler's operational HQ. OKL was split into two command elements; a forward operations HQ code-named Robinson, which would function in close proximity to OKW, and the second element comprising other departments, named Kurfürst, whose offices were located in and around Berlin. Finally Asien Ic, the intelligence officer stationed aboard Goring's personal train, Sonderzug Asien.'

7. *Evening Post*, Saturday, 29 June 1940.
8. *Ibid.*
9. Donald P. Journeaux, *op. cit.*, p.2.
10. Anon, *Hitler's British Islands: The Channel Islands Occupation Experience by the People Who Lived Through It*, p.13.
11. *Ibid.*
12. 'Report of Service on the 29th day of June 1940, Lifeboat – 0N 672 Stationed at St Peter Port', RNLI Archives.
13. *Ibid.*
14. *Alfred and Clara Heath* remained in Guernsey and operated in her normal role for two or three weeks before being officially commandeered by the German forces for use as a harbour patrol boat, having a machine-gun fitted on the foredeck. *Alfred and Clara Heath* was in such a poor condition at the end of the war that it had to be scrapped. As for *Howard D*, she was used by the Germans in Jersey in the role of a lifeboat and it is understood to have saved some thirty-four lives during the Occupation. The vessel survived and some sixty years after the war, having been refurbished, was put on public display in Jersey.
15. It is known that Harold's son Tony was present at the meeting with Obermeyer, the latter being 'described by him as a friendly, family man, sitting Tony on his knee and allowing this young boy of three to play with his medals while the negotiations took place'.
16. Cruickshank, *op. cit.*, p.28.

Chapter 9. 'The Mad Murderer of Berchtesgaden'
1. William M. Bell, *op. cit.*, p.91.
2. *Ibid*, p.92.

3. *The Times*, 29 June 1940.

Chapter 10. 'Marching against England'

1. Alan Wood and Mary Seaton Wood, *op. cit.*, pp.309-10.
2. George Forty, *Channel Islands at War: A German Perspective* (Ian Allan Publishing, Shepperton, 2005), p.29.
3. Personal 'War Diary' of Kenneth Lewis, in the archives of the Channel Islands Occupation Society.
4. Personal account of Albrecht Lanz in the author's collection.
5. In his recollections, Lanz pointed out that Koch, 'two days after the outbreak of war … had brought this proud ship, by night, with lights extinguished, safely into his home port, with 700 foreign passengers aboard. It was an unusual pleasure to talk to this old seadog, who, with his dry wit, and hearty manner, knows how to establish quickly the most cordial of relations.'

Chapter 11. 'The first landing on English soil'

1. Ambrose Sherwill, *op. cit.*, p.96.
2. Roman Gastager and Wendy von Well, *The Easter Bunnies: Long-Distance Reconnaissance by the German Luftwaffe over Poland, France, England & the Atlantic 1938-1945* (Trafford Publishing, Oxford, 2006). The term 'Easter Bunnies' was the nickname *Staffelkapitän* Liebe-Piderit gave to a group of five young men who joined *Fernaufklärungsgruppe* 123 in Hanau am Main at the end of March 1940. Aside from Roman Gastager, the other four 'Easter Bunnies' did not survive the war.
3. *Ibid*.
4. 'Policing During the Occupation 1940-1945', a talk by Albert Peter Lamy MBE, BEM, QPM. On 16 March 1942, Lamy was appointed Acting Deputy Inspector (Deputy Chief Officer) and four months later, on 30 July 1942, was appointed Acting Inspector (Chief Officer). Lamy therefore had the most unenviable task of leading a depleted police force in an Island under German occupation.
5. Frank Falla, *op. cit.*, p.17.
6. *Ibid*, p.18.
7. William M. Bell, *op. cit.*, p.97.
8. Simon Hamon, 'First Days Under the Jackboot', *Britain at War Magazine*, Issue 92, December 2014. In 1942 Inspector Sculpher, being British, was deported to Germany along with other UK-born residents. After the war he returned to Guernsey and resumed duty as Chief Officer on 9 August 1945. Albert Lamy was appointed as his deputy. On 11 December 1945, Lamy was awarded the British Empire Medal for services rendered during the Occupation. On Schulpher's retirement on 23 January 1946, Lamy was appointed Chief Officer.
9. Ambrose Sherwill, *op. cit.*, p.96.
10. *Ibid*.
11. *Ibid*, pp.97-8.
12. Frank Falla, *op. cit.*, pp.18-20.
13. Imperial War Museum, Department of Documents, Accession No.11109.
14. TNA, HW 5/3 (Operations in North-West Europe, Mediterranean and Africa, with Analyses of Orders of Battle and GAF communications and Signals).

15. *War Illustrated*, Volume 3, No.46, 19 July 1940, p.40.
16. *Hauptmann* Reinhard Liebe-Piderit was killed a few days after the Guernsey landings, on 19 July 1940. In his memoirs, Roman Gastager described what happened, having first explained that the actual aircraft in which Louis Blériot crossed the Channel on 25 July 1909 was located at his unit's base at Buc: 'The Blériot XI was a real museum piece for the entire squadron and our mechanics never gave up trying to get it fit for flying once again. Through ambition, ability, diligence and an incredible amount of patience, the mechanics eventually succeeded in getting this machine ready for action. The oldest and best pilot of the squadron, *Oberfeldwebel* Arkenhausen, actually circled the airfield in it a few times. Our *Staffelkapitän* [Liebe-Piderit] was so inspired by this that he also wanted to give it a try. Tragically, he crashed during his second turn and was killed on impact.' See Roman Gastager and Wendy von Well, *The Easter Bunnies*.
17. William M. Bell, *op. cit.*, p.99.
18. The 'Spitfire' referred to here was in fact an Avro Anson of the RAF's recently-departed School of Reconnaissance. It had developed engine trouble and when spares could not be flow in one member of groundcrew, Harry Lawrence, was ordered to render the aircraft useless. When he spoke to the author, he stated that, 'It was the only time while I was in the RAF that I wasn't put on a charge for damaging a 'plane!'
19. William M. Bell, *op. cit.*
20. *Ibid.*
21. Imperial War Museum, private papers of P. Girard, Accession No.10992.
22. 'The Arrival of the Occupying Forces', an account provided by historian John Goodwin.
23. Personal account of Albrecht Lanz in the author's collection.
24. The German flag was hurriedly made, at the request of German troops, by staff at Creasey's, a well-known local outfitters which, located in St Peter Port, is still trading to this day.
25. William M. Bell, *op. cit.*
26. Personal 'War Diary' of Kenneth Lewis, in the archives of the Channel Islands Occupation Society.
27. Quoted in Brian Cull, *First of the Few: 5 June – 9 July 1940* (Fonthill Media, Stroud, 2013).

Chapter 12. 'Strike the flag'
1. H.R.S. Pocock (Compiler), *The Memoirs of Lord Coutanche: A Jerseyman Looks Back* (Phillimore & Co, Chichester, 1975), p.16.
2. P. Le Sauteur, *Jersey Under the Swastika* (Streamline, London, 1968), p.14.
3. *Sonderführer* Hans Auerbach, *Die Kanalinseln; Jersey, Guernsey, Sark* (printed Jersey 1941).
4. H.R.S. Pocock, *op. cit.*, p.17.
5. Personal account of Albrecht Lanz in the author's collection.
6. H.R.S. Pocock, *op. cit.*, p.17.
7. *Ibid.*
8. Barry Turner, *op. cit.*, p.44.

9. *Ibid.*
10. Sonia Hillsdon, *Jersey Occupation Remembered* (Seaflower Books, Bradford on Avon, 2004), p.35.
11. Donald Journeaux, *op. cit.*, p.4.
12. *The Evening Post*, 2 July 1940.
13. F.A. Le Sueur, *Shadow of the Swastika* (The Guernsey Press, Guernsey, 1992), pp.15-6.
14. An account by Brian Ahier Read, dated 17 September 1997, and quoted on http://timewitnesses.org.
15. *Ibid.*
16. 'Legion Condor in the Channel Islands', an unpublished personal account of Dr. Ulrich Kaser.
17. In his account, Dr. Ulrich Kaser details further deployments by *Legion Condor*: 'To further bolster the Islands' anti-aircraft defences, on 11th July the 4th Battery was loaded in Cherbourg on to the captured ship the S.S. *Holland*. However, due to storms she remained in harbour, finally departing for St. Peter Port on 14th July. After off-loading nine 20mm Flak 30 the same day, the S.S. *Holland* then set course for Jersey with the one remaining troop of three guns from the 4th Battery. On the night of 15th July 1940, both the 4th and 5th batteries shot down a Bristol Blenheim over flying Guernsey. On the 21st July, the S.S. *Holland* was again employed, this time transporting the searchlights of the 5th Battery from Granville to St. Helier, Jersey. Finally, on the 9th August, having spent just over five weeks in the Channel Islands the 4th and 5th batteries were re-embarked and returned by ship to Cherbourg Querqueville. In 1941, I./Flak-Rgt.9 *Legion Condor* was sent east to Russia.' Note that no Blenheim losses are recorded for the night of 15/16 July, however the Operations Record Book for RAF Thorney Island, then a Coastal Command station, notes at 03.30 hours on the 16th, eight Blenheims of 59 Squadron reported 'intense tracer and Pom-Pom in region of [Guernsey] aerodrome, two searchlights held aircraft in beam until out of range. Nothing further of interest.'
18. Quoted in Barry Turner, *op. cit.*, p.36.
19. Sonia Hillsdon, *op. cit.*, p.36.
20. *Ibid*, p.37.
21. Personal account of Albrecht Lanz in the author's collection.

Chapter 13. 'Breeches, jackboots and forage caps'

1. NARA, Washington, D.C., T311/231 frame 1176.
2. NARA, Washington, D.C., T311/231 frame 1173. The 'planes referred to in this message were in fact examples of the Fieseler Fi 156 Storch, a highly versatile liaison aircraft. Note that in many accounts it is stated that the Germans landed on Alderney on 2 July 1940. In their book *The Alderney Story 1939/49*, the authors M. St. J. Packe and Maurice Dreyfus write: 'On July 2nd, the Luftwaffe had landed at Alderney airport, and taken possession of the deserted island.'
3. M. St. J. Packe and Maurice Dreyfus, *The Alderney Story 1939/49* (Alderney Society and Museum, Alderney, 1971), p.31.
4. Personal account of Albrecht Lanz in the author's collection. Lanz's statement

that a pair of Ju 52s was used to transport part of the Alderney garrison to the island is interesting in that earlier in the very same paragraph he made this comment: 'A few days later I made enquiries about the possibility of aircraft landing in Alderney, most northerly of the islands. According to what I heard, the existing airfield was unsuitable for heavy machines and it was not possible to land there.'

5. Martin J. Le Page, *A Boy Messenger's War: Memories of Guernsey and Herm 1938-45* (Arden Publications, St Peter Port, 1995), p.27.

6. Herm History, 16th to 21st Centuries, retrieved from www.herm.com. It is stated that the mock landings were made on Shell Beach using infantry from Guernsey's garrison.

7. Peter J. Rivett, *Brecqhou – A Very Private Island* (Planetesimal Publishing Limited, Paignton, 2002), p.151. The four Irishmen were James Hanafin, a labourer aged 22, his brother Terry Hanafin, aged 21, Henry Giles, a labourer aged 25, and Albert Lyons who, aged 39, was described as a gardener.

8. Ralph Durand, *op. cit.*, p.118.

9. Dame Sibyl Hathaway's words are taken from her autobiography, *Dame of Sark* (Heinemann, London, 1975).

10. Charles Cruickshank, *op. cit.*, p.48.

11. Quoted in Brian Aheir Read, *op. cit.*, p.18.

12. Personal account of Albrecht Lanz in the author's collection.

13. Michael Marshall, *Hitler Invaded Sark* (Guernsey Lithoprint, undated), p.11.

14. *Ibid*, p.12.

15. Personal account of Albrecht Lanz in the author's collection.

16. *Ibid*.

17. Sibyl Hathaway, *op. cit*, p.118.

18. Michael Marshall, *op. cit.*, p.14. In his book, Marshall adds the following observation regarding the German flag: 'Bel Air Hotel and the enemy flagpole at the top of Harbour Hill were so exposed to the skies that the Germans often kept their "Swastika" in its "box", fearing an attack by British fighter 'planes. This hiding the flag of Nazism away was an act somehow symbolic of the whole five years Occupation of Sark.'

19. Richard Le Tissier, *Mined Where You Walk: The German Occupation of Sark: 1940-45* (Seaflower Books, St Helier, 2008), p.25.

20. Julia Tremayne, *War on Sark: The Secret Letters of Julia Tremayne, A Personal Account of the German Occupation 1940-1945* (Webb & Bower, Exeter, 1981), p.15.

21. The first German representative on the island who held the title of *Inselkommandant* Sark, and who in turn was subordinated to the Commandant of Guernsey, was also officially appointed on 4 July 1940. Holding the post until 1942, his name was *Oberleutnant* Stefan Herdt.

Chapter 14. 'A heavy yoke'

1. Barry Turner, *op. cit.*, p.48.

2. K.M. Bachmann, *The Prey of an Eagle* (Burbridge, Guernsey, 1985), p.3.

3. Roy McLoughlin, *op. cit.*, p.25.

4. TNA, CAB/65/14/2.

5. *The Times*, 10 July 1940.

Chapter 15. 'It's the finish for all of us'
1. TNA, CAB/65/8/3.
2. Simon Hamon, 'Operation *Aerial* – The Evacuation of the Channel Islands', *Channel Islands Occupation Society Review*, No.39, 2011.
3. After the official evacuation, both *Hantonia* and *Isle of Sark* continued to operate their normal scheduled passenger ferry service between the Islands and Southampton. *Hantonia* last sailed to the Islands on 25 June and the *Isle of Sark* on 28 June, only to become embroiled in the German air raids.
4. David Kreckeler, 'Escapes from Guernsey and Alderney during the Occupation', *Channel Islands Occupation Society Review*, 1978.
5. The passengers were: George and Marjory Best; Mrs. E.J. Bougourd and her son, Edward, and daughters Mrs. Irene Le Gallez and Mrs. Doris Le Parmentier; Frederick Cohu; Mr. and Mrs. R. Claybourne; and Miss M. Le Prevost and her sister and Mrs E. Talbot. It is believed that *Florida III* was used as a patrol boat by the Royal Navy at some time during the war.
6. The *Mayflower* escapees were: Falla and his wife Vera; Mr. and Mrs Sid Robilliard and their daughter Mary Robilliard aged 5; Mr. and Mrs. R.H. Waymouth and their son Frank and Mrs. Waymouth's sister Miss Noel; Mr. and Mrs. A. Olliver; Wilfred Duquemin; Mrs. Guille and her two sons Horace and Winston, together with their wives Zoe and Violet; Frank Le Page; Leonard Le Page; Brian La Farge; Desire Le Chavetois; Fred Lowe; the brothers Claude and Arthur Mann; Peter J. Olliver; Harold Despointes; Ernest Ernest Rive; and an Austrian girl.
7. *The War Illustrated*, 19 July 1940, p.51.
8. TNA, FO 371/24392.
9. *Ibid*.

Chapter 16. 'Flushed with victory'
1. 'Policing During the Occupation 1940-1945', a talk by Albert Peter Lamy MBE, BEM, QPM.
2. *Ibid*.
3. Copies of the proclamation are held in the archives of the Channel Islands Occupation Society.
4. Imperial War Museum, Department of Documents, Accession No.11109.
5. The diary of Reverend Robert Douglas Ord, in the archive of the Channel Islands Occupation Society. The suicide mentioned by Ord in his account was probably that of Emile Cecil Carré. A report on the inquest was published in *The Star* on 2 July 1940. It stated that Carré was 'a 51-year-old grower of La Planque, Castel, who was found shot in the body at 11 o'clock on the morning of June 28. The [Police] Inspector said that when last seen alive Carré was quite normal. A baker's roundsman later discovered his body, near which were lying a shotgun and a piece of wood, the latter having apparently been used to manipulate the trigger.'
6. Personal account of Albrecht Lanz in the author's collection.
7. Kurt G. Stolzenberg, 'Der Erste Griff Nach England,' *Siegeszug Durch Frankreich. Kleine Kriegshefte Nr. 5-6* (Munich: Zentralverlag der NSDAP., 1940). The

translation has been kindly been provided by Randall Bytwerk. In the early years of the war, the Nazi Party's publishing unit produced a series of twelve booklets on various aspects of the war. No.5/6 detailed the victories in the West, particularly France.

8. *Ibid.*
9. It was inevitable that the invasion of the Channel Islands would have a disastrous effect on their agricultural industries. On 15 July 1940, for example, *The Times* carried the following piece of 'News in Brief': 'It is estimated that three-quarters of the Guernsey tomato crop has been lost owing to the German invasion.'
10. 'Occupying My Mind 1940-1945', the unpublished personal memoirs of Frank Hubert.
11. Imperial War Museum, Department of Documents, Accession No.11109.
12. Madeleine Bunting, *op. cit.*, p.40.
13. Dr Alistair Rose, *op. cit.*
14. Molly Bihet, *op. cit.*, p.71.
15. *Ibid*, pp.90-1.
16. *Ibid*, p.28.
17. Personal account of Albrecht Lanz in the author's collection.
18. Donald Journeaux, *op. cit.*, p.4.

Bibliography and Source Information

Books

Anon, *Hitler's British Islands: The Channel Islands Occupation Experience by the People Who Lived Through It* (Channel Island Publishing, Jersey, undated).

Aufsess, Baron von, *The Von Aufsess Occupation Diary* (Phillimore and Co, Chichester, 1995).

Bachmann, K.M., *The Prey of an Eagle* (Burbridge, Guernsey, 1985).

Bell, William M., *Guernsey Green* (The Guernsey Press Co. Ltd, Guernsey, 1992).

Bihet, Molly, *A Time for Memories* (Privately published, St Peter Port, 2005).

Birchenall, Peter and Mary, *Occupation Nurse: Nursing in Guernsey 1940-45* (Woodfield Publishing, Bognor Regis, 2001).

Bourgourd, Tony C., *Stolen Childhood* (self-published, Guernsey, 2002).

Briggs, Asa, *The Channel Islands Occupation and Liberation 1940-1945* (B.T. Batsford Ltd, London, 1995).

Bunting, Madeleine, *The Model Occupation: The Channel Islands Under German Rule, 1940-1945* (Harper Collins, London, 1995).

Carey, Violet, with Evans, Alice, *Guernsey under Occupation: The Second World War Diairies of Violet Carey* (Phillimore and Co, Chichester, 2009).

Cortvriend, V.V., *Isolated Island: A Factual Account of the German Occupation of Guernsey, one of the Channel Islands, 1940 to 1945* (Guernsey Star and Gazette Limited, Guernsey, 1947).

Coysh, Victor, *Swastika over Guernsey* (Guernsey Press, Guernsey, 1958).

Cruickshank, Charles, *The German Occupation of the Channel Islands, The Official History of the Occupation Years* (The Guernsey Press, 1991).

Cull, Brian, *First of the Few: 5 June – 9 July 1940* (Fonthill Media, Stroud, 2013).

Durand, Ralph, *Guernsey Under German Rule* (The Guernsey Society, London, 1946).

Falla, Frank, *The Silent War, The Inside Story of the Channel Islands Under the Nazi Jackboot* (Burbridge, Guernsey, 1981).

Forty, George, *Channel Islands at War: A German Perspective* (Ian Allan Publishing, Shepperton, 2005).

Gastager, Roman and von Well, Wendy, *The Easter Bunnies: Long-Distance Reconnaissance by the German Luftwaffe over Poland, France, England & the Atlantic 1938-1945* (Trafford Publishing, Oxford, 2006).

219

Ginns, Michael, OBE, *Jersey Occupied: The German Armed Forces in Jersey 1940-45* (Channel Island Publishing, Jersey, 2009).

Hathaway, Sybil, *Dame of Sark* (Heinemann, London, 1975).

Hillsdon, Sonia, *Jersey Occupation Remembered* (Seaflower Books, Bradford on Avon, 2004).

Jorgensen-Earp, Cheryl R., *Discourse and Defiance under Nazi Occupation: Guernsey, Channel Islands, 1940–1945* (Michigan State University Press, Michigan, 2013).

Journeaux, Donald P., *Raise the White Flag: A Life in Occupied Jersey* (Ashford, Buchan & Enright, Leatherhead, 1995).

Keiller, Frank, *Prison without Bars: Living in Jersey Under the German Occupation 1940-45* (Seaflower Books, St Helier, 2000).

King, Peter, *The Channel Islands War 1940-45* (Robert Hale, London, 1991).

Le Moignan, Luke, *Stories of an Occupation* (La Haule Books, Jersey, 1995).

Le Page, Martin J., *A Boy Messenger's War: Memories of Guernsey and Herm 1938-45* (Arden Publications, St Peter Port, 1995).

Le Quesne, Edward, Deputy, *The Occupation of Jersey Day by Day* (La Haule Books, Jersey).

Le Sauteur, P., *Jersey Under the Swastika* (Streamline, London, 1968).

Le Sueur, F.A., *Shadow of the Swastika* (The Guernsey Press, Guernsey, 1992).

Le Tissier, Richard, *Mined Where You Walk: The German Occupation of Sark: 1940-45* (Seaflower Books, St Helier, 2008).

Mahy, Miriam M., *There is an Occupation* (The Guernsey Press, Guernsey, 1993).

Marshall, Michael, *Hitler Invaded Sark* (Guernsey Lithoprint, Guernsey, undated).

Maugham, R.C.F., CBE, FRGS, FZS, *Jersey Under the Jackboot: A First Hand Account of the Island's Ordeal in the Grip of Nazi Occupation* (New English Library, London, 1968).

Mawson, Gillian, *Guernsey Evacuees* (History Press, Stroud, 2012).

McFadyen, Alec E.W., *A Diary of the Jersey Centre St. John Ambulance Association* (Jersey, undated).

McLoughlin, Roy, *Living With the Enemy* (Starlight Publishing, Jersey, 1995).

Mollet, Ralph, *Jersey Under the Swastika* (Hyperion Press, London, 1945)

Nettles, John, *Jewels and Jackboots: Hitler's British Channel Islands* (Channel Island Publishing, Jersey, 2012).

Packe, St. J., and Dreyfus, Maurice, *The Alderney Story 1939/49* (Alderney Society and Museum, Alderney, 1971).

Pantcheff, T.X.H., *Alderney, Fortress Island* (Phillimore & Co, Chichester, 1981).

Pocock, H.R.S. (Compiler), *The Memoirs of Lord Coutanche: A Jerseyman Looks Back* (Phillimore & Co, Chichester, 1975).

Quin, Olive, *The Long Goodbye* (Guernsey Press Co Ltd, Guernsey, 1995).

Read, Brian Aheir, *No Cause for Panic: Channel Island Refugees 1940-45* (Seaflower Books, St Helier, 1995).

Rivett, Peter J., *Brecqhou – A Very Private Island* (Planetesimal Publishing Limited, Paignton, 2002).

Roussel, Leslie, E., *Evacuation* (New Horizon, Bognor Regis, 1980).

Sanders, Paul, *The British Channel Islands under German Occupation 1940-1945* (The Jersey Heritage Trust, Jersey, 2005).

Sauvary, J.C., *Diary of the German Occupation of Guernsey 1940-1945* (Self-Publishing Association, 1990)

Sherwill, Ambrose, *A Fair and Honest Book* (Lulu, 2006).

Sinel, J.P., *German Occupation of Jersey: A Diary of Events from June 1940 to June 1945* (Jersey, 1945)

Tremayne, Julia, *War on Sark: The Secret Letters of Julia Tremayne, A Personal Account of the German Occupation 1940-1945* (Webb & Bower, Exeter, 1981).

Turner, Barry, *Outpost of Occupation: How the Channel Islands Survived Nazi Rule 1940-45* (Aurum, London, 2010).

Walters, Guy, *The Occupation* (Headline, London, 2004).

Winterflood, Herbert, *Occupied Guernsey: July 1940-December 1942* (Guernsey Press, Guernsey, 2002).

Wood, Alan and Wood, Mary Seaton, *Islands in Danger: The Fantastic Story of the German Occupation of the Channel Islands 1940-1945* (Four Square, London, 1967).

Wyatt, Horace, *Jersey in Jail, 1940-45* (Ernest Huelin, Jersey, 1945).

Articles

Hamon, Simon, 'First Days Under the Jackboot', *Britain at War Magazine*, Issue 92, December 2014.

Hamon, Simon, 'Operation *Aerial* – The Evacuation of the Channel Islands', *Channel Islands Occupation Society Review*, No.39, 2011.

Hamon, Simon, 'The Guernsey Guns', *Britain at War Magazine*, Issue 70, February 2013.

Kreckeler, David, 'Escapes from Guernsey and Alderney during the Occupation', *Channel Islands Occupation Society Review*, 1978.

Kurt G. Stolzenberg, 'Der Erste Griff Nach England,' *Siegeszug Durch Frankreich. Kleine Kriegshefte Nr. 5-6* (Munich: Zentralverlag der NSDAP., 1940).

War Illustrated, Volume 3, No.46, 19 July 1940.

Imperial War Museum, Department of Documents

Fletcher, R.E.H., Accession No.2986.

Girard, P., Accession No. 10992.

Hamel, Edward J., Accession No.12219.

Le M. Mainé, A., Accession No.11109.

Simon, Mrs E.M., Accession No.13251.

The National Archives

CAB/66/8/27.
CAB/66/8/38.
CAB 65/7/57.
CAB/65/7/58.
CAB/65/7/67.
CAB/65/8/3.
CAB/65/14/2.
FO 371/24392.
HW 5/2.
HW 5/3.

BIBLIOGRAPHY

National Archives and Records Administration
T311/231 frame 1173.
T311/231 frame 1176.
T311/231 frame 1206.
T311/231 frame 1208.

Channel Islands Occupation Society Archives
'A Startling Experience for Both Sides, Alderney and Guernsey 1940', the personal recollections of E.V. Clayton, published in the Channel Islands Occupation Society Review, No.28, 2001.
Dr Alistair Rose, 'Impressions of the Occupation of Guernsey' in the *Channel Islands Occupation Review*, No.28, 2001.
My Occupation Memories', a personal account by Roy Burton in the archives of the Channel Island Occupation Society.
'Occupying My Mind 1940-1945', published personal memoirs of Frank Hubert Channel Islands Occupation Society Review, No.28 2001.
Personal diary of A.C. Robins, in the archives of the Channel Islands Occupation Society.
The diary of Reverend Robert Douglas Ord, in the archive of the Channel Islands Occupation Society.
Personal 'War Diary' of Kenneth Lewis, in the archives of the Channel Islands Occupation Society.

Newspapers
Evening Post.
Evening Press.
Evening Times.
The Guernsey Press.
The Methodist Recorder.
The Times.

Private Records
Goodwin, John, 'The Arrival of the Occupying Forces', an account.
Harris, Jill, BBC WW2 People's War Archive, Article ID 01/A38447601.
Harvey, Betty, BBC WW2 People's War Archive, Article ID 01/A2871939.
Kaser, Dr. Ulrich, 'Legion Condor in the Channel Islands', an unpublished personal account.
Lamy, Albert Peter, MBE, BEM, QPM, 'Policing During the Occupation 1940-1945', a talk.
Lanz, *Major* Dr Albrecht, recollections in author's archive.
Woodland, Malcolm, BBC's People's War Archive, Article ID A3992349 and in person with author.

Index

The Channel Island Occupation Society was formed to study all aspects of the German military occupation of the British Channel Islands during the Second World War.

The society organises guided tours, excursions and talks throughout the Islands and France. It also continues to build up an extensive sound, documentary and photographic archive. Practical projects include the restoration of the Naval Signals H.Q. bunker at St. Jacques on the outskirts of St. Peter Port. Regular CIOS events take place, a list of these can be seen on its website.

If you would like to know more about the Channel Island Occupation Society, or perhaps become a member of the society, then please contact us. New members are always welcome.

The flagship publication of the Society is the annual *Channel Island Occupation Review*, which is sent free to members. Published alternately by the Guernsey and Jersey branches, it is produced to a high, professional, standard. All articles are meticulously researched and accompanied by numerous plans and photographs. In addition to this, members will receive three newsletters updating them on the latest news and events.

You can get more information by writing to the Secretary CIOS at
PO Box 338, St Peter Port, Guernsey, GY1 3UJ, or visiting:
www.ciosguernsey.org.gg